CW00523743

DISCOVER

TURKEY

Cover picture: Bodrum's western bay from the castle ramparts

DISCOVER
TURKEY

Terry Palmer

**HERITAGE
HOUSE**

DISCOVER TURKEY
First published March 1988
ISBN 185215.0106
Typesetting by:
Essex Phototypesetting, 2 Pace Units, Stephenson Rd, CLACTON on SEA, CO15 4XA
Printed by:
Colorcraft, Hong Kong
Distributed in the UK and major outlets overseas by Roger Lascelles, 47 York Road, BRENTFORD, TW8 0QP
Published by: Heritage House (Publishers) Ltd, 5, King's Road, CLACTON on SEA, CO15 1BG

© Terry Palmer, 1988

All rights reserved. No part of this publication may be reproduced, stored in a retrieval system, or transmitted in any form by any means (except for brief extracts for review purposes) without the written permission of the publisher.

For further reading:

Bible, The
Bodrum and Environs, the town guide, Bod-Info Turizm ve Ticaret Ltd, Bodrum
Classic Myth & Legend A. R. Hope Moncrieff, Gresham Publishing, c 1930
Ephesus, Selahattin Erdemgil, Net Publications, Istanbul 1986
National Geographic Magazine, Nov 1987: Süleyman the Magnificent
National Geographic Magazine, Dec 1987: Oldest known shipwreck
Pamukkale, Sabahattin Türkoğlu, Net Publications, Istanbul, 1986
Penguin Atlas of Medieval History Colin McEvedy, Penguin, 1961
Pergamon, Wolfgang Radt, Türkiye Turing ve Otomobil Kurumu, Istanbul 1984
Sites Bibliques de Turquie Everett Blake & Anna Edmonds, Redhouse Press, Istanbul, 1978 *(in French)*
Turkey, Freya Stark, Thames & Hudson, 1971
Universal Encyclopedia, Educational Book Co, London, undated and long out of print

Acknowledgements:
Norman & Margaret Arrowsmith, Tiptree, Essex; *Sonya Durrell*, Colchester, Essex; *Miss H. Dawson*, King's College Hospital, London; the Turkish Tourist Office, London. And in Turkey: *Mrs Melek Özden, Mr Yasar Tanzan, Mr Kenan Yilmaz.*

Further titles in the "Discover" series include:
DISCOVER MALTA
DISCOVER TUNISIA
DISCOVER GAMBIA
DISCOVER GIBRALTAR
ISBN 185215.0106 £4.95 in the UK

CONTENTS

INDEX TO MAPS

Is this really Turkey? The author at Kuşadası

Terry Palmer was born in the Fenlands of eastern England and has been in search of a mountainous environment ever since, preferably with a sparkling blue sea not far away. Add a mild climate, interesting scenery, a bit of history to stimulate the mind...and the answer, he agrees, is somewhere on the Turkish coast not far from Marmaris. But would he like to live there permanently? "The threat of earthquakes would make me hesitate to buy a house. You don't get many 'quakes in the Fens."

LOCATION MAP

WHY TURKEY?

Turkish delights

TURKEY IS A FASCINATING LAND of strong contrasts, attracting visitors of widely differing interests. The country has many good beaches backed up with landscape of rugged grandeur, and it has some splendid unspoiled resorts still small enough to explore in a day on foot.

But beyond that Turkey has some of the most outstanding Roman architecture in the world — think of places such as Troy, Ephesus, Pergamon, Halicarnassos, Aphrodisias and others; it has that legendary city of İstanbul where east meets west with the world's only intercontinental bridge; it has the troglodyte community of Göreme where seventh-century monks hewed caves from columns of volcanic ash; and it has the Dardenelles and Gallipoli of First World War associations.

It also has a fantastic people: Muslims who live by the Christian calendar, Asians who think of themselves as Europeans, and far to the east those mystic people the Whirling Dervishes.

Şiş Kebap Turkey is also the land of şiş kebap and yoğurt (shish-kebab and yogurt to the west, but we'll follow Turkish spelling in this book), of magic carpets and of steaming baths. The Turkish people are among the friendliest on the shores of the Mediterranean and will go out of their way to help a visitor, sometimes at their own expense. Put the whole package together and you have one of the most interesting holiday locations within easy reach of northern Europe — and that must be a true Turkish delight in itself.

Area The Republic of Turkey, Türkiye Cumhuriet (toor-kee-ya jum-hur-yet), stretches 1,050 miles (1,700 km) from west to east, and 415 miles (650 km) north to south, covering 300,947 square miles (779,452 sq km) and making it marginally smaller than France and the United Kingdom together.

In terms of latitude and longitude, Turkey reaches from 25° 42' E at the island of Gökçeada (gurk-chada), to 44° 22' E at the spot where it touches both Iraq and Iran. Its northernmost cape is at 42° 5' N near Sinop on the Black Sea — the same latitude as Beijing and Detroit — and at its southernmost, at Anamur Point, it registers 35° 57' N, equal to Tanger and the Grand Canyon.

Mount Ararat Its highest point is the celebrated and out-of-bounds territory of Mount Ararat, soaring 16,916 feet (5,165 m) skyward and the legendary resting-place of Noah's Ark.

One of the few countries to straddle a continental divide, Turkey has 97% of its area in Asia, the Asia Minor of ancient times, and the remaining section, Thrace, in Europe. The coastline, covering more than 5,000 miles, is virtually tideless, stretching along the Black Sea (Kara Deniz), the Sea of Marmara (Marmara Denizi), the Aegean (Ege Denizi — aygay deneezee) and the Mediterranean (Ak Deniz). *Ak*, by the way, means 'white.'

Lakes and Mountains The landscape has certain similarities with that of Spain in that the majority of the country is a high but rugged plateau with baking summers and frigid winters. The similarity ends there as Turkey has several large lakes, notably Lake Van (Van Gölü, van gur-loo) in the east and Tuz Gölü south of the capital, Ankara. The main mountain ranges are the Taurus by the Mediterranean, divided into the Batı Toroslar (bat-uh tor-os-

The much-photographed Celcus Library at Ephesus

lar — lar or ler being the Turkish way of forming the plural) behind Antalya, the Orta Toroslar towards Adana, and the Güneydoğu Toroslar (goo-nay-doh-uu) running north of Syria: they are, respectively, the west, central and south-east Taurus ranges, geologically recent and still subject to earth tremors.

The Pontine Mountains, fringing the Black Sea coast, are known to the Turks as Kuzey Anadolu Dağları (daa-lar-uh): Anadolu is the local name for Anatolia and Dağları is the genitive plural of *dağ*, 'mountain.'

Rivers Turkey, basically a dry land, has some rivers which have helped mould early civilizations due more to their strategic importance than their size. The Euphrates, known locally as the Fırat (fuhrat) rises near Erzurum in the east of the country, and the Tigris forms near Batman, south of Erzurum, from two small streams.

In the west the Büyükmenderes (büyük, boo-yook, means 'big' and is a word you should learn) follows a meandering course to enter the Aegean between Kuşhadası (koo-sha-da-suh) and Bodrum (bod-rum). The river's sinuous course is to be expected when you realise that Menderes has become anglicised to *meander*, and gave us that verb.

Turkey's neighbours are a motley collection of countries: Bulgaria and Russia in the Communist block; troubled Iran; Iraq and Syria in the Arab world; and Greece, with whom Turkey has had frequent differences of opinion over the ages, most recently in Cyprus.

Although 98.2% of its population is Muslim, Turkey uses the Christian (Gregorian) calendar. The switch-over began on 1 March 1917 with the calendar's introduction and was completed on 26 December 1925, when the Moslem calendar was dropped. The official day of rest is Sunday though Friday is the holy day; there is equality of the sexes in theory and in practise; and if you see a veiled woman in the streets you can bet she's a foreigner.

Turkey and Egypt are the only Moslem states to maintain diplomatic relations with Israel, and there's a Jewish community in İstanbul as well as a few Christian churches around the land. Turkey is, to put it mildly, unique.

BEFORE YOU GO

Doing your homework

A FIRST JOURNEY TO TURKEY needs careful preparation. This chapter gives an essential background to your planning.

PASSPORTS and VISAS

All foreigners visiting Turkey need a valid passport. Citizens of the USA, Canada, Australia, New Zealand and all western European countries including Greece, Iceland and Malta *but excluding Sweden* may enter without a visa; all but the Portuguese may stay three monnths. The Portuguese may stay for two months while the Swedes, like the Israelis, need a visa for their three-month entitlement. Holders of South African and Greek Cypriot passports may have visas stamped on a loose-leaf insert on request.

There is no restriction on entry for people who have visited Israel or South Africa and have the relevant frontier stamps in their passports.

For interest, citizens of Iran may enter with merely a passport but Iraqis, Syrians, Soviets and Bulgarians, whose countries also border Turkey, need visas.

For further information, contact your Turkish Information office.

INFORMATION OFFICES

United Kingdom and Ireland: First floor, 170 Piccadilly, LONDON W1V 9DD (01.734.8681-2).

United States and Canada: 821 United Nations Plaza, NEW YORK, NY 10017; 2101 Massachusetts Ave NW, WASHINGTON, DC 20036.

Belgium: Rue Montoyer 4, 1040 BRUXELLES.

Denmark: Vesterbrogade 11A, 1620 V KØBNHAVN.

Germany: Baselerstrasse 37, 6000 FRANKFURT am MAIN 1.

Netherlands: Herengracht 451, 1017 BS AMSTERDAM.

Sweden: Kungsgatan 3, 111 43 STOKHOLM.

Spain: Torre de Madrid piso 13°, Plaza de España, MADRID 28008.

MONEY MATTERS

The Turkish lira, shown as TL on price tags, is a moderately hard currency: you can buy it at your bank before setting out and sell any surplus when you return. It's advisable to take some lira as there's little scope for changing currency at the airports, particularly on night flights.

There's no limit to the amount of currency you can take into Turkey, but you may export no more than US$1,000 worth in any currency, though as the dollar slips this figure may be revised.

You should keep receipts for money changed as there's a small risk of being asked to show them if you convert surplus lira before leaving the country; you may also have to establish the origin of your lira if you take home a carpet or item of similar value. In the unwise and unlikely event that you brought in all your spending money as lira, you should carry the receipt issued by your bank at home.

There's no shortage of banks in Turkey. The principal one is the Merkez Bankası (mer-*kez* bank-a-suh), the Central Bank, but there are 44 others, many of whom advertise on hoardings in the countryside. The Yapı ve

Credi (yap-uh vay credee) is a leading financier of house purchase as well as a prominent advertiser.

Exchange Most commercial banks have currency exchange counters with staff fluent in at least one European language. In the resorts they operate a rota so that one bank is open on Saturday morning, and some branches also open the exchange counter on a Sunday morning.

Business hours Banking hours are nominally 0900 to 1200 and 1300 to 1700 Monday to Friday.

Banks will accept a wide range of currencies in notes and travellers' cheques, and many will cash cheques on European banks with the appropriate guarantee card, but finding who will cash whose can be tiresome.

Perhaps the easiest and safest way is to draw lira as required on Visa, Access or American Express cards (but read on!), subject to domestic regulations, with the bank taking a 2% commission.

Post Offices The PTT or Post Office is heavily into the currency exchange business and as the telephone agencies of the larger PTTs never close — officially, that is — it's theoretically possible to change currency outside banking hours, but within reason.

Leading hotels and travel agents offer competitive rates for changing currency but they deduct a larger commission. Money changers in Turkey are licensed and you could find yourself in trouble if you're caught changing money elsewhere.

There's a black market in foreign currency but as it's an internal matter you're not likely to come in contact with it. The government is desperately short of hard currency and has therefore put severe restrictions on the amount of lira its own people can spend abroad. This has put pressure on traders to accept dollars and Deutschmark in place of lira to sell at a premium to intending travellers, but there's no incentive for the visitor to pay in 'hard' cash, and the fall of the dollar has added another complication to the problem.

Credit and charge cards

Access, Visa and American Express are easy to use in banks, with Diners Club less acceptable. They're also convenient for hiring cars from the firms of international repute but, beyond that, their use is restricted with many hotels even in the three-star category not accepting every card and some not accepting any.

Plastic money is useless for buying petrol and bus and train tickets, though at the other extreme there are many backstreet souvenir shops in the top resorts whose proprietors have caught onto the plastic-card craze, mainly with Access and Visa. You'll certainly be able to buy your carpet with a card.

Place little reliance on the lesser-known credit or charge cards but be prepared for the exception as Turkey is very much a land of surprises.

Currency

Banknotes in circulation are for 50, 100, 500, 1,000, 5,000 and 10,000 lira and there are coins for 10, 25, 50 and 100 lira. The kuruš, or piastre, worth a hundredth of a lira, has fallen victim to inflation , and in practise you may be in Turkey several days before you see your first coin. You will need a purse or money-belt to hold your wad of low-denomination banknotes, unless the Government revives its plan to bring in a 100-for-one issue.

Inflation was rife in the 1970s, reaching 130% per annum, and this table shows it's still a long way from being under control.

October 1982, £1 300TL   October 1983, £1 245TL
October 1984, £1 500TL   October 1985, £1 790TL
October 1986, £1 700TL   October 1987, £1 1,500TL

STUDENT DISCOUNTS

Despite the plunging lira, holders of International Student Identity Cards can get discounts of 10% on almost all services operated by THY, the Turkish Airlines, by Turkish Maritime Lines, and Turkish State Railways.

There are identical reductions available on the coach services connecting İstanbul with Munich and Vienna, and a 20% reduction for ISIC holders on the Paris coach, provided they are not older than 26.

Cinemas and concert halls grant up to 50% discount for ISICs, but this is little inducement as most of the performances are in Turkish.

In addition, THY offers 50% discounts for groups of sportspeople and for children from 2 to 12, with a 90% discount for toddlers who don't occupy a seat.

Other cards also qualify for reductions, but the response is less predictable.

The granting of ISICs has become a racket in certain parts of the world and they are available for around five Egyptian pounds in Cairo on production of a letter of introduction from a university: fake introductory letters are also available for a small sum. There are black markets for ISICs in a number of European cities.

TOUR OPERATORS

This list of British tour operators offering holidays in Turkey is compiled from the *ABC Holiday Guide* and the *St James's Press Holiday Guide*. It's not exclusive, and is offered as an indication of what's available. Travel agents have further details and addresses.

Key:

A	archaeological	S	traditional package summer holidays
Aa	architectural		
AP	art & painting	SC	self-catering
C	city holidays	T	tailor-made
Ca	camping	W	holidays in winter (not winter sports)
Cu	cultural		
F	flight only	WS	water sports
FD	fly-drive (but not exclusively so)	X	specialist
		Y	yachting and sailing
H	historical	(B)	featuring Bodrum
M	coach holidays	(C)	featuring Çeşme
P	pilgrimages & religious	(K)	featuring Kuşadası
R	rail tours	(M)	featuring Marmaris
RW	rambling & walking	(O)	featuring Ölüdeniz

The tour operators:

Aegean Turkish Holidays
FD,M,S,T,(B),(K)
Allegro Holidays S,W,(C),(M)
Arrowsmith Holidays S,(B),(M)
Balkan Holidays
M,S,(B),(C),(K)
Beach Villas SC,(B)

Biggles F
Bladon Lines S,(B)
Cambrian S,(B),(K)
Camper & Nicholson S,W,Y
Castlemain Marine S,W,Y
Celebrity Holidays
F,M,S,(B),(K),(M),(O)
Contiki (18-35) X,M,S
Cosmos Tourama M,S

11

Cresta F,W
CV Travel Cu,SC,(B),(O)
Dema F,S,W
Enterprise M,S
Excalibur X (exclusive luxury)
Europcar M,S
Fairways & Swinford A,H
Falcon Sailing WS,Y,(B),(M)
First Resort Holidays SC,(O)
Global Tours S
Golden Horn Travel
FD,T,W,(B),(C),(K),(M)
HF Holidays AP,RW
Halsey Marine S,W,Y
Horizon S
Intasun S,(B),(K)
Inter Church Travel Cu,H,P,W
Island Sailing Y,S
Jasmin Tours W
Karounides X (air tours)
Kuoni R
Lancaster S,(B),(K)
Lamington Travel M,S,Y,(K)
McCabe Travel P
Mark Warner WS,S,(B),(K)
Metak Holidays F,S,W,(B),(C)
Olympic R,Y
Panorama S
Poundstretcher S
Orientours P
Panorama S,(M)
P&O Air Holidays R

Premier Faraway Holidays R
Ramblers M,S
Regent Holidays
F,M,W,X,(B),(K),(M)
Saga M,S,X
Serenissima & Heritage
Aa,Cu,H,R,S
Skyworld S
Slade Travel C,W
Society Expeditions W
Sovereign M,S,W
Steepwest Holidays
SC,(B),(K),(M)
Sunmed S,SC,(B),(K),(M),(O)
Sunquest FD,M,S,W,(B),(C),(K)
Sunstart S,(M)
Swan Hellenic AP,Cu,W
Thomson C,Cu,S,W
Timsway S,(B),(K)
Top Deck Travel S,W,X
Touropa, W,X,(K)
Trafalgar Travel M,S
Transglobal X,S
Travelscene S,W
Trek Europa X
Twickers World H,S,W
UK Express F,M,W,(K)
Vivair F,W
Voyages Jules Verne R,X
Wings,M,S,(B),(K)
YHA Travel Ca

WHERE, WHAT AND WHEN?

Turkey has such a vast range of attractions that this is no easy question. Luckily it's possible to combine several interests in one visit.

Beach holidays

If your holiday plans centre around a beach, you should head for the popular resorts on the Aegean and Mediterranean: Kuşhadası, Bodrum, Marmaris, and Fethiye for the Ölüdeniz, the 'Dead Sea.' Slightly less known are Çeşme, Datça, and Kaş overlooking the Greek island of Kastellorison, then Çavuş and Alanya.

Less favoured for Europeans are the Black Sea resorts of Şile, 70 km east of İstanbul and a weekend favourite for the city dwellers, Zonguldak, Sinop and, in the far east, Trabzon.

These resorts face north and the coastal scenery is less exotic, which are good enough reasons for them to be less favoured by the sun-seeking Europeans, therefore there's less English spoken. You could consider them if you're adamant about a Turkish holiday, must come in high season, but dread excessive heat.

There are several small beach resorts, some of them difficult to reach and with an obvious dearth of night-life. You need a basic knowledge of Turkish or should be a lover of isolation to appreciate these locations.

Swimming The swimming season along the Mediterranean coast extends from early April to mid October, with high summer sometimes very hot as in August 1987 when shade temperatures exceeded 100°F (44°C) for several days. On the Aegean the season is from mid April to early October, and on the Black Sea from June to September.

Caution The waters around Turkey may be nearly tideless, but they still have currents. Don't swim out to sea from a headland, and be wary of undercurrents, particularly within range of the Bosporus's outlet to the Black Sea.

These are sample temperatures — air,sea — in degrees Celcius:

	January	April	July	October
İzmir	8,11	25,15	27,26	17,21
Antalya	10,17	16,18	28,27	20,25
Trabzon	7,10	11,10	23,24	16,20

Archaeology

Turkey's ancient relics are in the same class as Egypt's Pyramids and Peru's Machu Picchu, but they haven't had the same publicity. Ephesus, near Kuşadası, is so well restored that some of the buildings could be made habitable simply by reroofing, yet the city was thriving 2,700 years ago. Pergamon is a hilltop metropolis covering many acres; Hierapolis still has a well-preserved Roman theatre, as do Kaunus, Milet, Asklepion, and many more, though the most famous of them all, Troy, can offer little more than a few stones and a modern wooden horse.

Without exception, these ancient cities are either within sight of the Aegean or are an easy coach ride inland. Even if you've never bothered with ruins before, it would be a pity to visit Turkey and not see at least one site, preferably Ephesus.

History

Turkey's early history focused on such unknown peoples as the Urarti and the Hatti as well as the better-known Hittites, all of whom lived in remote communities in Anatolia. Then came the Greek and Roman tribes who populated the Aegean and Mediterranean coastlines, followed by Byzantines, Seljuks, Persians, Arabs and Ottoman Turks, who have all left their mark on the country and its peoples.

History features such fairytale characters as Midas, Croesus and Darius, the warriors Alexander and Constantine who both earned the epithet 'Great,' the saints Peter and John with the Virgin Mary, classical heroes Antony and Cleopatra, and finally the Ottoman Sultan Süleiman the Magnificent.

In most countries you can ignore history if it doesn't interest you, but Turkish history stimulates its own interest and astounds you with up to 200 Graeco-Roman theatres, cities that are thousands of years old, and a heritage of castles and caravanserais dotted across the country.

Culture and Folklore

The most unusual and picturesque examples of Turkish folklore are undoubtedly the Whirling Dervishes, centred on Konya. Their founder was Celaleddin Rumi, born around 1207. The son of an Islamic scholar, Rumi created his own meditative and quasi-religious sect when he withdrew from worldly affairs after his spiritual mentor had been murdered. He devised a form of worship-dance in which the performer spins on the left heel with right palm raised to receive God's bessing, left palm turned down to pass the blessing to earth.

The Mevlevi, 'followers of the guide,' spread into Syria and Egypt with several factions mutilating themselves or swallowing burning coals or live snakes.

The Turkish Dervishes had great influence in the Ottoman Empire but Atatürk saw them as a threat to unification of the modern state and banned their religious activities. They survive today as a cultural attraction rather than a cult, and the Mevlana Festival in December and the green-tiled mausoleum of Mevlana Rumi are the main points of interest in modern Konya.

The cave-dwelling community of Göreme near Kayseri is another major attraction. In the valley of the Kızılırmak River, red and yellow volcanic ash from nearby Erciyes Dağı (3,917 m) has been eroded over the millennia to leave tall conical pillars of soil, each protected by a naturally-occurring boulder. Monks dug their chapels into these cones which not only dominate the conventional houses lying between them but give a surrealist atmosphere to the region. Students of religious history can see the story of early and medieval Christianity in the chapels' decorations.

Turkish culture includes several folk-dances whose merit has been overshadowed by the Dervishes. Among them, the Spoon Dance, Kaşık Oyunu, is perfomed in the Taurus Mountains between Silifke on the coast, and Konya; and the Sword-and-Shield Dance, the Kılıç Kalkan, is kept alive in Bursa.

The Dervishes go on international tours, which is probably the best opportunity of seeing them as Konya is more than 3,000 feet high on the Anatolian plateau and the December weather is harsh.

Skiing

Turkey is some way from entering the big world of organised winter sports as can be seen from the very limited amount of accommodation available at its resorts and the almost total absence of après-ski. Not a single British winter sports operator features Turkey and, bearing in the mind the difficult motoring conditions in Anatolia in winter and the remoteness of some of the resorts, it's doubtful whether many of them will ever graduate into the next league, no matter how good they may be. By the way, the Turkish for 'ski' is *kayak*.

There are two ski centres which might interest western Europeans eager for a bit of aventure: Köroğlu and Uludağ.

Köroğlu The resort is near the junction of the E80 İstanbul to Erzurum highway and the E89 turnoff for Ankara, 125 km from the capital and the nearest railway and airport. The two hotels have 400 beds, a swimming pool, and ski lift to the slopes lying between 1,900 and 2,200 m. Equipment and instructors are available.

Uludağ The Turkist Tourist Office considers this the best resort in the country, with appeal enhanced by its name, Great Mountain, and the mountain itself was formerly called Olympus of Mysia. At 36 km south-east of Bursa on the Sea of Marmara it's easy to reach from western Europe (three hours travelling time by bus from İstanbul), has 3,000 beds available in accommodation ranging from good hotels to family chalets, and is the only resort to offer après-ski. There are three chair lifts, three ski-lifts, slalom courses, nursery slopes, and a small hospital for the unfortunate. The resort lies high on Ulu Dağ from 2,000 m almost to the summit at 2,543 m. Equipment and instructors are available and the season runs from January to April.

Thermal Resorts

Turkey is in an earthquake zone (though you'd never believe it on seeing some of the concrete-skeleton buildings currently going up), and the geothermal activity has created around 1,000 hot springs, mainly in the western part of the country.

Çeşme, whose name in English is 'fountain,' and Pamukkale, are described in detail in the relevant section, but there are other centres where thermal springs have been commercialised.

Bolu A 250-bed spa near Bolu on the E80 170km north-west of Ankara. Waters at 44°C hold calcium and sulphates and benefit sufferers of rheumatism and gynaecological disorders.

Bursa Spas for sufferers of rheumatism and skin disorders with waters containing sulphates, sodium and magnesium up to 78°C.

Gönen North of Balikesir, Gönen has a 150-bed resort for treating skin, nervous and urinary complaints. The waters reach 82°C.

Harlek By the village of Ilica, north of Küthaya, which is south-west of Eskişehir. Waters from 25°C to 43°C suitable for drinking or bathing, for sufferers of rheumatic, nervous and urinary disorders, contain calcium and magnesium.

Hüdayi Near Sandıklı, south-west of Afyon, a 100-bed resort with fluoride, bromide and sodium in its waters; treats metabolic disorders.

Ilğin At 87 km from Konya on the Afyon road this resort is short on accommodation but has a good clinic. Radioactive waters at 42°C treat a wide range of disorders.

Kızılcahamam On the Bolu road, 86 km north of Ankara, this spa is 975 m above sea level. Its waters, at 50°C, are used in treating rheumatic and digestive problems.

Sakar North of Eskişehir near Sarıcakaya. Sciatica and rheumatism are among the ailments treated with these 54°C waters.

Caution Some motor policies don't cover drivers 'travelling for the purpose of obtaining medical treatment.'

Sightseeing There's plenty to see in Turkey, and not only because it's such a large country. In addition to the archaeological sites there's a wealth of interest in Istanbul, starting with the Topkapı Palace; the Blue Mosque of Sultan Ahmet; the Haghia Sophia Mosque, now a museum; the Grand Bazaar; the Bosphorus Bridge; two sets of city walls, and many other attractions.

Göreme and Pamukkale should figure on the list, as should the coastal scenery and the open plateau of Anatolia untouched by tourism. And in the east, there's Lake Van, the Monastery of the Virgin in Trabzon, and the chance to glimpse Mount Ararat, though not to climb it.

Family Holidays

Family holidays with young children would naturally centre on the coastal resorts where life has less surprises, where English is widely spoken, and where there are beaches, restaurants, comfortable hotels, and ice cream. The list of British tour operators indicates those who offer conventional holidays in or near Bodrum, Çeşme, Kuşhadasıı, Marmaris and Ölüdeniz. The season is from April to mid October in the south, slightly shorter on the Aegean, and July and August are not only the hottest but also the busiest months; avoid them if you can.

Beach activities at Kadınlar, Kuşadası

WHAT TO TAKE

The English word 'supermarket' can be seen over a few shops in Turkey but the concept of the supermarket has not yet arrived. Prepacking of food is still in its infancy, which may not be a bad thing, but it means there's very little which is familiar to western European eyes. If you want your own suntan lotion or even a special cereal and can carry it, take it. If you want your own brand of coffee, by all means take it as the Turkish variety has a flavour which isn't immediately palatable. Many restaurants offer *kahve* (coffee) and *Nescafé* as if they're completely different items; in Turkey that's not far from the truth.

Take all the film you need as it's expensive in Turkey and is sometimes left on display in shop windows in the full sun for months. The X-ray scanners at the airports don't harm film of rating lower than 1,000 ASA; I've had a film scanned four times with no ill effect.

People intending to travel beyond the bounds of the resort should take a small water bottle with a good cap — it's surprising how quickly you can become thirsty on a hot day — and a toilet roll. Don't ask why: you'll probably find out!

And for those intending to travel further afield, a lightweight sleeping bag is useful. In the cheaper pensions and hotels the sheets are changed only when they get dirty.

DISABLED

Turkey is a difficult destination for anybody confined to a wheelchair. There are so few in use in the country that there is no provision at all for the disabled. Kerbs are up to a foot high; pavements, even in cities, are for the nimble-footed; and shops, hotels and offices have anything from one step to twenty outside the door.

It is virtually impossible for a disabled person to board a bus, including those serving the airports, and there are far too many passengers in the average dolmuş (mini-bus, explained later).

Given sufficient determination a disabled person could see a limited amount of the country and enjoy the beaches, provided there is always a strong helper at hand. Transport would need to be by hired car or taxi from the airport and back to it and it's advisable to check with the tour operator *and* with the hotel that all conveniences are accessible. Despite these constraints, several tour operators cater for the handicapped.

WOMEN TRAVELLING ALONE

Turkey is surprisingly safe for a western woman travelling alone, provided she takes the same precautions she would at home. Indeed, she will probably be safer in Turkey than in many other countries, including her own.

Turkish men treat their womenfolk with respect but some of the youths like to proclaim their supposed superiority, the most effective response being to ignore them completely.

Despite its equality, the female half of the Turkish population goes out alone far less than women of the Teutonic races, and teenage girls are almost never seen on the street on their own. It's the result of convention and the teachings of Islam, rather than the fear of being molested.

It's stating the obvious, but a solitary woman should never dress provocatively and should behave as if she's totally competent to look after herself, which she certainly needs to be in the remoter areas — but so does a man.

Turkish women don't travel long distances alone and it's inconceivable for one to book into a hotel without a companion. This puts a strain on the European woman travelling solo as she may find herself the only female staying in a small pension with a motley assortment of men, some in their long underpants washing at a communal basin early in the morning. However, a growing number of young women are backpacking on their own around Turkey with no special problems caused by their sex, in fact some of them believe the older Turkish men admire them for their audacity.

HEALTH

There is no need for any precaution against cholera, typhoid or polio and Turkey is two thousand miles from the malaria belt, though it has its share of mosquitos and other annoying insects: women with sensitive skins may care to take an insect repellent.

Rabies is here as in most of Continental Europe but the risk of contracting the disease is minuscule; there were 21 deaths in Turkey in 1986 from a population of 50 million. The precaution is simple — don't become involved with animals, particularly the large number of stray cats and kittens.

The malady which is most likely to strike is the Turkey trots, the local variation of Spanish tummy or Delhi belly, which on one occasion a few years ago affected almost every foreign visitor at a certain location on the second day. The authorities concerned did their best to trace the origins of that outbreak, but the problem is still there.

Provided the illness is nothing more than diarrhoea there is little to worry about, although it can be extremely inconvenient. The cause could be any of several: the calcium in the water loosening the bowels, the chlorine in the water upsetting the digestive system, bacteria in pre-cooked food not being killed on re-heating, or one's natural lack of immunity to the bugs in this part of the world.

The remedy is simple: switch to mineral water — Niksar is a popular brand and has no more than 2.5 mg of calcium per litre — and eat only the most basic of foods such as bread and honey for a day or two.

If the problem persists into the second day, go to a chemist — the word is *eczane* (ej-zah-ner) — for some Kemicetine capsules (take one every six hours) and some Becozyme C forte (they're also available in Europe: take one after meals). 200mg of Emedur taken two or three times a day, half an hour before meals, is the prescription for vomiting. This recommendation, supplied by a Turkish doctor, will cost around 3,000TL.

And if that doesn't do the trick, go see the doctor yourself. He'll almost certainly have done some of his training in Europe or USA so there'll be no language barrier and while he'll make a charge it won't be exhorbitant. Nor will a day or two in a state hospital, though you'll be expected to pay more if you go to the excellent American Hospital (Amerikan Hastanesi) at Güzelbahçe Sok, Nişantaşı, in İstanbul.

Should you be among the very few people to contract food poisoning, don't ignore it. The symptoms are headache, fluctuating temperature, diarrhoea and stomach pains. The remedy is to go to bed for a day or two, keep warm, drink as much as you can, preferably weak tea without milk, and to eat as little as possible.

COST OF LIVING

Turkey is a ridiculously cheap country for European visitors, but the story is somewhat different if you happen to be a Turk. These prices were noted when the lira stood at 1,500 to the pound sterling (1,000 to the US dollar) and allowances must be made for subsequent inflation.

Man's shirt, cheap, in market	2,500TL
Man's leather slip-on shoes	4,000-4,500TL
Turkish coffee powder, sold loose	10,000TL/kg
Standard loaf	100TL
Seasonal produce: large melon	50-150TL
tomatoes	200-400TL/kg
grapes	400-600TL/kg
apples	400-600TL/kg
pears	800-1,000TL/kg
Cigarettes, pack of 20 imported	800TL
Cigarettes, pack of 20, Turkish	300TL
75cl bottle Scotch (any brand) in shop	4,500TL
50cl bottle of beer in shop	450-500TL
(600TL in a bar, 1,000TL in night club)	
Minimum letter rate to Europe	200TL
Coach journey, İstanbul to Göreme	7,000TL
THY flight, İstanbul to Antalya	42,500TL (basic)
Night for 2, no breakfast, average pension	7,000TL
Dinner for 2, smart restaurant, with wine	20,000-30,000TL
Dinner for 2 in locanta, no wine	5,000-7,000TL
Gin and tonic in bar	1,500TL
Handmade silk rug 15"x21," excellent quality	340,000TL
Rent for smart house Bodrum for season	7,500**DM** monthly
Purchase of ditto	50,000,000 to 90,000,000TL
Skilled tradesman's basic income	*25,000TL weekly*
Peasant's average income	*45,000TL monthly*

LANGUAGE

So you don't speak a word of Turkish? No problem. In the resorts everybody whose trade *depends* on tourism speaks English and German to some degree, often to fluency. French is in a comfortable third place with no other language worth mentioning, not even Greek or Arabic, though exceptionally you may meet somebody with a flair for languages who has mastered Swedish or Norwegian.

Note, however, that the operative word is 'depend': police, bus drivers, clerks at the PTT and similar people seldom know more than 50 words of another language.

Beyond the resorts the situation is different. During the days of the German economic miracle, many young Turks drifted westward to work, and these former Gästarbeiter, now in their 30s and 40s, will often be your only linguistic contact — in German, and with varying degrees of fluency.

The lycees, the better-class secondary schools, teach English, but conversation with a ten-year-old boy who is still puzzled by *sing-sang-sung* will seldom produce answers to the vital questions of the day. Turks recognise the importance of English as a world language and a few people from many occupations are managing to learn something of it, but their vocabulary is limited.

Many older men of wealthier families, particularly in Cappadocia (eastern Anatolia) still speak the French they learned at school, which can frequently be useful. As far as Turkish interests are concerned, Spanish doesn't exist.

Off the beaten track, then, you'll often be reduced to sign language. Have no fear; it's surprising how quickly you can communicate basic needs without uttering a word.

Tartar The Turkish language originated in central Asia and is in a separate linguistic family with Tartar and Kirghiz. As the Turks moved south-west to their present homeland they came into contact with Islam and borrowed a number of Arabic words along with the script. Kemal Atatürk introduced the Latin alphabet in 1928, and in 1932 a language purification society, Türk Dil Kurumu, began creating a unified language and finding Turkish equivalents for Arabic words. Despite the *dil kurumu*, which is still at work, Turkish is borrowing European words to create its *fabrika, istasyon, lastik, oto* and *sandviç* (factory, station, tyre, car, sandwich).

The language today is spoken throughout Turkey, in the Turkish Republic of Northern Cyprus, eastern Bulgaria, and beyond the Caspian Sea in the southern USSR: the name of the soviet republic of Kara Kalpak south of the Aral Sea translates into English as 'black fur cap.'

Alphabet The Turkish alphabet has 29 letters. It has dropped Q, W and X and has added Ç, Ğ, İ, Ö, Ş and Ü, which have their own set places in the order of things so that *şah*, 'shah,' comes after *su*, 'water.'

All letters are pronounced as in English *except:*

C, as 'J' in 'jam;' **G**, always hard, as in 'gun;' **J**, as 'ZH' or the French 'J;' **U**, as 'U' in 'murder.'

The extra letters: **Ç**, as 'CH' in 'church;' **Ğ** has no sound; it lengthens the consonant in front of it, thus the Turkish word *yoğurt* should be pronounced 'yooort.'

Ğ never begins a word. **I**, lower case ı is unstressed, as the 'e' in 'the man,' thus *Topkapı* is really 'top-kap-uh.' Note, therefore, that what we consider the normal lower case i, has as its capital, İ.

Ö, a longish 'er,' as the German Ö; **Ş**, as 'SH' in 'shop;' **Ü**, as 'OO' in 'too;'
The circumflex, ˆ over a character doesn't constitute a separate letter; it

19

modifies the pronunciation. With â, î and û (that's an 'i', by the way, not an 'ı'), pronounce them as 'ya,' 'yi' and 'yu.'

As the difference between I and İ has such an influence in pronouncing Turkish, we have tried to retain the correct spelling throughout this book even though it meant dotting every İ by hand. Our typesetter has the capacity to handle all the other accents we throw his way.

Turkish is not an easy language for a European as it's not like any other he's likely to know. Obviously the vocabulary is a major problem with every word needing to be learned, but there are compensating factors. The pronunciation is totally regular, there are no genders to complicate nouns and adjectives, and there is no word for 'the.'

However, the agglutinating character of Turkish makes it formidable on the printed page. Core words can have all kinds of suffixes tagged onto them, changing an adjective to a noun to a verb, and even to the equivalent of an English phrase, yet it is still just one word.

The plural of nouns is -ler or -lar, which is also the third person plural of verbs, hence 'the girls (daughters) have come (came)' is *kızlar geldiler*, which is some consolation towards simplicity.

Foreign words inevitably creep into Turkish and are spelled phonetically. *Oto* is easily recognised as 'auto' but would you recognise these as a British world statesman and an American make of car: *Çörçil, Şevrole*? There's perhaps a hint of humour in the word *sözcü*, meaning 'spokesman.' Sez you?

BASIC VOCABULARY

This is no place to begin teaching Turkish but it's very useful to have access to a basic vocabulary. If you want to learn the language, get *Elementary Turkish* by L. V. Thomas, Dover Pub'ns, Sep 1986, and a Langenscheidt dictionary: the pocket size is useful for when you're travelling.

Turkish is like French in that each syllable should carry equal stress; for English speakers, who tend to emphasise the beginning of the word, it has the effect of making it sound as though Turkish words are stressed at the end.

1	bir	bee-r	21	yirmi bir,	etc
2	iki	ee-kee	30	otuz	oh-tuz
3	üç	ooch	40	kirk	kurk
4	dört	durt	50	elli	el-lee
5	beş	besh	60	altmiş	alt-mush
6	altı	al-tuh	70	yetmiş	yet-mish
7	yedi	ye-dee	80	seksen	sek-sen
8	sekiz	se-keez	90	doksan	dok-san
9	dokuz	doh-kooz	100	yüz	yooz
10	on	on	101	yüz bir,	etc
11	on bir,	etc	200	iki yüz,	etc
20	yirmi	yeer-mee	1,000	bin	been
			1,000,000	milyon	mil-yohn

(seen on taps on the roadside and in other public places:)

not drinkable	içilmez
drinkable	içilir

Railway station	istasyon
Train	tren
Bus station	otogar
Bus	otobüs
Hotel	otel
Pension	pansiyon
A cheap hotel	ucuz bir otel
Baggage	bagaj
Left luggage office	bagaj depositu
Airport	hava alanı
Ticket	bilet
single	gidiş
return	gidiş-donüş
Toilet	tuvalet
men's	bay
women's	bayan
Bread	ekmek
Cheese	peynir
Butter	tereyağ
Beer	bira
Wine	şarar
Gin	cin
Coffee	kahve
Tea	çay
Apple	elma
Pear	armut
Water	su
Sugar	şeker
Breakfast	kahvaltı
Dinner	esas yemek
Bill	hesap
restaurant	restoran
"	lokanta
pastry shop	pastane
pizzeria	pideci
meat ball restaurant	köfteci
kebab restaurant	kebapçı
bakery	ekmekçi

Yes	evet
No	hayır
Please	lütfen
Thanks	teşekkür ederim
"	mersi
Sorry (pardon)	affedersiniz
Hello	merhaba
Goodbye (said by person going)	Allaha ısmarladık
	(al-lah'smarla-duk)
Goodbye (response from person remaining)	
	güle güle
Good morning	çünaydın
Good day	iyi günler
Welcome	hoş geldiniz
(response:)	hoş bulduk

ISLAM

...and other religions

THE WORD 'ISLAM' means submission to God's will, and Islam is indeed a strict religion, demanding its followers show that submission in their daily life and prayers.

Islam is the faith first propounded by Mahomet, sometimes spelled Muhammed, and gathered into the holy book, the Koran. Mahomet's forcefulness set Islam on its course and it now has more than 460 million believers from Morocco to Indonesia, from Tashkent to Tanzania. Among them is 98 percent of the population of Turkey.

A key point in Islam, as in other monotheist religions, is the fundamental belief in the resurrection, and a world and a life beyond this one; adherents also believe that each person's life follows a preordained pattern and for a few this idea that "it is written" can become an excuse for indecision and inactivity.

The five "commandments" of Islam are the need for faith, as defined in the muezzin's chant from the mosque; the need to pray five times a day; the command for the wealthy to give 2.5 percent of their income to the needy; the observance of Ramadan, the ninth month of the Islamic lunar calendar, by refraining from eating, drinking, smoking, and sexual activity during the daylight hours; and to make a once-in-a-lifetime pilgrimage to Mecca, preferably two months after Ramadan — the Turks call it Ramazan — and dressed in simple clothes which give no hint of wealth or class.

Muezzin The visitor to Turkey will probably find the five daily calls to prayer by the muezzin (moo-ez-een) the most apparent sign that this is a Moslem state. The muezzin is not a preacher — Islam doesn't have priests in the sense that Christianity or Judaism do — but a messenger, who uses the public address system installed on a minaret of every mosque to call the faithful to prayer nominally at sunrise, noon, mid-afternoon, sunset, and late evening, though the first call often comes long before sun-up. The times of prayer are precise to the minute and vary day to day; they can sometimes be found in the newspapers.

There is no insistence that people need to pray at these set times, nor need they go to the mosque to do so, but on Friday, the holy day, they should comply if at all possible.

"La ilaha al Allah" The muezzin's chant is usually indecipherable but he is proclaiming in Arabic what, in English, would be: "God is almighty. I believe there is no god but God, and that Mahomet is his prophet. Come to pray. Come for redemption. God is almighty and there is no god but God."

Mahomet Mahomet was born in Mecca around 570AD and by the age of six was an orphan, raised by his grandfather. Around 612AD, married to a rich widow and with time to meditate, he began hearing the voice of God, giving him the final revelations and urging him to carry the word to all mankind.

When Mahomet tried converting the moon-worshipping Arabs they drove him from the city, and it is this exodus, the *hegira*, which is the starting-point for counting the years in the Islamic calendar. The Gregorian calendar of 365¼ days, now in use in Turkey, dates the event 1,365 years ago, but according to Islam's lunar reckoning we are in the year 1,409.

Mahomet set up home in Medina and began pursuing his God-given command to preach the new religion. He was so successful that eight years after his flight from Mecca he returned to the city as its conqueror and by his death two years later in 632 he was ruler of Arabia, his Koranic law becoming the civil law of the land, as it is today in Islamic fundamentalist countries — but not in Turkey.

At no stage in his life did Mahomet claim to be anything more than a divine messenger, and he has never been considered as a deity or the son of God. His teachings demand that his followers, in their daily prayers, must cleanse themselves spiritually and physically (which is why you always find water available in mosques), and address themselves directly to the supreme deity, not to any of his prophets nor to any idols. The faithful face Mahomet's birthplace as a mark of respect.

Turkey offers total freedom of religion to its citizens and among the 1.7 percent of non-Moslems there are Christians of the Orthodox, Gregorian and Armenian Apostolic sects; there are Chaldeans, Syrian and Greek uniats, Latins (with an archbishop in İzmir) — and there is a community of Sephardim Jews in İstanbul, with its Grand Rabbi.

Turkish mosques, based on the open-courtyard plan of Mahomet's home in Medina, are open to visitors of any faith, but one should avoid going in on Friday and on any other day when the muezzin is calling, and be considerate of anybody at prayer.

Women *must* cover their head and shoulders, and should wear long skirts or trousers, nor should men show much leg above the knee. As Islam demands cleanliness at prayer it is a sin to foul the prayer mats which the faithful will touch with their forehead and hands, therefore everybody must remove shoes at the door.

It's a distinct experience to see inside a mosque, but non-Moslems will find little of interest in any of those in the average small town. The building is used exclusively for religious purposes and lacks the tombstones, wall plaques and parish records of Christian churches, and the cemetery is always some distance away.

The Roman theatre at Hierapolis, by Pamukkale

GETTING THERE

Land, sea or air

THERE ARE SO MANY WAYS to reach Turkey from northern Europe that we are spoiled for choice. They can be divided into the options of overland, by land and sea, or by air, and we'll examine them in those groups.

OVERLAND

A quick glance at any map of Europe shows plenty of roads and railways, making the overland route tempting for someone with the spirit of adventure and a little extra time available. You'll need the time, and you'll certainly find the adventure whether you go by train, by bus, or drive your own car.

Train

The old-style Orient Express on which Agatha Christie planned one of her murders, would have taken us from London to İstanbul in comfort and in reasonable time, but the modern train journey is an ordeal. There are several variations of route but the most obvious one from the United Kingdom starts at London's Victoria at 1300 on Day 1, reaches Cologne at 0137 on Day 2 and goes via Munich (0900), Salzburg, Ljubljana (1700) to Zagreb, arriving at 2014 on Day 2 and departing at 0145 on Day 3. Then on via Belgrade (0724 to 0935) and Sofia (1922 to 2022) to Svilengrad (0118 on Day 4), the border town of Kapikule (0246 to 0425) and arriving in İstanbul at 1010 on Day 4.

There is also the complication of needing a Bulgarian transit visa *each way* which, at the time of writing, is available only in your country of origin and costs, in London, £20. You can avoid the visa requirement by diverting via Skopje and Thessaloniki, but it adds even more time. If you're travelling on a South African passport you'll need to divert anyway as the Bulgarians won't let you in.

The *Istanbul Express* is a series of trains starting daily from Munich, Salzburg, Vienna, Paris, Lausanne, Milan and Venice, and converging on Belgrade for the run through Bulgaria. It's also a long haul and the train is frequently late.

Bus

This is much more practical if you're still hungering for adventure; it's also the cheapest.

London

Euroline leaves London's Victoria Coach Station every Friday at 2000 for Brussels where passengers transfer to the İstanbul coach, arriving there on Tuesday at 1100. The return journey starts on Wednesday at 1500, reaching London at 0700 on Sunday, for a fare of £107 single, £177 return.

Amsterdam

The Magic Bus leaves from the Dam, in front of the Royal Palace, on Mondays and Wednesdays, taking two days to reach İstanbul. The 1987 cost was 70,000TL each way, or £50. The Magic Bus address was Incili Cavus Sok, İstanbul, but letters are now being returned.

Paris

Bosfur Turism combines with Eurolines for the route from Paris to İstanbul: contact address is 3 Avenue de la Porte de la Villette, 75019 Paris (40.34.36)

Strasbourg

Contact Varan Tourism, 37 Faubourg de Pierre, 67000 Strasbourg (20.03.87)

Munich

Bosfur Turism, Seidistrasse 2,2, 8000 München 2 (59.50.02). There are connections with other German cities, plus Netherlands, Scandinavia, London, Brussels and the Spanish Mediterranean coast.

Vienna

Bosfur Turism, 1040 Südbahnhof, Argentinierstrasse 67, Wien (65.06.44)

Varan Tourism, Südbahnhof, Südtrolerplatz 7,Wien (65.65.93)   (See "Student discounts" on page 11)

Drive Yourself

This really is asking for adventure, and the rarity of foreign-registered vehicles on Turkey's roads shows that few people have considered it viable. There are 2,000 or so miles between Paris and İstanbul, to be covered both ways — unless you opt for sea travel for some of the journey.

Officially, both Greek and Turkish customs officers enter details of your vehicle on your passport and you're not allowed to leave the country without the vehicle unless you've put it in customs bond: that could make it difficult to take a day trip to one of the Greek islands.

In practise, however, customs officers of both countries are not bothering with the private motorist who's obviously going to drive his car home again.

LAND AND SEA

The choices are, in essence, fourfold: travel overland by bus, train or car to (a) Piraeus, the port for Athens; (b) to Venice; (c) to Ancona on Italy's northern Adriatic coast; or (d) to Brindisi on the heel of Italy. Option (a) infers there's only one Greek port from which to sail to Turkey whereas there are seven, ranging from Rafina just east of Athens, to Alexandroupolis which is only a few miles from Turkey.

To Piraeus

No matter how you travel, it's a four-day journey from London to Athens. The rail service is marginally better as it doesn't get lost in the wilds of Bulgaria; it's a long haul in your own car; and neither Euroline nor the Magic Bus can shorten it.

The Euroline route from London (depart Mondays 2130) is: Paris, 0730; Aosta, 1900; Turin 2130; Milan 2359; Bologna, Florence, Perugia, Rome (0945 on Wednesdays). Then to Brindisi (1800) for the night ferry to Patras and arrive Athens 1930 Thursdays.

Now this is where it gets clever; open a map of the Aegean and make yourself comfortable.

From Piraeus the easier routes are to Chios (Hios) and across to Çeşme; or you can sail from Chios to Lesbos (Lesvos) and so to Ayvalık; or go to Samos and thence to Kuşadası.

Or you can island-hop down the Dodecanese from Patmos to Leros to Kalimnos, to Kos (Cos) and so to Bodrum; or you can continue down to Rhodes (Rodos) and make Turkish landfall at Marmaris.

For details of sailings within the Greek islands, contact the National

Tourist Office of Greece which, in Britain, is at 195 Regent St, London W1R 8DL (01.734.5998).

By whichever means you care to cross the Aegean, you will need to make that last leap to the Turkish mainland. These are the details:

Lesbos to Ayvalık:

The journey from Mytilini (Lesbos) with the Greek ferry takes 2½ hours, departing 1600 hrs and returning from Ayvalık 0830, Monday, Wednesday and Friday only, June to September. There's also a Turkish-owned ferry leaving Mytilini at 1330 and Ayvalık 0900, on the same days for the same season. The winter service from either ferry is once weekly at the most.

Samos to Kuşadası:

Departing daily at 1600 for a 2½ hour journey; leaving Kuşadası at 0830. With the direct link from Samos to Piraeus, this is the most popular island route: ferries leave Samos at 1815 Monday and Wednesday, at 1915 Thursday and Saturday, and at *both* times on Sunday. The single fare in 1987 was 1,750 drachma (roughly £7).

There is a daily ferry link for the 4 hour cruise from Piraeus to Patras (Patra) on the Peloponnese, from where a late-night car ferry sails to Brindisi and on to Ancona.

The Akdeniz Travel & Shipping Agency, Kordon Promenade, Kuşadası is among several local agents handling reservations.

Kos to Bodrum:

Karya Tours of Bodrum (tel 1759) operates the *Büyük Ortak Karyalı I* on the daily summer-only service to Kos, leaving Bodrum at 1030 Monday to Friday and giving 3 hours on Kos; and leaving 0930 on Saturday with 5 hours on Kos. Fares in 1987 were 10,000TL per person single, 15,000TL return, with 100DM (around £33) for a car each way.

In addition the Bodrum-based *Fahri Kaptan I* and *II* offer ferry services on the the Bodrum-Kos run from Neyzen Tevfik Cad 190 (tel 2870), and the *Bodrum Express* sails daily to Körmen and Kos from Neyzen Tevfik Cad 70 (tel 2309). The *Meander*, operated by Gino Tours at the Yat Limanı, (tel 2166) also operates a daily service to Kos.

Then there's the Turkish *m.v. Atalante* which leaves Bodrum at 1600 every Wednesday, June to September, calling at Kos and Piraeus on a Greek island cruise. Booking agency: Merhaba Travel, Iskele Meydanı 67 (tel 1086).

And a Greek-owned ferry has a stake in the market with its own daily summer-only service from Kos on the 1600-out, 0830-return basis.

Chios to Çeşme:

Daily service (excluding Monday) throughout summer; 1 hr crossing; 1600 from Greece, 0830 from Turkey.

Rodos (Rhodes) to Marmaris:

Daily summer service; 3½ hr crossing; 1600 from Rhodes, 0830 from Marmaris.

Where Greek-owned ferries operate the service to Turkey the fare is quoted in US dollars and ranges from $10 on the Bodrum to Kos run, to $25 for the Kuşadası to Samos crossing, per person, one way (discounts for return tickets). Cars are charged by weight, with an approximation being $50 one way.

The drachma lost half its value in five years; the Turkish lira has lost 80 percent in the same time, hence the tendency for operators to quote hard currencies such as the Deutsch Mark, the US dollar, and occasionally sterling. But the dollar is not so almighty after its autumn 1987 slump and the prices quoted will almost certainly be increased in 1988.

Regardless of the currency quoted, the Greek Government influences the fare charged by vessels flying its flag. That fare is prohibitive for the average Turk — not that he'd want to visit Greece, anyway — but the morning deparure from Turkish ports gives foreigners staying in Turkey the chance to visit Greece when the shops are open. The evening sailings from the islands are a deterrent to foreigners staying in Greece who would have to spend a night in Turkey, and see nothing.

From Ancona

The Karageorgis Line operates the service to Patras year-round, with a sailing time of 35 hours and using the ro-ro vessels *Mediterranean Sea* and *Mediterranean Sky*, only one of which sails in winter.

Sailings from Ancona: winter; Wednesday 1300, Saturday 2100. Summer; winter sailings *plus* Monday 2359, Friday 2100.

Sailings from Patras: winter; Friday 0200 (loading Thursday evening), Monday 2100. Summer; winter sailings *plus* Wednesday 2100, Sunday 1300.

Fares range from around £25 to £100; capacity, 800 passengers per ship.

United Kingdom agents: Mak Travel & Tourism, 36 King St, Covent Garden, London WC2 E8JH (01.836.8216).

From Brindisi

The Adriatica Shipping Line operates the year-round service to Patras with sailings on about one day in three in the off-season, on alternate days in June, and every day at Easter and in summer. The two vessels, the *Appia* of 6,100 tons and the *Espresso Grecia* of 5,200 tons, share the load, and are supplemented by a third ship in high season.

The basic timetable is: depart Brindisi at 2230 for Corfu and Igoumenitsa (on the mainland nearby), arriving Patras 1800 next day; the return sailing leaves Patras 2200, calls at Corfu and Igoumenitsa and arrives Brindisi 1700.

There's a high-summer fast service *in addition* which leaves Brindisi daily 2000 arriving Patras 1300; return from Patras 1800 arriving Brindisi 1000.

And from Patras there's the ferry to Piraeus (see earlier) or a bus to Athens, arriving 2200, and the option of all those Aegean routes.

There's a useful train, the "Parthenon," which leaves Paris's Gare de Lyon at 2003 from late June to early September, and connects with the Brindisi ferries.

From Venice

Perhaps you'd like to travel to Turkey in style? Proceed, then, to Venice, by train, bus (there are adequate services) or private limousine and embark on the Turkish Maritime Line's car ferry *Samsun*, which leaves port every Saturday at 2100 hrs.

In high season, late June to mid October, the ship arrives at İzmir on Tuesday at 1100, and at 1600 on Wednesday begins the return trip to Venice, arriving Saturday at 1000.

From early March to late June the *Samsun* leaves İstanbul 1700 Tuesday, calls İzmir 1200 to 1600 Wednesday and arrives Venice 1000 Saturday. Sails Venice 2100 Saturday; İzmir, 1300 to 1600 Tuesday; docks İstanbul Wednesday 1000.

Low-season fares (from İstanbul, and from İzmir from mid-September) range from around £100 to £240 per person; high-season from İzmir only, around £110 to £270; port tax and meals (except breakfast) extra. Cars cost from £80 one way.

For details of this and other Turkish Maritime Line's operations, *including the car ferries from İstanbul to Bandırma and to İzmir,* contact:

United Kingdom: Sunquest Holidays, 9-15 Aldine St, Shepherd's Bush, London W12 8AW (01.749.9933).

Netherlands: Antony Veder Co, Scheepmakers Haven 2, Rotterdam, postbus 1159.

West Germany: RECA-Handels GmbH, Hans Martin Schleyer Str 16, Stuttgart D-7032.

France: Worms cie, 30 Ave Robert Schumann, Marseille 13002.

Switzerland: Natural SA, Sanktjacobstrasse 220, 4002 Basel, Postamtfach 905.

Turkey: Türkiye Denizcilik İşletmeleri, Denizyolları Ac, Rıhtim Cad, Karaköy, İstanbul.

Orient Express

But there's yet another option, which is as much a holiday in itself as a means of travelling to Turkey. You can once more go all the way by Orient Express.

Not by train to İstanbul, of course: that closed some years ago. The much-publicised Venice-Simplon Orient Express which was revived in 1981 goes in luxury from London's Victoria and bills itself as "the world's most romantic adventure." From Venice it connects, much of the time, with the m.v. *Orient Express*, a 12,500 ton luxury ferry-cruiser which went into service in May 1986 on the İstanbul run, berthing within yards of where the old train used to terminate.

This new train-and-ship Orient Express is subject to the dictates of private charter but in essence operates this route:

The *train* leaves London Victoria 1100 Thursday, for Folkestone. In Calais passengers board another luxury train for the run through Paris, Zürich, St Anton, Innsbrück and Verona, arriving Venice 1830 Friday.

The 'Orient Express' arrives at Kuşadası

The *ship* leaves Venice 1800 Saturday for Piraeus (arrives Monday: stays five hours allowing the opportunity to disembark and island-hop to Turkey) and Istanbul (0900 Tuesday). Now things become complicated. The ship sails Tuesday evening for Kuşadası (1030 Wednesday, staying several hours), the Greek island of Patmos, then Katakolon in western Peloponnisos (it does not return via Piraeus), arriving Venice 0800 Saturday.

Further complications: the train goes to Vienna instead of Venice in high summer; neither service is year-round; and they start and finish on different dates. It's luxurious, but it's also expensive: the return train fare can cost more than £1,200 and the ferry could (but needn't) add another £1,000, per person.

For more details contact VSOE Reservations Office:

United Kingdom: 20 Upper Ground, London SE1 9PF (01.928.6000). **France:** phone Paris 47.42.36.28. **Benelux:** phone (02) 513.83.95. **Denmark:** phone (1) 141126; **Finland:** phone (90) 602.711. **West Germany:** phone (069) 230.911.

BY AIR

Thirty-nine airlines operate scheduled services into İstanbul from around the world, among them being such odd neighbours as El-Al and the airlines of Syria and Jordan. From here, Turkey's most prestigious airport, there are direct services to Amsterdam, East Berlin, Brussels, Cologne, Frankfurt, Geneva, Hamburg, London Heathrow, Munich, Paris, Rome, Vienna, Warsaw and Zürich.

Seventeen regional airports in Britain have flights into İstanbul with transfers at Heathrow or continental airports, and there's a flight from Dublin via Frankfurt.

Turkish Airlines, Türk Hava Yolları (toork ha-va yoll-ar-uh) also operates its internal services from İstanbul, serving Adana, Ankara, Antalya, Dalaman, İzmir and Kayseri, with connections to the other airports in Turkey.

İzmir Airport has direct flights to Amsterdam, Heathrow, Munich, Paris, Rome and Zürich, and even Dalaman can boast one international link — to Frankfurt.

Charter airlines concentrate on İzmir with lesser traffic to İstanbul and Antalya, while most package tourists fly to Dalaman (for details of airports, see "Arriving in Turkey," page *XX*)

Travellers looking for an economy seat should try those tour operators who also offer flight-only (see "Tour Operators," page *XX*), or contact the Air Traffic Advisory Bureau (London, 01.636.5000; Manchester, 061.832.2000; Birmingham, 021.783,2000). Both methods will also yield flights originating in northern Europe outside the British Isles.

In addition, travel agents may also have last-minute bargains from the tour operators, including flight-only deals. In this latter event the airport of arrival will usually be Dalaman.

Caution On the map, Rhodes Airport looks convenient for a holiday based in the south-west of Turkey. Resist the temptation. Everybody going to Greece on a charter flight must have genuine accommodation booked in Greece, which excludes the 'token accommodation' letout of most charter operators. This will either make your Turkish holiday more expensive or give you problems with the Greek authorities, or both.

CONNECTIONS TO NORTH CYPRUS

Car ferries and hydrofoils for the Turkish Republic of North Cyprus leave from Taşucu, 4 km west of Silifke, and from Mersin, 88km further east.

Marmaris: Paradise on earth?

Turkish Maritime Lines operates a car ferry between Mersin and Famagusta. Locally, make contact at the docks in Mersin; in Europe use the contacts listed above, 'from Venice.'

The Ertürk company operates the Taşucu to Girne (Cyprus) run; local contact is the bus station in Silifke or the Tourist Office at Atatürk Cad, Taşucu. From Europe with time to spare, write or phone the company's office in Bodrum (see 'Bodrum - tour operators') where you'll stand a better chance of an English-speaking contact.

The Uğur company runs a thrice-weekly hydrofoil service from Taşucu to Cyprus; on the spot information is available from the bus station or tourist office.

PACKAGE or INDEPENDENT?

For a family holiday with young children there is no option: you must buy a package. But for the traveller with the spirit of adventure, going independently either solo or in a small group, Turkey offers the type of challenge that is fast fading from our lives.

For the go-it-aloner the obvious problem — or challenge — is language. Turkish is a central Asian tongue and its only similarity with any European language is in a few borrowed words. The package tourist will avoid all difficulties with communication, and with food, accommodation and travel, but he will also lose some of the flavour of the true Turkey.

The language barrier becomes worse as you penetrate Anatolia or the remoter eastern provinces, but the adventurer will soon learn a few essential words, and sign language — if not rudimentary French or German — will fill in the gaps.

Package tourists will have a choice of excursions but will need to compromise on the time spent on each: you could spend a day at Pamukkale and not have the chance to see nearby Aphrodisias. The independent traveller will need to do his homework and even then may miss some locations, Troy being a prime example. However, Turkey is an easy country in which to travel, the people are friendly and appreciate the language barrier (it works both ways), and it's a real adventure to buy a train ticket or reserve a hotel room without speaking or understanding a word.

There are other compromises; the budget-conscious explorer could buy a package holiday and go adventuring for a few days, while the person with more funds might consider exploring remote Anatolia in organised individuality: Top Deck Travel, for example, operates double-deck buses retired from the London streets, and Golden Horn Travel will provide a tailor-made holiday, removing the hassle but leaving the adventure.

ARRIVING and DEPARTING

Turkish landfalls

AIRPORTS IN GENERAL are clean, modern, and have all the amenities you would expect: toilets, banks, restaurants and duty-free shops, *but there is seldom any provision for invalids or nursing mothers*. The busiest for scheduled flights is at İstanbul, the busiest for package holiday flights at Dalaman, and the busiest charter airport, İzmir.

İZMİR

İzmir's *new* Adnan Menderes Airport is at Cumaovası, 16 miles (24 km) south of the city. It opened in November 1987 replacing Çiğli, which was north-west of the city, and it's called ABD in the airline guides.

THY buses meet all flights, day or night, and ferry the passengers to the THY terminal in Gaziosmanpaşa Bulvarı (think of it as three words; Gazi Osman Pasha) in the centre of İzmir, convenient for the tourist office and the Büyük Efes Otel. The journey takes up to an hour and the fare is anybody's guess. In 1987 the tickets for the old airport at Çiğli were overprinted 700TL but conductors were asking up to 1100TL, though on some buses there was nobody to collect fares at all.

Departing The bus leaves from this same spot in İzmir to convey passengers back to the airport for all airlines at all times of the day or night; be here two hours before take-off time for international flights, 1½ hours for domestic flights.

ANTALYA

Antalya Airport is 5 miles (8 km) west of the town, just off the road to Adana; it's AYT on your luggage label.

The airport is smart and modern but handles less than a score of international arrivals in an average week and these will have buses arranged to transport passengers to the THY town office on Cumhuriyet Cad, opposite the old harbour. There's no scheduled bus service between the airport and the town but you can catch a dolmuş from the dolmuş-only station on Ali Çetinkaya Cad (keep going east on Cumhuriyet Cad from the THY office). The bus will drop you on the main road, leaving you a mile to walk so don't come expecting to walk straight onto a flight to Ankara, İzmir or İstanbul, the only internal airports served, as seats are booked several days in advance.

Package tours A considerable number of charter flights use Antalya in addition to the scheduled services. People on a package who have bought accommodation will have no bus worries in either direction, but passengers on a flight-only package may have to take a taxi.

İSTANBUL

İstanbul's Atatürk Airport is the country's largest. The new building is at Yeşilköy, 15 miles (24 km) west of the city centre, between the main road to Greece and the Sea of Marmara. Its code is IST.

Arriving Atatürk handles 39 airlines with direct services to 53 airports outside Turkey, and to hundreds through onward connections. THY buses meet every scheduled flight and carry passengers to the THY terminal at the southern end of Meşrutıyet Cad in the Tünel area of İstanbul near the Galata Tower; journey time is 25 minutes.

To make certain of catching the airport bus, go to the Domestic Terminal from where buses leave on a regular half-hour service to Şişhane in European İstanbul north of the Golden Horn.

Assuming you have been able to arrange car hire in advance you can collect your vehicle at the airport.

Departing The excellent bus service operates in reverse, from Meşrutıyet Cad, leaving two hours before take-off of international flights from Terminal 2, and 1½ hours before departure of domestic flights from Terminal 1: don't go to the wrong terminal.

DALAMAN

Dalaman Airport (DLM on your luggage) features large in the tour operators' brochures but occupies little more than an inch in the *ABC World Airways Guide* which lists only the scheduled flights to Frankfurt, İstanbul and Ankara. We are therefore looking at an airport almost totally geared to the package tourist.

Arriving Much as İzmir or Antalya, with a terminal about the same size, though major extensions start in 1988. There are several banks for currency change but little else.

Tour operators' buses meet the relevant planes and rush their passengers away, usually westward to Marmaris or Bodrum but also east to Fethiye and Kaş. People on a flight-only deal will need to take a taxi into Dalaman town, some three miles (4 km) away.

Departing There's a bank which occasionally runs short of foreign currency in the middle of the night, and toilets which are immaculate though some are of the hole-in-the-floor design. Beyond the check-in and the customs examination, usually quite rigorous as in all airports, there's a smart departure lounge with three duty-free shops open round the clock.

Transport to the airport is provided for the all-inclusive customer, otherwise it's that taxi again.

BODRUM

Bodrum? There's no airport at Bodrum! True, but work starts on one in 1988. There was one planned for Çeşme in the early 1980s which may also be realised one day, though it's rather close to İzmir.

ANKARA

Esenboğa Airport, called ANK in the international code and on labels, is 22 miles (35 km) north-east of Ankara at the end of a stretch of specially-built road. Buses operate a service to the THY offices in Hipodrom Cad, conveniently beside the railway station and 600 yards from the bus station.

SEA ARRIVAL

There are no special problems in this quarter. Ferries from the Greek islands dock in the centre of Kuşadası, Çeşme, Bodrum and Marmaris. Car ferries arriving in İstanbul moor by the Kennedy Caddesi at the entrance to the Golden Horn, ideally suited for the European railway station and for the ferries across and along the Bosphorus to the Asian railway station at Haydarpaşa and to the other places of interest along the waterway.

ACCOMMODATION

Hotel to hostel

TURKEY CAN OFFER THE TRAVELLER an almost limitless range and variety of accommodation, from the extremes of the Hilton Otel in İstanbul to hiring a tent for the night. Variations on this theme include a floating hotel in Marmaris, a bed in a hut looking like a chicken coop and, in the interior where tourists are thin on the ground, a fascinating array of hotels and pensions.

HOTELS and PENSIONS

At the top end of the market, Turkey's hotels are on an international standard as indeed they should be. But note that the price quoted will invariably be less than the price demanded as the management adds a 15% service charge and 12% KDV.

KDV? The words are Katma Değer Vergisi and the translation is Value Added Tax which, you realise, is levied at 12% in the hotel trade; elsewhere it's applied at 15%.

The Turkish word for hotel is *otel*, the dropped 'h' showing the French influence which is also to be seen in the word *pansiyon*. It would be logical to expect an otel to offer better class accommodation than a pansiyon but in the middle and bottom of the market the words mean the same. Indeed, there are occasional pensions which are equal to the best three-star hotels, offering immaculate rooms with private balcony, telephone, wall-to-wall carpeting, en-suite toilet and shower, and as much breakfast as you can eat, while billing much less than a hotel and not showing the service charge or the KDV as extras.

Conversely, some so-called hotels are utterly basic, providing a room, a bed, and somewhere on the establishment a toilet of the hole-in-the-floor variety, and a washbasin. Cold water, of course.

In many towns in the interior, this basic formula is all you can expect, whether the sign outside says *otel* or *pansiyon*. The sheets and pillowcases will be clean, but there's no guarantee they've been laundered since the last guest but ten slept in them. If you've any worries on this point it's better to take a sleeping bag and curl up in that.

Take a look under the bed. If you find a pair of simple, slip-on sandals you'll know you're in an establishment that caters mainly for Turks. These man-sized items of footwear are for your use on your expeditions to the toilet and bathroom.

Toilets This bizarre ground-level toilet, another sign of the French influence, needs closer examination. It's about two feet square, is recessed in the floor, and is usually the entire furnishing in the small room. The method of use is simple: prepare your clothing, paying particular attention to long skirts and items in trouser pockets, step backwards onto the two raised footrests, crouch, and...voilà! The first use of such a toilet can bring about minor cultural shock but it is in fact better than using a dirty pan, as the body doesn't come into contact with the earthenware.

Now come the complications. No toilet paper? You should have brought your own: *always* carry toilet paper on your travels in Turkey. And if you see a little plastic basket or tin can in the corner of the lavatory, drop your used paper in there rather than down the hole.

No flush? There should be a tap fixed six inches or so above the floor, trickling into a pint plastic mug. One mugful of water provides an adequate flush.

TOURIST COMPLEXES

Tourist complexes, otherwise known as holiday villages, are built specifically for the sophisticated Western holidaymaker and in most cases provide everything that a package visitor may need throughout his stay.

In other words: a clean and comfortable room, washing and lavatory facilities, often en suite and comparable with those you left at home, and the Turkish version of a continental breakfast. In addition to the accommodation, of course, there'll be the full range of amenities from telephone and television lounge to an on-site shop, particularly for visitors who're self-catering.

Expect prices for basic foods to be dearer than in the town, but the quality and display should also be better. But don't expect to find your favourite breakfast cereal either on the dining-room table or on the shop shelves. Kellogg is virtually an unknown word in Turkey.

CAMPING

The Turkish Tourist Office lists around 24 official camping sites in the country, some of which are detailed under the appropriate resorts. The Tourist Office adds that camping elsewhere is possible but not advisable, though experienced campers report that hazards in Turkey are less than in many parts of Europe.

There are no rules stating where you may not camp, and the usual precautions apply: don't make yourself too obvious, don't leave the tent unattended, and pay heed to the risks of being surrounded by goats or caught in a flash flood. And beware the unwelcome creaures of the wild, as poisonous snakes and scorpions are found in Turkey, though rarely.

Motor camping is considerably easier, safer, and more comfortable. Provided you're not too obtrusive you can stay a day or two in car parks in most of the resorts, though disposal of waste can soon become a problem.

Camping Gaz The 190cc cylinders of liquid butane, used on Camping Gaz burners, are not available in Turkey and are, of course, prohibited luggage aboard aircraft. You can buy LPG in 12.4kg cylinders but there could be problems of incompatibility with your pressure reducer.

HOSTELS

There are several hostels for young people and students carrying ISIC, Interail and some other cards:

Topkapı Atatürk Student Centre at Londra Asfaltı, Cevizlibağ Durağı, Topkapı, İstanbul;

Kadırga Student Hostel, Cömertler Sok 6, Kumkapı, İstanbul;

Cumhuriyet Youth Hostel, Cemeci, Ankara;

Atatürk Student Hostel Inciraltı 1888, Sok 24, Inciraltı, İzmir;

For reservations at these, write Yüksek Kredı ve Yurtlar Kurumu Genel Müdürlüğü, Kıbrıs Cad 4, Kurtuluş, Ankara.

Intepe Youth & Boy Scout Hostel, Güzelyalı Mevkii, Tusan Moteli Yanı, Çanakkale;

Hasanağe Youth & Boy Scout Hostel, Küçük Kumla, Bursa.

For reservations here, write in good time to Millı Eğitin Gençlik ve Spor Bakanlığı, Gençlik Hizmetleri Genel Müdürlüğü, Millı Müdafa Cad 6, Kızılay, Ankara).

The Fluted Minaret in old Antalya

THE COST?

Those hotels which are registered with the Ministry of Culture and Tourism qualify to use the description 'touristic,' and to charge accordingly, plus the extras. Their service and quality are, as you would expect, of international standard.

Other places, inspected and listed by the belediye, the local council, have to conform to standards which are much lower. This is the realm of budget accommodation, where 12,000TL buys luxury for two people and where 7,000TL is the average asking price for bed and breakfast...though usually there's no breakfast.

It's possible to find a basic but adequate room for two for 4,000TL, and some hotels will let you sleep on the flat roof for 1,000TL a person.

Hostels ask around 3,000TL per person per night, or 2,000TL per person for group travellers, but be prepared for all these prices to rise as the lira sinks in value.

FOOD and DRINK

Eating out

A MEAL IN A TURKISH RESTAURANT can undoubtedly be one of the high spots of the day, no matter whether you're watching your waistline or your pocket. The first might suffer; the second won't.

Turkish cuisine is renowned from the Balkans to north Africa, and began to make its impact in western Europe long before the tourists found Turkey. The dishes were originally the simple food of a semi-nomadic peasantry, but through the centuries culinary skills have improved, fresh ingredients have been added, and latterly the French and Italian influence has appeared.

As Turkey is essentially a dry land with limited pasture, fruits and vegetables are the most important ingredients: for example, the Turks know 40 ways of preparing the humble aubergine. Meat is usually chopped into small pieces to go further, and well-cooked to overcome its inherent toughness. Hence you find tiny pieces of roast meat — *kebap* — done on a spit — *şiş*. It'll be beef or mutton, or maybe goat, but in a Moslem land you'll go a long way before you find pork, ham or bacon.

Breakfast A Turkish breakfast, *kahvaltı*, is the simplest meal of the day and often the servings are bigger as the hotel or restaurant is cheaper. Expect fresh white French-style bread, butter, and jam, and in addition you'll have either black olives, ewe-milk cheese, tomato or a tiny marrow.

The smart hotel may serve coffee, but it won't be Turkish as that's reserved for the main meal and is rather expensive; it's probably *Amerikan*, a weaker brew that leaves a fine sediment. It's not unknown for guests to take their own instant coffee to the table and ask for hot water.

The cheaper hotel may concentrate on tea, which is reasonably priced — it's grown in the country — and comes in a large pot. Add milk and sugar to taste.

The *lokanta* or *restoran*, which usually opens for breakfast and closes around midnight, give or take a few hours, will normally have *Nescafe* on the menu, but at a higher price.

Apple tea, *elma çay*, is an optional high-summer breakfast drink that goes down extremely well at any time of day and is frequently offered in the carpet shops to anybody who might remotely become a customer. It's made by pouring hot water onto a desiccated apple powder which dissolves. Sugar is added as required, but the drink has its own inbuilt sweetness.

Tea and coffee are served in small, waisted glasses without handles, so your fingers will instantly warn you if the fluid is too hot to drink.

There is a pleasant alternative breakfasting place in the *pastane* or *pastahane*, the pastry shop, which specialises in delicious but fattening cream and fruit pasties.

Main meal Lunch, *öğle yemeği* and dinner *esas yemek* are interchangeable as the main meal and unless you're eating in your hotel you'll have a choice of four types of establishment in which to dine; the conventional *restoran*, the *lokanta* which is a little down-market, and the specialist *köfteci* and *kebapçi*. The first of these concentrates on the köfte, the meat ball, and the second on roast meat — and there's no misprint with the word endings, -ci and -çi. You'll also find -cı and çı.

The *restoran* is much as you'd expect to find it in Europe, with tablecloths, smart waiters, and prices to correspond. The *lokanta* is more like a cafeteria, usually overflowing onto the pavement, and in both types of establishment you'll frequently be able to watch the speciality meats being cooked.

A typical *lokanta* menu on the Aegean had this *fiyat listesi* (price list, in TL) in the summer of 1987:

soğuk mezeler	600	cold snacks; hors d'oeuvre
salata	500	salad, usually assorted
midye	1000	mussels (dolması is 'stuffed')
kalamar	3000	squid
ahtapot	2500	octopus
şiş kebap	1500	small pieces of meat spit roasted
pirzola	1500	lamb chops
köfte	1200	meat balls
ciğer	1200	liver
biftek	1800	beefsteak, but don't expect top grade
bonfile	2400	fillet steak
karışık ızgara	2500	mixed grill
piliç (½)	3000	roast chicken
sicak mezeler	600	hot snacks, unspecified
meyve	600	fruit, *unspecified*
tatlı		desserts, *as specified:*
70'lik Yeni Rakı	5000	bottle of Rakı
35'lik Yeni Rakı	2500	half-bottle of Rakı
70'lik kalite şarap	3000	bottle of 'quality wine'
35'lik kalite şarap	2000	half-bottle; note the price
duble Rakı	1000	a 'double' Rakı
tek Rakı	500	a standard serving
bira	500	beer
meşrubat	300	drinks, *unspecified* (Cola, etc)
Nescafe	500	any instant coffee
kahvaltı	1000	breakfast

Order any of the main dishes and it will automatically come on three plates, the other two holding chunks of delicious crusty bread, and a pile of boiled and flaky rice, *pilav*.

Fish This menu is typical in that it doesn't specify the fish — mullet, swordfish, bass, tunny, etc — as supplies of these are unpredictable. Don't ask for a fish menu; ask instead what fish is available and go and look at it on the slab. Remember, too, it's sold by weight.

A restaurant will offer a wider range of dishes at a higher price, but you'll be paying for the service and the décor rather than any increase in the quality or the quantity of the food. The menu will feature some of these specialities:

arnavut ciğeri	fried liver and onions
baklava	flaky pastry with nuts and syrup
balık çorbası	fish soup
beyaz peynir	white cheese
bulgur pilav	rice with cracked wheat
çerkes tavuğu	cold chicken with garlic and walnut
çik köfte	çik is raw: so are the meat balls
dondurma	ice cream

düğünçorbası	meat and egg soup
iç pilav	rice with nuts and currants
iskembe çorbası	tripe soup
patlıcan kızarmatsı	fried sliced aubergine in yogurt
sade pilav	the basic pilav: boiled rice
sebse çorbası	vegetable soup
sütlaç	cold rice pudding
tavuk çorbası	chicken soup
yayla çorbası	yogurt soup, but 'yayla' is 'pasture'

Kebaps certainly deserve a mention. Apart from the standard spit-roast *şiş kebap* there is the popular *döner kebap* in which a leg of mutton is roasted over charcoal and thin slices peeled off as the joint cooks. *İskender kebap*, named from the man who created it, is döner kebap slices laid on unleavened bread and covered with tomato sauce and hot butter. There are variations of kebaps all over the country reflecting local tastes.

Beer, wine and spirit Despite the dictates of Islam, the Turks like their alcohol. The local company Efes and the international giant Tuborg brew delicious lagers in Turkey, and the state monopoly company TT produces its *Tekel Birası*, 'Monopoly Beer,' but few European palates put it in the same class.

Local wines are good and cheap, with *Kavaklıdere* and *Doluca* dominating the market. The national drink is Yeni Rakı, made by TT from anise and resembling Pernod or the Spanish Anis. It should be drunk with an equal quantity of water and its flavour is one you'll either love or loathe.

TT also produces *cin, kanyak, votka* and *viski*, and is the sole importer of spirits including the better-known gins, brandies, vodkas and whiskies. Considering Turkey's grave shortage of foreign currency, TT's monopoly, and the attitude of Islam towards alcohol, it's astounding that whisky sells in Turkish shops considerably cheaper than it does in Britain.

Look at the label on a bottle of imported scotch. Beneath the words 'printed in Scotland' you'll find TT's name, *Tekel Tarafından İthal Edilmistir* ('import monopoly') and then the price, *fiyatı TL 6500*, or whatever inflation decrees.

Snacks Turkey has plenty of fast-food barrows, known in the singular form as *büfe* and *kuru yemis*; the latter is literally 'dried fruit' and describes its wares perfectly.

A word of caution Dining the Turkish way can be the most memorable part of your holiday...for two reasons. Some foreign digestive systems adapt to Turkish food slower than others, and a few don't adapt at all. Minor stomach upsets are common, and I have a none too pleasant recollection of having to stop my bus four times in a three-hour journey and run behind a hedgerow. Unfortunately there aren't many hedges in Anatolia.

Victim of inflation: the 100TL banknote.

TALKING TURKEY

Facts and figures

AFFILIATIONS

Turkey is a full member of the United Nations, NATO, and the OECD, and is an associate member of the European Economic Community with aspirations towards full membership — the only non-European, non-Christian candidate — despite considerable objection from a vociferous section of the community.

BUSINESS HOURS

Shops Shops throughout Turkey are open whenever there's the likelihood of earning money. This means that in rural towns untouched by tourism they're open from dawn until dusk. In the resorts a *lokanta* may serve breakfast from 0800 and still be open at 0300 the next day. Shops catering for the townspeople close at dusk.

Neither the Moslem holy day nor Sunday, the official day of rest, affects shop opening hours in the resorts, but in the interior many trade shops close on Sunday. Food shops and bars everywhere invariably open every hour that Allah sends, as does the *ekmeçi*, the baker.

Banks Banks have core business hours of 0830 to 1200, 1330 to 1700, Monday to Friday, but there's usually one open for currency conversion on Saturday and Sunday in the resorts and the larger towns.

Tourist offices Tourist offices have set business hours but seldom do any two have the same hours, and even then they'll be varied at whim. It's safe to assume the offices will be open from 0900 to 1700 but you should allow an hour or more for lunch and don't expect them to be open on Sundays — though some will.

Post Offices The postal side of the PTT business opens shop at 0800 Monday to Saturday. Each office closes at its own set hour, but the times vary from 1230 in high summer in a small town *and the main resorts* to 2359 in the larger towns. It's not all gloom, however: at least one office in town will remain open until 1730. Sunday trading is from 0900 to a maximum of 1900.

The telephone counters are usually open around the clock — but they won't sell you stamps at 0300!

Museums Museums and archaeological sites not only have standard opening hours of 0830 to 1700, but a standard admission fee of 500TL on 'normal' days, reducing to 250TL on 'public holidays' which really means weekends. However, there are the inevitable variations.

Most museums are closed on Monday, and palaces on Monday and Thursday, but Topkapı is closed only on Tuesday.

Government offices From 0830 to 1230, and 1330 to 1730, Monday to Friday; in Aegean and Mediterranean regions they'll not open on high summer afternoons. I can't give you the dates because they're set each year at provincial level.

CINEMAS

There's an adequate network of cinemas, including several open-air ones in the main resorts, but they show films with Turkish sound-tracks. Excellent if you're learning the language.

COMMERCE and INDUSTRY

Turkey has an agricultural economy with 10 million people over the age of 18 working on the land. There are 23.7 m hectares of land growing wheat, cotton, tobacco, fruits for drying, and a few bizarre crops such as liqorice root, sesame, and mulberries for the Bursa silk industry. Twenty million hectares are under forest, mostly conifer, and this is where Turkey produces most of its honey; and there are 2.9 m hectares growing vines and orchard fruit including the figs and almonds of the Büyükmenderes valley, and gums.

İzmir is the centre of the tobacco industry with 60% of the crop going to the United States. The Turks smoke the remainder with no regard to signs saying *sigara içilmez* (no smoking).

In 1985 the country had 40 m sheep, 17 m cattle, 13 m goats, 1.2 m asses, 623,000 horses and 544,000 buffalo. The sheep keep the carpet weavers busy while the goats, many of them Angoras — the name is a corruption of Ankara — produce mohair. And the buffalo still haul the ploughs.

There's oil in the south-east near the Iraqi border, with a 494-km pipeline running from Batman to İskenderun; there's another runnng from deep in Iraq to İskenderun as well. Turkey extracted 2.11 m tons of crude in 1985, as well as 30 m tons of lignite, 3.8 m tons of coal, 222,000 tons of chromite and 38,000 tons of sulphur, most of the latter the gift of ancient volcanoes.

EDUCATION

School attendance is co-educational, compulsory to the age of 12, and free. There was 67% adult literacy in 1980, a great increase on the 1928 figure when Arabic script was dropped. There are 27 universities, and non-Moslems run their own private schools in İstanbul.

ELECTRICITY

It's 220v, 50 cycles, as in Continental Europe, but with two-pin power sockets, each pin 4mm in diameter and with 15mm between them. This means they're incompatible with everything British, including electric shavers, and there's little from the continent that will fit. Take an adaptor.

FAIRS and FESTIVALS

This calendar lists a few of the annual events around Turkey, concentrating on those of interest to tourists.

January, Selçuk. Camel wrestling, mid-month at Selçuk, and at Aydın and district on the four weekends following.
Apr-May, Selçuk. Ephesus International Arts Festival; folk-dancing in the Epheus theatre.
Spring, İstanbul. Tulip Festival.
May-June, Edirne. Kırkınpar wrestling, the Turkish national sport with wrestlers covered in oil.
June,Rize. Tea Festival.
June, Marmaris. Art and Tourism Festival.
June-July, İstanbul. International Arts and Culture Festival, lasting 25 days with every aspect of performing arts represented.
Summer, Erzurum. Javelin contest.
Foça, July. Folklore and watersports Festival
July, Kuşadası. Pop Music Festival.
July, Samsun. International Folk-dance Festival.
July, Çeşme. Sea Festival.
August, Çanakkale. Troy Festival.

Sept 22, Çanakkale. Parades marking the defeat of the British in 1915.
September, Bodrum. Art and Culture Week, held in the castle.
December, Konya. Mevlana Festival with Whirling Dervishes.

GAS

As already mentioned, the 190cc canisters of Camping Gaz and similar makes are not available. Ipragaz is on sale in 12.4kg cylinders, but you'll need that only if you're towing a caravan.

GOVERNMENT

Mustafa Kemal Atatürk, whose statue is in every town square and whose profile dominates the currency, created the modern Republic of Turkey from the ruins of the old Ottoman Empire. With the slogan 'peace at home, peace abroad,' he began shaking the people out of their lethargy and introduced major reforms beginning in 1923 with the creation of a civil republic, free from religious interference and governed by a two chamber parliament, the lower chamber of which was elected with free vote by all men and women aged 21 or more.

Caliph In 1924 he abolished the caliphs who had held political and religious office for centuries, and followed with the suppression of the Dervishes in eastern Turkey. He brought all schools, religious or not, under government control and in 1932 introduced the reading of the Koran in Turkish; until then it had been exclusively in Arabic.

He had already weakened the religious hold on the people by replacing the Islamic legal system with one based on the Swiss method, by introducing the Italian penal code and German commercial practises. Marriage became a civil contract with divorce permitted on equal grounds (divorced women can now give their children their own maiden name), the Gregorian calendar replaced the Islamic one, and Sunday became the official day of rest.

Surname Another break with the Arab influence came with the introduction of the surname, passed on down the male line and replacing the use of first name plus a description, often cruel, as in Ahmet Topal, 'Ahmet the Cripple.'

In 1928 Arabic script was dropped in favour of the Latin alphabet, then in 1934 Turkey went metric and women gained complete equality with men — and the elections of 1935 brought 17 women into government.

Today this westernisation continues, with the Turks seeing themselves as Europeans who happen to live in Asia; as prospective full members of the EEC, the only non-Christian state to be elected; and a Moslem people sorely embarrassed by the actions of their neighbours in Iran, Iraq and Syria. And, for that matter, in the Soviet Union as well.

Atatürk was president from 29 October 1923 to 10 November 1938 when President İnönü took over, lasting until 21 May 1950.

Martial law Democracy flourished with some difficulty until civil unrest brought down the government in the late 1970s. The Turkish Grand National Assembly was dissolved on 12 September 1980 and the National Security Council — martial law — took over. In October 1981 the Consultative Assembly began work on a new constitution to replace that of 1961, and at a referendum in November 1982 98% of the voters supported it.

Democracy returned with the election on 6 November 1983 for the 399 members of the lower house of the Grand National Assembly in which the Motherland Party won 211 seats, the Populist 117, and the National Democrats 71.

41

In the November 1987 elections the Motherland won 292 seats, the Populist movement 99, and the True Path Party 59, making 450 seats.

Local government Turkey is divided into 67 provinces, known in the singular as *il*, subdivided into districts (*ilçe*) and towns (*bucak*). The word *belediye* which you'll see on everything from ambulances to dustcarts, means 'municipality.'

NEWSPAPERS

British, French, German, Italian and US European editions of newspapers are on sale in the main resorts the day after publication, but at prices that carry the cost of air freight.

The *Turkish Daily News*, founded in 1961, labels itself as Turkey's first and only English-language daily and is an excellent newspaper costing a modest 200TL for 12 broadsheet pages, giving world as well as national news.

The problem is that it's not easy to find. It's on the newsstands in the main resorts and in Ankara and Istanbul, but you'll be lucky to find it elsewhere, though many Turks buy it to help them with their studies of English.

The same publishing company caters for the French-speaking market with the *Orient Express* of similar quality.

The Turks serve themselves well with newspapers. There are 13 titles published daily in Ankara, 29 in Istanbul and 5 in Izmir.

POLICE

There are four types of police in Turkey, the *polis* being by far the most noticeable. They fill a general role, mainly controlling traffic and settling minor issues. Their white caps and green uniforms make them distinctive, their white cars have the word *polis* in large blue letters, and they're the men and women you'll need if you lose your passport or have your camera stolen by another tourist, but seldom will you find one who speaks more than a few words of English. If sign language won't solve the problem they'll usually call on the staff of the tourist office for translation.

In certain places there are officers of the tourism police whose main role is helping the visitor.

The *jandarma* is an armed force allied to the military and has conscripts among its numbers. It's far less in evidence and is there for the heavy work of catching the hardline criminal. Jandarmes who wear white helmets with *As Iz* are military police.

The men in blue are the *belediye zabıtası*, who are really weights and measures inspectors pretending to be policemen.

POPULATION

Turkey's populatin is exploding in slow motion, but at the moment there's no shortage of space. In 1927 there were 13.6 million Turks; in 1935 16.1 m; in 1945 18.7 m and in 1950 20.9 m. Then the increase accelerated: by 1960 27.7 m; 1970 35.6 m, 1980 44.7 m and in 1985 50.6 million.

A league table of the largest towns, with population in thousands, reads:

1	İstanbul	5,494	2	Ankara	2,251
3	İzmir	1,489	4	Adana	776
5	Bursa	614	12	Samsun	280
13	Antalya	258	21	Denizli	171
22	Trabzon	155			

POST OFFICES

The PTT (pay tay tay) shows distinct signs of its French ancestry from its name which is, in Turkish, *posta, telefon, telegraf*, to its use of the *jeton* or token coin — the Turks have borrowed that word as well — for making a phone call. Offices are sited prominently in towns and the orange-and-black PTT sign is easily visible (see 'business hours').

Posting a letter is simple. In the larger offices stamps are available at separate counters designated in English — but the clerk won't necessarily speak anything but Turkish.

Making a phone call is a little more complicated. Disregard any instructions you may read in poor English in the automatic-dialling boxes: this is the procedcure.

Buy a good supply of *büyük jetonu*, big jetons, at the telephone counter; they'll come in handy for later calls and you can cash in any you don't use. Go into one of the many kiosks sited anywhere in town and labelled 'international' in English. Look for the tiny red light; if you can't see it, the phone should be working. Lift the receiver. You will at once hear the dialling tone, a continuous purr. Put two or three jetons in the appropriate slot and dial 99 to escape from Turkey. Without pausing (but it doesn't matter if you do) dial your country code, then your home area code (omitting the first 0 for UK calls) and finally your subscriber's number.

An interrupted tone signifies engaged, which will almost certainly be the result of too much traffic for Turkey's inadequate number of international lines. Replace the receiver and your jetons will automatically be spilled into a slot at the bottom of the orange equipment box. Try again.

The worst time to make a call is from around midday to early evening, and any time on Sunday when rates are 20% cheaper; the best is up to mid-morning or in late evening — but remember the time difference for the folks at home.

When you get a connection you can thrust more jetons in as you talk and reclaim the unspent ones at the end. If there's a mosque close at hand, try not to make your call when the muezzin is about to summon the faithful to prayer or you may not hear yourself speak.

It's possible to phone via the manual system from a cubicle inside the PTT, theoretically at any time of the day or night. You'll certainly have to wait for a connection, you'll have no control over the cost of the call as you'll pay later over the counter, and you'll pay at the higher operator rate. But you'll be free of traffic noise which can be a problem in the kiosks.

Stamps and jetons are on sale at newspaper stalls where you see the sign *telefon jetonu posta pulu satiliciği*.

International codes from Turkey are:

Canada and the USA	1	Iceland	354
United Kingdom	44	Ireland	353
Australia	61	Netherlands	31
Belgium	32	New Zealand	64
Denmark	45	Norway	47
Federal Germany	49	Sweden	46
Finland	358		

PUBLIC HOLIDAYS

New Year's Day	Jan 1
National Independence Day	Apr 23
Atatürk's Memorial Day	May 19
Victory Day (defeat of 1922 invaders)	Aug 30
Republic Day	Oct 29

PUBLIC TOILETS

There is an adequate but not generous supply of public conveniences. In resorts they are usually near the waterfront or on the main square, and are labelled either *WC* or *tuvalet*. Often in the backwoods you'll see them signed *bay* and *bayan*: gents go in the first, ladies in the second.

Lavatories are also on bus and railway stations, occasionally near a market, and frequently in an accessible position in a mosque courtyard. Most are free but some have an admission charge of 50TL.

But what awaits you inside? Conditions range from the excellent to the overpowering, and the old French-style hole-in-the-floor receptacles are quite common. For further thoughts on these see 'toilets' on page 33.

RADIO and TELEVISION

Türkiye Radyo ve Televizyon broadcasts news in English, French and German on 88MHz and 99.2MHz around 0100 and 0700 hrs; you can catch them in any of the coastal resorts. There are also foreign-language weather forecasts for sailors:

Turkish radio's music output is mostly in traditional style and passengers on long-distance buses soon develop an ear for its strange, sad, downward-lilting cadences. There's plenty of western pop as well.

The two television channels operate from around 1900 to midnight, plus or minus an hour, with news in English at 2130 on channel two. Most of the programmes are imported and you might see some of your BBC favourites...dubbed into Turkish.

In 1983 there were 6 million television sets in the country, and in the remote villages the only screen is in the *lokanta*, which means few women will ever see it.

1,000TL buys the cheapest lodgings in Bodrum

RESIDENCE QUALIFICATIONS and BUYING PROPERTY

Moving in

There is no standard qualification for a Turkish residence visa. People planning to stay in the country longer than three months at a time (or two months if that's your allowance) should contact the Turkish Consulate General of the country they're living in and state their case; each application is judged on its merits. In effect, if you can support yourself financially and are not an undesirable alien, you'll get the visa. But you won't be allowed to take a job unless it's one no Turk is capable of doing.

Buying a home

The logical extension of having a residence visa is to buy a house. No problems at all, provided you're a citizen of a country which will allow a Turk to buy property there. In effect, if a Turk may lawfully buy your house, you may buy his. If not — not.

The price of property in Turkey varies enormously, with the coastal resorts and the Bosphorus suburbs of Istanbul being among the most expensive, but still much less than the corresponding property would cost in southern England.

The first step for a UK citizen is to contact the British Council and find a lawyer in Turkey; you should also engage a competent solicitor back home to oversee the deal. The Turkish lawyer will put you in touch with an estate agency if you haven't decided on the actual property you want, or you could try the agency at Değir Menler Sok 44, Eski Çeşme, Bodrum (tel 1920) or the many others on İnönü Caddesi, İzmir, or the adverts in the *Turkish Daily News*.

You'll need to be able to raise the entire purchase price and transfer it to Turkey through banking channels; that way you'll be able to export the same amount of money when you sell the property although at the moment you'll not be allowed to export any capital gains.

In addition, you'll need another 10% of the price for public participation — consider that the legal fees — and up to 4% for property tax.

If *I* were buying a house in Turkey I'd want to know exactly how it was built, bearing in mind the country is in the earthquake belt and Fethiye was flattened by a 'quake in 1958. Do make certain you're fully insured.

SOUVENIRS

You'll not escape from Turkey without buying some souvenirs. At the bottom of the market a gilded tea glass, with spoon and decorative saucer, costs around 1500TL, while at the top end you could pay more than a million lira for an antique carpet and probably find you couldn't take it out of the country.

Let's look at carpets and kilims first, the kind of souvenir you'll be offered a dozen times a day, every day. A kilim is a rug or carpet that's hand made from wool, using a technique that virtually hides the knots so the finished article lies flat.

The price depends upon several things: the closeness of the weave, the material used, the age of the article, its size, and your ability to haggle.

Closely-woven work obviously takes much longer, but it produces a work of art. Close-weave kilims use the much finer fibres of the angora goat in preference to sheep wool, and the most delicate of all are made from silk.

Surprisingly, an old carpet or kilim is usually worth considerably more than a new one, and you can make a rough estimate of its age by holding it in front of you and dropping it. If it falls stiffly, it's new; if it collapses like a wet blanket, it's old.

So it's new. Now check it by opening the pile and comparing the buried and the exposed colours for indications of fade. Wipe it with a damp white tissue to see if the colours wash off; they won't if they're genuine vegetable dyes of the kind that have been used for generations.

Or is it old? In that case, check it even more carefully for evidence of repairs which could reduce its value, remembering that Turkish carpet repairers are as skilled in their craft as are the weavers.

You may well wonder why an old carpet is on sale? Indeed, why there are so many old carpets on the market? The answer is that the drift from the countryside to the city is gaining momentum, families don't have enough space in their city apartments for their heirlooms, and they probably need to raise some cash to pay the moving expenses.

Kilims and carpets, by tradition, were made by the womenfolk, and the smaller rugs were prayer mats for their children and not intended for sale at all. The craft continues today in the hands of semi-illiterate nomads in Anatolia who work to their own individual designs, each of which reveals a strong link with the Koran if you know where to find it. Many patterns have stylised whirling Dervishes, others have camel heads arranged in a broad V shape, which should point towards Mecca when the mat is laid out for prayer.

Colours have a significance as well; blue for the evil eye, green for paradise and red for abundance. And if you're careful, clever, or lucky you'll be able to see the five commandments of Islam potrayed on your new-old prayer mat.

Size is of minor concern. A handmade silk rug around 15 inches by 21 inches (say 40cm by 55cm) could represent eight weeks' work for the weaver, while a 3ft by 6ft (1m by 2m) wool rug could be made well within a month.

If the kilim really is old you may have difficulties with the customs as you try to leave Turkey. Get your salesman to write, on headed notepaper, a letter stating that it is not an antique (though he may have spent an hour persuading you that it is), or be prepared to forfeit it at the airport.

Don't try taking an obvious antique such as furniture, jewellery or an archaeological find out of the country, no matter what pack of lies the salesman writes for you: Turkey forbids the export of its heritage and that's final.

Other sensible and useful souvenirs include leather goods, copperware and meerschaum carvings (the world's largest deposits of magnesium silicate or meerschaum — German for 'sea foam' — are found near Eskişehir). But don't be duped into buying quasi-antique copper; if the customs officers let it through without a query you'll realise just what you've wasted your money on.

STREET CRIME

Crime is noticeable not only by its absence but by the assumption of most Turks that it's not a hazard worth consideration.

Tourists walk the streets carrying shoulder bags and cameras in manners that would incite snatch-thieves within minutes in some other Mediterranean countries we could mention, and shopkeepers in the bazaars often leave their stock out all night with just a tarpaulin thrown over it.

As tourism expands, this attitude will inevitably change for the worse. At the moment the entire crime in the Turkish resorts mounts to no more than a few score incidents, usually involving tourists losing things or stealing from each other.

Elsewhere in the Mediterranean a tourist accosted in the street should instantly be on guard. This is not so in Turkey where the native is almost always genuinely trying to help with no thought of reward. He may even be out of pocket by his generosity.

TELEPHONES — see 'post office'

TIME

Turkey is two hours ahead of GMT. It was three hours ahead until November 1984 when the government brought it into line with Continental Europe. Since then the country has adopted summer time or 'daylight saving' and changes its clocks when the Continental Europeans do. Britain, of course, insists on choosing its own dates for the annual ritual.

TRANSPORT

There were 55,296 km of surfaced roads in the country in 1985, with almost 31,000 km of them being state highways, so giving an adequate network of main roads. Many small villages deep in the countryside have only grit-road access and this is therefore one aspect of the true Turkey that the visitor will often miss.

There were 983,700 cars, 418,000 lorries and vans, 135,000 buses and dolmuşes and 288,000 mopeds, for a population in excess of 50 million — one car for 50 people.

There were 8,400 km of railway track, at 1.435 m gauge, which carried 136 million passengers. And THY operated 31 aircraft.

WATER

Is it safe to drink? Yes, but in some parts of the country it's so heavily chlorinated as to be unpalatable.

Despite the absence of rain from May to October there's no apparent water shortage. Shopkeepers dampen their pavements each morning and some petrol stations have sprinkler-type fountains playing all summer.

Water is available on tap in almost every town and village, but certainly not in every home. There are adequate public taps and fountains along the roadside, but watch for those words *içilmez* for 'not drinkable' and *içilir* for that which is 'drinkable.' You'll see these signs in public toilets as well.

If you're ever desperate for a drink, remember that every mosque has an array of taps for worshippers to wash their feet before praying; there's no objection to a Christian cupping his hands or filling a bottle at any of these spots, though preferably not just before a call to prayers. It's a pity, but few other Moslem lands are this lenient.

Several brands of mineral water are available for when the chlorine becomes overpowering, and most long-distance buses carry adequate stocks in bottles or plastic sachets which the conductors issue free to passengers.

WEATHER

Turkey's climate is more predictable than that of northern Europe. From May to October it's going to be dry everywhere except for the occasional summer storms, and on the Aegean and Mediterranean coasts it will be hot — very hot. Anatolia will be hot by day but cooler by night, and in the remote eastern mountains of Cappadocia it will be cold at night all the year through.

Winter is wet everywhere, with snow falling on much of the central plateau from November to March and even Istanbul will see a light dusting during the winter.

These are the average *maximum* temperatures for Istanbul (top line)and Ankara in °F/°C:

JAN	FEB	MAR	APR	MAY	JUN
46/8	48/9	52/11	61/16	70/21	71/21
39/4	42/5	52/11	63/17	73/23	78/26

JUL	AUG	SEP	OCT	NOV	DEC
77/25	83/30	75/24	68/20	59/15	52/11
86/30	87/31	78/26	70/21	56/14	42/6

(see also *swimming*, page 13 for air and sea temperatures)

WHAT YOU WON'T LIKE

Nowhere is perfect, but I've probably given the impression that Turkey comes nearer to it than many other places on earth. Nevertheless, there are aspects of Turkish life which *I* don't enjoy, though they may not disturb you at all.

There are stray cats by the hundred thousand. I haven't seen any signs of cruelty and the animals are certainly not afraid of humans. They all scrounge for a living, which is natural for felines, and many people put spare food out for them.

But there are scarcely any cats at all in İzmir, İstanbul or Ankara, stray or otherwise. Why not? Because the government introduced a rabies-prevention programme to eliminate strays and in these cities the bounty hunters killed every cat and dog on sight.

Traffic Morning and evening commuter traffic in the western suburbs of İstanbul is diabolic. On some roads, buses and dolmuşes come in like an invading army while on other roads nearby the traffic is snarled to a standstill — and this in a country with a very low level of private motoring. As car ownership increases, *somebody* in İstanbul will need to do something.

Driving The standard of driving is not the worst I've seen, but it's rather disconcerting to be the front passenger in a bus that's doing 90 kph with a mere two feet (60 cms) clearance between the back of the lorry in front.

Nor is it any fun being behind the wheel of a car doing a steady 70 kph on a straight and empty road only to have a bus creep up behind you and the driver blast his horn for no apparent reason.

The bus driver would see it differently. His defence would be that car drivers are so irresponsible they're quite likely to indicate a right turn and then make a left one — or that they'll turn left into a side road without giving any warning or checking in their mirror. Regrettably, the bus driver has a valid argument.

The lesson, therefore, is simple. If you're travelling by bus, beware the danger seat, although it offers the best view. And if you're driving a car, keep a careful watch in your mirror and, for the sake of Allah, beware the almighty bus!

TRAVELLING IN TURKEY

Road, rail, air or sea

BY FAR THE EASIEST way to travel in Turkey is by road, and from the choices that throws open, the most expensive way is by hire car.

ROAD

Hire car With less than a million cars and taxis in a land of 50 million people, it's obvious that Turkey isn't equipped for mass private motoring. Add to this the fact that package tourism has only just arrived and is set to expand rapidly, and you have the unhappy situation which makes hire cars rare and expensive.

For a motoring holiday in peak season it's as well to make hiring arrangements at least four months ahead, and even out of season you should complete the deal a month in advance, whether you're travelling independently or taking a fly-drive package. Adding the cost of committed hiring to the cost of your holiday shows that you'll also need to insure against cancellation.

Avis, Hertz, Europcar and Budget are all in Turkey: in the UK you can arrange the hire by phoning 01.848.8733 for Avis; 01.679.1777 for Hertz; 01.950.5050 for Europcar; and 0800.181.181 for Budget. There are several small car-hire businesses in the coastal towns with rates slightly cheaper than the international companies but as they're not organised it's impossible to contact them in advance. They cater mainly for the local trade and are also booked up days or weeks in advance.

CostLet's look at the cost first. A one-day-hire contract for a Renault 12 costs 12,000TL plus 120TL per km; for a Jeep Wrangler, 25,000TL plus 250TL/km; and for a Mercedes 230E, 95,000TL plus 950TL/km.

Contracts for two days or more don't carry the kilometer charge; for a three-to six-day hire the Renault would cost 32,000TL, the Jeep 66,000TL, and the Mercedes 237,000TL — all per day. This rate drops by around five percent for contracts covering seven days or more. VAT of 10% is included in these figures.

In addition, the hirer buys all petrol; pays a 20,000TL deposit which is returned if he surrenders the car with a full tank (he would have started with it full); pays another deposit equal to 130% of the estimated total rental cost; and pays 4,200TL for collision damage (6,500TL for the Jeep and the Merc). He has the option of paying 1,500TL per day as personal accident insurance. And after all that, the hirer finds he's not insured for broken windscreens or damaged tyres. The prices are at 1987 levels, but the shattered windscreen is a continual risk.

Licence The legal requirements are blissfully simple. The driver must have held a full licence for a year, and be aged 21 or more. He does *not* need an International Driving Licence.

Once on the road, things become easier — apart from the hazard of horn-blaring bus drivers, absent-minded lorry drivers, and animals wandering on the minor roads. It is compulsory to wear seat belts but few Turks bother outside the town limits despite the possibility of police spot checks.

In view of these hazards, plus the absence of marking at the edge of the road, it's not advisable to drive at night.

Parking Parking is ridiculously easy. There are no yellow lines along the kerbs and no parking meters even in the cities, but you might occasionally find the international no-parking sign: in case you've forgotten, it's a red circle with a red diagonal stripe on a blue ground.

Speed limit The speed limit is 50 kph in towns and 99 kph on the open road.

Petrol Petrol stations and their pumps are modern, easy to see, and there's often round-the-clock service. There's no shortage of petrol stations in the tourist areas but on the main roads of Anatolia and Cappadocia you can travel miles without seeing one. Shell, BP and Mobil share the market with Petrol Ofisi and Türkpetrol, offering 'petrol' of 91 octane at 69TL per litre or around £2.15 per Imperial gallon. 'Super Benzin' costs 74TL per litre, or around £2.34 per gallon. Bear in mind that oil prices fluctuate and the lira is steadily declining in value.

Bus and dolmuş

The Turkish for 'bus' is *otobus*, but the English translation of *dolmuş* is 'filled to capacity,' which frequently describes the interior of these 15-seat minibuses.

In Turkey the bus is the long-distance vehicle, usually clean and well-appointed, and if you're on an inter-city *ekspres* run, you'll probably travel in near luxury. But avoid the back row of seats in the Mercedes buses: they're not recliners. Fares, by European standards, are token payments.

The dolmuş is the short-haul workhorse, operating routes within the larger towns and cities, and connecting the city centre with the surrounding villages. While the bus operates to a set timetable, the dolmuş leaves when it's full or, occasionally, when the driver is fed up with waiting. The dolmuş driver may pull out of his loading bay on the bus station and cruise slowly around town while his conductor solicits more custom.

Ticket touts As you walk into the *otogar* (think of it as a corruption of the French *auto gare*, 'vehicle station') you'll probably be accosted by ticket touts demanding to know your destination and then pointing or leading you to the appropriate ticket office.

Don't be fooled. The touts are selling tickets for a particular company and not for the next bus scheduled for a particular destination. If you're unlucky you may buy your ticket only to find you have a two-hour wait, while a rival company's coach sets out with empty seats.

Bus tickets Unless you board your coach as it's leaving the otogar or you wave it down on the open road, you'll need to buy your ticket at the company office rather than on the vehicle. The ticket will not only tell you the company's name, your destination and the date and time of departure, but will also specify your seat. If you have any preferences try to make them known in the ticket office.

There's keen competition on the bus routes and in normal circumstances you'll not have to wait long for a vehicle, but at peak holiday times it may be advisable to buy your ticket the day before you intend travelling.

And when you're on that bus going, for example, from Bodrum to Marmaris on an August day, take a note of the high number of obvious non-Turks among your travelling companions and spare a little sympathy for the long-suffering locals!

Dolmuş tickets Dolmuş passengers pay the driver or conductor either during the journey or at the end. When there are 23 passengers, including three rucksack-toting foreigners and the conductor, in a vehicle designed to carry 15, paying the fare becomes a matter of passing money from hand to hand and watching in trepidation as the driver sorts out his change without stopping.

Luggage All vehicles have luggage compartments. There's enough space under the bus floor to stow 50 large suitcases, but the dolmuş's trunk at the rear of the vehicle is often too small to cope. It's fairly uncomfortable to squeeze into an already-full dolmuş while wearing a rucksack, then sit on the edge of the seat for 10 weary miles: one quickly learns the need to travel light.

Almost every bus carries a supply of drinking water in bottle or sachet, which the conductor will distribute free during the journey or on request. He'll also go to each passenger with a bottle of toilet water and squirt a little into cupped hands as a welcome refresher on a hot day.

Bus and dolmuş stations In a small town such as Bodrum or Marmaris the otogar is not only the bus station but also the pick-up point for the dolmuş, and frequently for the taxi as well. In a town the size of Antalya the otogar caters exclusively for buses and there's a separate *dolmuş garaj*; if you're lucky there's even a dolmuş service between the two. İzmir, for example, has its vast otogar beside the Atatürk Stadium in the north-east, but buses for Çeşme leave from a much smaller otogar in the western suburbs, 8 km away. There's a dolmuş service connecting them, but it's more convenient though more expensive to go by taxi. To make matters more complicated, there's a dolmuş station near the city centre where you can board a minibus for Çeşme.

Taxi

The Turkish taxi is usually distinguished by the yellow-and-black bands along its sides and by the word *taksi* on the roof. Fares are set by the municipality for standard journeys and you should ask the driver for his *tarife*; if you're proposing to go adventuring by taxi off the beaten track then agree the fare, on either a time or a distance basis, before you get into the car.

The old harbour is now Antalya's marina

A point to remember is that if you're looking for a taxi, you normally pay the driver what he asks. If, however, the driver solicits you for custom you're in a strong position to bargain and you may reduce the asking price by half.

Most taxi drivers have a smattering of English, and some speak decent German as a result of being *Gästarbeiter* during the grim sixties. Many of the taxis themselves were bought with the proceeds of those years of expatriot labour.

RAIL

Rail travel is more comfortable than the most luxurious coach can offer, but it's slower and more expensive. Exactly how much more depends on whether you opt for second class, first class, or the ultimate of a private first-class sleeper, though the fare will never equal what you would pay in western Europe for a comparable journey.

It's advisable to buy tickets for daytime travel in advance, preferably no later than the day before travelling, and it's essential to book all sleeping comartments. Türk Devlet Demiryolları (dem-eer-yoll-ar-uh, literally 'Turkish State Iron-roads') is not computerised so it's not possible to buy a ticket for a journey starting in a place other than where you are.

Ekspres Don't consider travelling anything other than *ekspres* or *mototren* as you'll not only forfeit most of your comfort, you'll also be going slower than the bus.

A glance at a physical map of Turkey shows the severe problems which confronted the German rail-builders; even now, the only railway stations on the Mediterranean coast are at Mersin and Iskenderun in the extreme east, and the only Aegean station is at Izmir, though there are stations at Selçuk and Söke, in the Kuşadası hinterland.

Trains you might consider using include the Mavi Tren (Blue Train), a first-class-only daily service each way between İstanbul and Ankara, and the nightly İzmir Ekspresi which links Ankara with the Aegean, both ways.

AIR

THY operates a network of flights connecting all the country's airports. Fares are cheap even by United States' standards but there's nothing approaching a shuttle service: intending passengers need to book several days in advance.

SEA

Turkish Maritime Lines operates a web of car ferries based on İstanbul and including the weekly high-summer cruise to Antalya, the year-round Black Sea route to Trabzon (see page 141), and the İzmir-İstanbul link of the weekly cruise to Venice (see page 27). The company also runs the Sirkeci (İstanbul) to Bandırma car ferry, which has an infrequent service.

Bosphorus ferries Four ferry routes link old Istanbul in Europe with its newer suburbs in Asia, and other routes zigzag across the Bosphorus towards the Black Sea. Fares for the direct crossing from near the Galata Bridge start at 120TL, which buys a *jeton* valid for a single crossing. It's a non-stop service.

Dardanelles ferries Two ferries link Europe and Asia across the Dardanelles: the Gelibolu (Gallipoli)-Lâpseki and the Eceabat-Çanakkale routes. Both are drive-on, no-booking services which sail on the hour every hour, day and night, for the 30-minute crossing at fares of 120TL per person, 200TL for a motor-cycle, and 2,000TL for everything else.

DISCOVER TURKEY

Turkish delights

IN THE FOLLOWING CHAPTERS we examine the attractions of modern Turkey region by region: the **Aegean**; the **Mediterranean**; central **Anatolia**; the **Black Sea**; **Istanbul** and environs.

For each of the major resorts there's a list of British tour operators offering holidays in the area, compiled from the *ABC Holiday Guide* and the *St James's Press Holiday Guide*. The lists are not exclusive and are offered purely as an indication of what's available; by their length they also show how popular each resort is with British package holidaymakers.

A minaret of the Blue Mosque, Istanbul

THE AEGEAN

Çanakkale to Bodrum

ÇANAKKALE

ÇANAKKALE IS A CLEAN, SMART and quiet town, but there's nothing here to make the tourist linger: no beach, no night life, no restaurant of repute. There's a naval shore station here, guarding the approaches to the Dardanelles, and the town centre memorial lets nobody forget 18 March 1915, the day the British and French started their ill-planned Gallipoli campaign. And on 22 September the town celebrates the defeat of the invaders by holding a massive street procession with everybody and everything that's mobile, from an air force flypast to the town dustcart.

There's also the Troy Festival from 15 to 18 August when a young Helen of Troy is hostess to folk dancing and concerts.

A *çanak* is an earthenware pot, and *kale* means 'tower;' the tower in question is the 15th century fortress built by Sultan Mehmet II and as it's still militarily sensitive, tourists aren't allowed on the battlements. There's a small military museum in town.

Beaches? The best in the neighbourhood is at İntepe, near the supposed burial mound of King Dardanos, great-grandfather of Ilus, builder of Ilium, Truva, or Troy.

Troy

Troy is difficult to reach with public transport. Perhaps the best way is to take the bus south from Çanakkale, get off when you see a yellow signpost proclaiming TRUVA 5 and pointing down a minor road. Yes — it's a ten kilometer hike, counting the return. If you stay on the bus to Taştepe the next sign threatens TRUVA 35, which is daunting.

The other option is to take a taxi from ạnakkale, preferably sharing it with two or three other people to ease the cost, because you'll almost certainly be disappointed with Troy.

Compared with other ancient ruins in Turkey, Troy is little more than a heap of stones. Yet there isn't just *one* city: there are several, each built on the ruins of its predecessor. University of Cincinnati archaeologists claim to have separated 47 distinct layers but it's widely acknowledged there are nine cities on the site with Troy VI or VIIa (c1275BC-c1240BC) being the one that Homer knew.

The earliest layer, Troy I, was a Bronze Age settlement established around 2,500BC, and the topmost strata, tentatively labelled Troy IX, was built in the 6th century AD and known as Ilium Novum.

Heinrich Schliemann, who began excavations here in the 1870s, discovered fire-stained stones which he attributed to the sacking of Troy after the citizens of Ilium took in the notorious wooden horse; a modern reconstruction of the horse is here as well, dominating the site. But Helen's jewels, the Spartan treasure which the youth Paris stole, aren't here any more — if they ever were. Schliemann, anxious for recognition for his labours, claimed to have found the jewels and after some years of deliberation he presented them to the Berlin Museum. The museum is now in East Berlin and the jewels are somewhere in the Soviet Union, yet another reason why the Turkish Government totally forbids the export of antiques.

Achileum The ancient city of Achileum is further down the road towards Kumkale ('sand tower'), but has even less to show than does Troy.

HOTELS

Anafartlar Hotel, Kayserili A Paşa Cad (tel 4451); two star, the town's best hotel.

Bakır Hotel, Yalı Cad 12 (tel 4088)

Mola Hotel, Güzelyalı İntepe (tel 22)

Ozan Hotel, Güzelyalı (tel 66)

Truva Hotel, Yalıboyu (tel 1024)

Tusan Hotel, İntepe (tel 1461); Mar — Sep

Yaldız Hotel, Kızılay Sok 20 (tel 1793)

PENSIONS

Gönül Pension, İnönü Cad 21 (tel 1503)

Gürbüz Pension, Atatürk Cad (I arrived at this pension at 1am and found impeccable service up to the standard of some three star hotels)

TOUR OPERATOR

The Troy-Anzac Travel Agency in Çanakkale (tel 1440) runs tours to the war cemeteries in the area.

EDREMIT

Edremit, at the head of its gulf, is a distinct contrast to Çanakkale. It's an old, undeveloped, and as yet unspoiled town despite its closeness to the sea. Here you will see asses hauling carts of farm produce through narrow streets lined with old houses, and in summer you may see heaps of melons stacked on the pavements, waiting for the buyer who never comes.

The town has a number of squares, linked by a maze of rambling streets humming with life at a really basic level. If you're 'doing' the Aegean and want to see Turkey as it really is without venturing deep into the interior, then come to Edremit.

If you stay overnight, be prepared for basic accommodation. The Doğan Palas is convenient for the bus station; perhaps a little too convenient at 5am.

To the west, the coast road runs through some spectacular scenery, particularly the descent into Küçükkuyu. There are several stretches of narrow and shingly beach by the villages of Altınulok and Akçay, with a choice of basic pension accommodation or even more basic 'camping,' in one instance in small wooden huts. Perfect if you want instant access to sheltered waters for swimming.

Five miles east of the town is a motel which draws on the waters of a hot spring, said to help sufferers of rheumatism.

And in the hills to the south-east is the site of Adramittium Thebe: the name has an obvious connection with Edremit, but this isn't the famous Thebes — that's in Egypt.

The road south bypasses **Burhaniye** and **Karaağaç**, a newish village full of white houses which look like holiday homes, but they're not.

Pyrrha On a lonely headland to the north-west is the site of yet another ancient city, Pyrrha, named from the mythical daughter of Epimetheus. She and Deucalion, son of Prometheus, were the only humans to survive a terrible Flood which, according to Greek mythology, the god Zeus inflicted upon the world to punish mankind. As the Flood receded, Pyrrha and Deucalion scattered human bones at Zeus's bidding and so re-created humanity.

This legend predates Christianity but has an obvious connection with the Old Testament story of what was presumably the same Flood. While the Greek account doesn't place Pyrrha's story at Pyrrha, it's worth noting that the ancient city site is at the opposite end of Turkey to Mount Ararat where Noah's ark grounded as the Biblical Flood receded.

AYVALIK　　Avyalık is a fishing village that is gradually gaining a reputation as the focal point for a cluster of small village resorts. It's a pity that the quayside to the west of the town centre has an olive oil refinery and a soap factory, each with tall chimneys. Avyalık itelf has few pensions, no night life, no beach, and not many long-distance buses leave the main road to make the five-mile detour into town.

Yet it's an interesting place, inhabited by Greeks until around 1920 when they were repatriated and their place taken by Greek-speaking Turks from Cyprus. The mosques began life in the 16th and 17th centuries as Greek Orthodox churches.

From Avyalık town centre you can take the Monday, Wednesday or Friday 1700hr Greek boat to Lesbos, but this town is more enterprising than some and there's a Turkish ferry as well, operating a more favourable timetable with an 0900 departure — yet still on those same three days. Both services drop to a once-weekly schedule in winter.

Boats leave the town quay for Ali Bey Island, just across the bay, though it's possible to go by dolmuş as a causeway connects Ali Bey to the mainland. There are around 22 other islands within easy reach, none of them inhabited.

Sarımsakli Plaji — Garlic Beach — to the south of town has the best sand in the neighbourhood, with a wide range of motel accommodation; just north of the beach is Şeytan Sofrası, the 'Devil's Table,' a hill that offers a spectacular viewpoint.

HOTELS

Avyalık Palas, Avyalık	Elif Hotel, Avyalık
Billurcu Hotel, Sarımsak	El Hotel, Avyalık
Ankara Hotel, Sarımsak	Kantarcı Hotel, Avyalık
Başhent Hotel, Sarımsak	Murat Reis Hotel, Tuza
Berk Hotel, Sarımsak	Özel Hotel, Avyalık
Canlı Balık Hotel, Avyalık	Sefa Hotel, Avyalık

AYVALIK

PENSIONS

Akbaş Pension, Sarımsak
Akkoç Pension, Avyalık
Altay Pension, Ali Bey
Atün Pension, Ali Bey
Balcı Pension, Ali Bey
Barbaros Pension, Ali Bey
Deniz Pension, Ali Bey
Fıçıcı Pension, Avyalık
Günay Pension, Ali Bey
Güneş Pension, Ali Bey
Murat Pension, Avyalık
Sayak Pension, Sarımsak
Şebi Pension, Sarımsak Sedef
Pension, Ali Bey
Uûr Pension, Ali Bey
Yıldız Pension, Ali Bey

MOTELS (a selection from those available)

Ahi Motel, Sarımsak
Altınkum Motel, Sarımsak
Angel Motel, Sarımsak
Avyalıktaş Motel, Sarımsak
Batı Motel, Tuzla
Çavdar Motel, Sarımsak
Çinar Motel, Sarımsak
Ege Motel, Sarımsak
Erbil Motel, Sarımsak
Karakaş Motel, Sarımsak
Kıyı Motel, Avyalık
Samanyolu Motel, Sarımsak
Şeref Motel, Sarımsak
Sevo Motel, Sarımsak
Uğrak Motel, Sarımsak
Varol Motel, Sarımsak
Yonca Motel, Sarımsak

CAMPING

Ada Kamping, Ali Bey
Çamlık Kamping, Çamlık

RESTAURANTS

'E' Restaurant, Altınova (20 km south)
Efes Birhanesi, Merkez Meydanı, Ayvalık

ENTERTAINMENTS

The option is confined to a choice of discos in Sarımsaklı Plaji.

BERGAMA

Bergama is one of the smartest and cleanest towns in Turkey, and the reason is plain to see. Modern Bergama is not only a market town serving a fertile coastal plain, but the ruins of ancient Pergamon put on the itinerary of every well-heeled tourist doing a guided tour of the archaeological sites of Asia Minor, and of passengers on luxury cruises to the Aegean who are landed at Dikili, 25 km to the west, for a guided tour of the one of the largest cities of ancient time to have survived into the modern age. (Dikili, by the way, is a small town that's growing and likely to feature in the holiday brochures in a few years. It has a small port — and a good beach.)

Bergama, therefore, is pristine, with some of the smartest roadside restaurants in the Aegean, with an immaculate marble-floored public lavatory on Hükümet Cad, the main street — but with few good hotels as most of the visitors are day trippers.

Pergamon Pergamon, the acropolis or hilltop city, dominates the summit of the 350-metre rugged mound to the north-east of town, while an early-day hospital, the Asclepion, nestles on the side of a gentle valley several kilometers away to the west.

There's no public transport to either place so the solo traveller faces the choice of a long hike — allow all day to see both places — or a taxi ride. If you opt for the taxi, pay it off at the Acropolis and come down to modern Bergama on foot, through the ruins of the Roman-era upper and lower markets: at least, you'll have seen something that the well-heeled travellers in their air-conditioned coaches must inevitably miss.

The ancient city's first recorded mention was in 399BC after the Spartans defeated the Athenians in the Peloponnesian War; the next mention was in

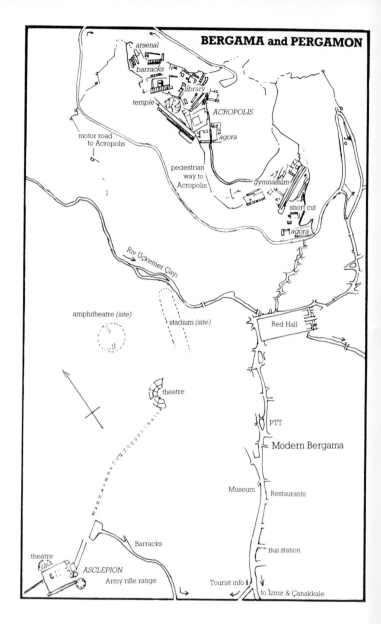

BERGAMA and PERGAMON

arsenal

barracks

library

temple

ACROPOLIS

agora

motor road
to Acropolis

pedestrian
way to
Acropolis

gymnasium

short cut

agora

Rıv Üçkemer Çayı

amphitheatre *(site)*

stadium *(site)*

Red Hall

theatre

PTT

Modern Bergama

Museum   Restaurants

Bus station

Barracks

theatre

ASCLEPION

Army rifle range

Tourist info **i**

to İzmir & Çanakkale

323BC after the death of Alexander the Great. Alexander, king of Macedonia, had conquered the western ports of Asia Minor in 333BC and had left one of his generals, Lysimachus, in control. With Alexander's death in battle his empire collapsed and Lysimachus assumed control of the western end of Asia Minor, plus a fortune from the spoils of many of Alexander's campaigns.

Lysimachus Lysimachus deposited his treasure in the rather primitive hilltop fortress of Pergamon and in 281BC went off to fight the Syrian king Seleucis to gain the remainder of Anatolia. He, too, was killed in battle, and Philetarus, custodian at Pergamon, inherited the region by default, much as Lysimachus had done.

Philetarus Philetarus, a eunuch, used his fortune wisely, giving some to neighbouring potentates to buy peace, and using some to enlarge the acropolis and its defensive walls. The eunuch's nephew Eumenes I (263-241BC) inherited Pergamon as its first king, in fact if not in title, and continued the expansion of the hilltop city.

His son Attalus I, self-styled king and saviour of Pergamon, extended his boundaries far to the east and helped the Romans in their conquest of Seleucia, Seleucis's kingdom on the Tigris. Attalus's son, Eumenes II (197-159BC), reaped the benefit of these favours when the Romans were reluctant to take control of their new territories, and Eumenes found himself ruler of a region extending from Troy to Ephesus to Konya.

Parchment The mighty king created himself a mighty capital at Pergamon by rebuilding the upper citadel, extending the city onto the southern slopes of the hill, and throwing a three-mile-long curtain wall around the fortress, enclosing lowland areas beside the river Üçkemer Çayı (Selinos). A true patron of the arts, he built the large library which was reputed at a later stage to hold 200,000 volumes, and when the Egyptians, fearing a rival to the library of Alexandria, cut off his supply of papyrus reed — it's that which gave us the word 'paper' — his scribes came up with a writing-material made from animal skin which they called *pergamen* from the city's name. We still use the same word but we pronounce it 'parchment.'

Attalus II, Eumenes's son, continued expanding his domains and founded the city of Attaleia, the present-day Antalya. But *his* son, Attalus III, was scarcely fit to rule a kingdom. A sadist, he cultivated poisonous plants and tried their toxins on condemned prisoners, and in 133BC, a mere five years into his rule, he died without heirs, bequeathing his kingdom to Rome.

Rome was now ready to accept the territory and it became the Province of Asia — not Asia *Minor*, but *Asia* — taking its place with the provinces of Lydia, Mycea, Bithnia (Bursa), Phrygia, Caria, Lycia, and others. And as a final act of degradation, Mark Anthony ransacked the Pergamene library to replace volumes lost to fire in the great library of Alexandria.

During the second century AD under the emperors Trajan and Hadrian, the city expanded down the slopes and onto the plain where it saw the building of a Roman temple dedicated to Egyptian gods: its gaunt ruins, called the Red Hall or Kızıl Avlu before their true purpose was known, stand amid the ordinary houses of modern Bergama.

Blood To the west, the Romans added the Asclepion, a vast hospital named from Aesculapius, the Roman god of medicine whose symbol was a snake: as the snake shed its skin, so would the Asclepion's patients shed their illnesses. The physician Galen (131-210AD) who practised here after studying in Alexandria, pioneered research into the circulation of blood which was not pursued until 1623 by William Harvey. Much of Galen's other work, which included herbal remedies, diet control, exercise, and dream analysis, formed the basis of medicine for a further 1,500 years.

The last of Pergamon's great works, the theatre at the Asclepion, the stadium, plus another theatre and an amphitheatre which lie midway between Asclepion and Acropolis, completed the scene.

As the Roman influence faded, so Pergamon declined, with a Byzantine wall being built around the citadel on the southern slopes of the hill. By the time the Arabs attacked in the 8th century, there was little worth defending.

PERGAMON TODAY

Much of Eumenes II's city still stands atop this rugged hilltop, having survived more than 2,000 years. German archaeologists started the excavation of the 30,000-acre site but Turkish specialists have taken over and are restoring the theatre and the Temple of Athena, arguably with too much enthusiasm.

Guides are available, both the human and the printed kind, but if you prefer to wander at random you can try following a series of blue dots which are intended to lead you round the site. Notice-boards with detailed plans of the various sections are a greater help.

Mains water At the northern tip of the ancient city by the ruins of the arsenal, look out across the open country towards the mountain of Madra Dağ, 45 km away. That's where Pergamon's water came from in the Roman era, in earthenware and lead pipes that came over three passes, crossed two hills and descended to the plain, carrying water under gravity and at times exerting a pressure of 20 atmospheres on its pipes.

The water supplied the public fountains, the cisterns, the baths, and the public sewerage system, and allowed the traders in the markets on the southern slopes to keep their wares clean and fresh.

If you're fairly fit, come down to Bergama via this southern route, passing the Attalid city's cemetery and the Roman sanatorium, its two gymnasia and the two agoras, or markets. You'll now welcome the blue dots as they lead you along a patch which at times becomes precipitous.

Asclepion Almost nothing remains of the Asclepion save the foundations, a tunnel, and the Sacred Well which still gushes with refreshing water, perfectly drinkable though there's no sign saying *içilir,* 'drinkable.'

You'll see the theatre from a long way off and will probably be tempted to photograph it, but there are signs in several languages, including English, hanging on a barbed wire fence and announcing that photography is forbidden as the valley contains an army rifle range.

Theatre The theatre, which has excellent acoustics, is much restored with a new marble proscenium, and cement patching in the seats to the left of the proscenium, the western side. This completely ruins the sense of history but it has allowed someone to calculate with a fine degree of certainty the original seating capacity: 2,500 people, in a hemispherical theatre with 23 rows of seats. Use this as a guide to calculate the seating capacity of other theatres you'll see on your travels and be sceptical of claims to audiences of 25,000.

For your mental ready-reckoner, the top row of the theatre would have held 170 people and each succeeding row would hold five more than the row beneath. It would take another 10 rows to double the seating capacity by which time the rate of increase would be compounded...

Museums Back on the main road to town you'll see two museums on your left. The Archaeological Museum holds most of the sculptures which the early German archaeologists never carried back to Berlin (and so, in 1945, to the USSR), but it has little appeal to anybody not studying the subject. The Ethnological Museum is more interesting to the casual visitor as it shows some of the carpets made in Bergama and some of the local costumes.

HOTELS
Balar Hotel, Hükümet Cad (basic)
Bergama Hotel, just off Hükümet Cad (absolutely basic)
Park Hotel, Hükümet Cad (basic)
Şehir Hotel, Hükümet Cad (basic)

PENSION
Akinci Pension, just off Hükümet Cad(basic)

MOTEL Tusan Bergama Motel, Bergama-Izmir Yolu (road to Izmir) (tel 1173)

CAMPING
Kleopatra Kamping, between Asclepion road and main coast road.

RESTAURANTS
Bergama Restaurant, Hükümet Cad
Doyum 2 Restaurant, near Balar Hotel, Hükümet Cad
Kardeşler Restaurant, Uzun Çarşı Cad
Sayın Restaurant, Uzun Çarşı Cad (part of Hükümet Cad)
Şehir Restaurant, Hükümet Cad
Tea Gardens, Hükümet Cad

AEOLIAN RESORTS
South from Bergama there are several small resorts and ancient city sites, all but one of which are several miles from the main road. **Çandarlı** is a small fishing-village on the site of the ancient city of Pitane, of which nothing remains. Pitane was founded by the Greeks when this part of the coast was

Bergama from the Acropolis of Pergamon

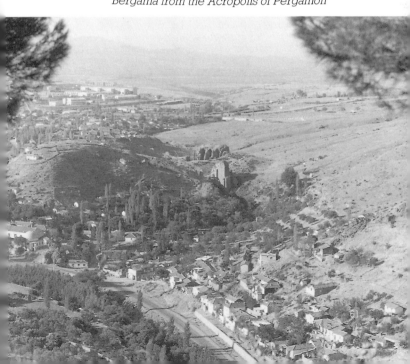

their colony of Aeolis, named from Aeolus, their god of the winds. Çandarlı's greatest attraction, apart from peace and quiet, is its 14th century fortres built by the Genoese who also held Lesbos and Chios islands.

On the other side of Çandarlı Bay, the ruins of the Aeolian cities of Gryneum and Myrina lie between the road and the coast, but there's nothing to see of them either, beyond a few scattered stones.

Aliağa Aliağa is the only town on this main road, and as it has its own little bay with a small beach, it's now a resort in the making: perhaps the Donmez Hotel may induce you to stay for the night. The original town was built from stones cannibalised from **Kyme**, in its time the largest city of ancient Aeolis and more important that Ephesus. Once again there's little to see of the old city, and the modern refinery certainly provides no inducement to linger.

Foça Twenty-five kilometers off the main road, Foça lies on a rugged headland overlooking the approaches to the Gulf of İzmir. Founded by the Ionians as Phocaea, though it was in the province of Aeolis, the town prospered so much that in the 6th century its inhabitants captured the ports of Nice and Marseille. The French have now returned the compliment by building a Club Mediterranée holiday village on the edge of town which, despite this intrusion, is an attractive fishing community with another of those Genoese fortresses.

HOTELS in Foça

The Hanedan, Palmerai and the Sultan hotels are on or near Büyükdeniz Cad in the town centre; Club Mediterranée (May-Sep) is on the edge of town. Small **restaurants** specialise in locally-caught fish.

IZMIR

For the third largest city in Turkey, there's surprisingly little to see in İzmir as wars, fire, and earthquakes have destroyed much of it. A quick glance at a street map would infer that the city centre is 9 Eylül Meydanı, Ninth-September Square, which commemorates the recapture of Smyrna by Atatürk's troops on that date in 1922. If not, then it's surely Cumhuriyet Meydanı, Republic Square, where Atatürk's statue looks proudly out to sea and towards the defeated Greeks.

Konak It's neither. The centre is marked by the Arab-styled clock tower towards the southern end of Cumhuriyet Bulvarı in the district known as Konak. Konak means 'government house' and here stands the building in question.

Bazaar A pedestrian footbridge allows for easy crossing of the very busy Cumhuriyet Bulvarı and leads you almost directly into Anafartlar Caddesi, İzmir's fascinating bazaar area. Here you will find small but smart shops selling spices, leather goods, jewellery, and many other items which could tempt the souvenir-hunter. There is also a wide range of lokantas and köftecis.

Agora Anafartlar Caddesi twists through the maze of old streets, crosses the main Gaziosmanpaşa Bulvarı and now, devoid of interest, heads east and then north to Eylül Meydanı. From the southern side of this duller section, sidestreets numbered 938, 940, 941 and 943 lead to the site of the Roman market-place, the Agora, now restored and with many of the columns re-erected as if they're just waiting to take the weight of the roof.

Look south-east from here — or, indeed, from many parts of the city — and you'll see the crags of the Greek Mount Pagos topped by the fortifications of Alexander the Great's Kadifekale.

Kadifekale It's a moderate walk from the Agora — the option is to take a

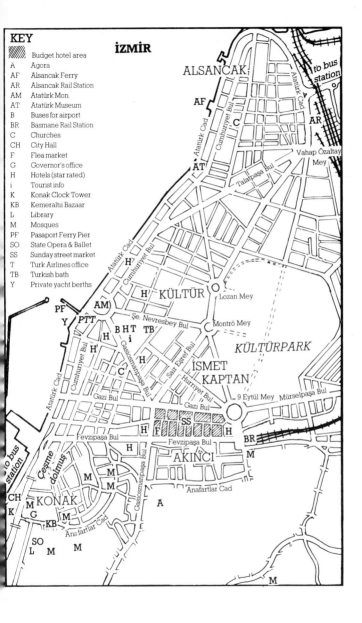

İZMİR

KEY

/////	Budget hotel area
A	Agora
AF	Alsancak Ferry
AR	Alsancak Rail Station
AM	Atatürk Mon.
AT	Atatürk Museum
B	Buses for airport
BR	Basmane Rail Station
C	Churches
CH	City Hall
F	Flea market
G	Governor's office
H	Hotels (star rated)
i	Tourist info
K	Konak Clock Tower
KB	Kemeraltı Bazaar
L	Library
M	Mosques
PF	Pasaport Ferry Pier
SO	State Opera & Ballet
SS	Sunday street market
T	Turk Airlines office
TB	Turkish bath
Y	Private yacht berths

ALSANCAK

to bus station

AF

Atatürk Cad

Cumhuriyet Bul

C

AR

Vahap Özaltay Mey

AT

Talatpaşa Bul

Atatürk Cad

Cumhuriyet Bul

H

KÜLTÜR

Lozan Mey

PF

AM

Y PTT

Şe. Nevresbey Bul

Montrö Mey

H B H T

i TB

KÜLTÜRPARK

Cumhuriyet Bul

H

Gaziosmanpaşa Bul

Sair Eşref Bul

İSMET

KAPTAN

Atatürk Cad

C

Gazi Bul

Hürriyet Bul

9 Eylül Mey

Mürselpaşa Bul

Gazi Bul

H F SS

H

Fevzipaşa Bul

to bus station

Çeşme dolmuş

Fevzipaşa Bul

BR

AKINCI

M

H

Anafartlar Cad

CH

M

M

Gaziosmanpaşa Bul

A

KONAK

K

G

KB

M

Anafartlar Cad

SO

L M

M

M

Sunday street market in Izmir

dolmuş from the bus station by the Konak Clock Tower — but the reward justifies the effort. This is the oldest surviving part of the city, Kadifekale, the 'Velvet Castle,' built by Antigonus and Lysomachus, the generals whom Alexander left in charge of the region shortly after he conquered Asia Minor in 333BC. It is also the spot the Aeolians had chosen around 1,200BC for their city of Myrina, which had the same name as their other city south of Bergama. *That*Myrina died; this one survived to become Smyrna and ultimately İzmir.

It's easy to see why Mount Pagos assumed such importance. The view from this spot is spectacular, encompassing almost all the sprawling modern city including the suburbs that swing around the northern shore of the Gulf of İzmir, but in ancient times Mount Pagos was vital for the view it gave down the narrow waterway that leads out to the open Aegean. Climb to the Velvet Castle at any time of day, but come if you can as dusk approaches and the lights twinkle out across the city and around the bay. The occasional jet airliner circling overhead on its approach to the new Adnan Menderes Airport, 16 miles away, adds to the illusion of Wonderland.

Kültürpark Back down at street level, 9 Eylül Meydanı offers an escape into the Kültürpark. For most of the year the park is purely for relaxation, offering a zoo, botanic garden, fairground, golf, tennis, an open-air theatre, a parachute tower and the Archaeological Museum, but from 20 August to 20 September, comfortably spanning that date of 9 Eylül, the Kültürpark is home to the Izmir International Trade Fair.

Tourist office 9 Eylül Meydanı also offers three tempting routes into modern, post-revolutionary İzmir, all of which lead in the general direction of Cumhuriyet Meydanı. The central road is Hürriyet Bulvarı — note the spelling of Hürriyet, meaning 'freedom,' compared with Cumhuriyet meaning 'republic' — which leads to Gaziosmanpaşa Bulvarı where, in smart new concrete and glass buildings that could be anywhere, you will find the head office of THY, the Turkish state airline; the tourist information office; the Bulvarıüyük Efes Hotel; and Budget rent-a-car. This is where the airport buses drop off and pick up their passengers.

Spare parts South-west of 9 Eylül Meydanı and bounded by Fevzipaşa Bulvarı and Gazi Bulvarı is the district for budget hotels and motor mechanics. It's the place to come if you need to buy, swap or repair a spare part for almost any make of car or truck; if you can't find what you want you'll find a mechanic who can make it, but if even that fails, come back on a Sunday when the central street called 1369 becomes an open-air market with anything and everything on sale. You want a new shirt, a left-handed thingummy, or even a broken watch? You'll find it here.

HOTELS

Anaba Hotel, Cumhuriyet Bulvarı 124 (tel 144380)

Babadan Hotel, Gaziosmanpaşa Bul 50 (tel 139640)

Billur Hotel, Basmane Meydanı 783 (tel 136250); near station, mid-range

Büyük Efes Hotel, Gaziosmanpaşa Bul 1 (tel 144300); five-star, with 296 rooms.

Etap İzmir Hotel, Cumhuriyet Bul 138 (tel 144290); four-star

İzmir Palas Hotel, Vasıf Çinar Bul 2 (tel 215583)

Karaca Hotel, 1379 Sok 55 (tel 144445)

Karaoğlu, 1369 Cad; basic

Katipoğlu Hotel, Fevsipaşa Bul 41 (tel 123373)

Kaya Hotel, Gaziosmanpaşa Bul 45 (tel 139711)

Kilim Hotel, Atatürk Bul (tel 145340)

Kismet Hotel, 1377 Sok 9 (tel 217050)

Yeteroğlu Hotel, 1369 Cad; basic

Yumukoğlu Hotel, Şair Eşref Bul 10 (tel 136565)

PENSIONS

Pansiyon Fa, 1375 Sok, 24, near Cumhuriyet Cad (tel 215178)

There are several small pensions scattered in the suburbs, but none is convenient for access to the city centre.

CAMPING

Incıraltı Kamping, on edge of city on the road to Çeşme.

RESTAURANTS

Bergama Restaurant, Cumhuriyet Mey

Büyük Efes Hotel Restaurant (see above)

Çin Restaurant, Necatibey Bul, 1379 Sok 57 (tel 257357)

Kordelya Restaurant, Atatürk Cumhuriyet (tel 148686)

Park Restaurant, Kültürpark (tel 141311); top of the market

Yengeç Restaurant Cumhuriyet Bul 236 (tel 217364)

There are plenty of lower-priced places at which to eat, particularly along the Anafartlar Cad as already mentioned.

ENTERTAINMENTS

The major hotels offer their own entertainments, and the summertime cabaret at the Büyük Efes is open to non-residents. Otherwise, from May to October, try the Kültürpark where you will find the Kubana and the Mogambo nightclubs.

TRANSPORT

There are numerous ways to travel in and around Izmir. The main bus station is to the north-east of the city and beyond the limits of our street plan: from here you can take buses to anywhere in the country *except* the Çeşme peninsula.

For destinations around Çeşme you need the much smaller bus station to the west of our street plan; it's by Fahrettin Altay Meydanı, where İnönü Cad meets Mithatpaşa Cad.

For a dolmuş to either bus station from the city centre, go to the Konak Clock Tower; this smaller bus station is also a handy starting point for bus trips to the Kadifekale and other places in the city, including the main Basmane rail station.

It's not really practical to take the train from Izmir unless you want the experience and are heading for Ankara or İstanbul. See the section on rail travel on page 52.

There are ferries from Konak and Alsancak to the suburbs on the other side of the bay; you can also sail from Izmir to Istanbul and the Black Sea, or south to Antalya, or across the Aegean to Greece and Italy; see 'Getting There' on page 26.

And you can go by air on THY to Ankara daily at 0800 or to İstanbul on up to eight flights a day — but you will need to book in advance. You'll recall that the THY office is on Gaziosmanpaşa Bul (reservations, phone 258280 and speak in English), and that's also where you get the airport bus.

BEYOND İZMİR

Manisa Manisa, 50 km north-east of İzmir, has been the town of mosques since 1922 when the invading Greeks destroyed much of the wealth of architecture that had endured earthquakes and other wars since Roman times. Strangely, the Greeks left the mosques of which the oldest is the Ulu Camii, the Great Mosque, dating from the early 14th century. The impressive 16th century Sultan Mosque was the gift of Ayşe Sultan, mother of Süleiman the Magnificent, and is the setting for a religious festival every April.

Nearby are the ruins of the Lydian city of Magnesia ad Sipilum — Sipil is the nearby mountain and national park — named thus to distinguish it from the Magnesia ad Maeandrum on the banks of the Menderes River, and a few miles to the east is the legendary location of the Rock of Niobe. Niobe was the mythological wife of Amphion, King of Thebes, and proud mother of twelve children. She mocked the goddess Leto who had only two offspring, the twins Apollo and Artemis, at which Leto ordered the twins to kill Niobe's family of twelve and turn Niobe herself into a stone which was to weep in perpetual remorse for her lost children. The rare metal niobium is named from her.

Magnet But it's the third Magnesia, in Greece's Thessaly, which has given us the word 'magnet' from the large amounts of iron ore which were found nearby. Early navigators learned that a chunk of the rock was sufficient to act as a compass needle when hung on a thread and this *lithos*, 'rock,' has come to us as the word 'lodestone.' Oh, yes — magnesium was also found in Thessaly.

Sardis The site of Croesus's city, Sardis, is 90 km east of Izmir near the modern village of Sart which lies to the south of the main road, Euroroute E96 and E881. The ruins are impressive and as they cover many acres it's worth considering coming here on an organised day trip from Izmir or Kuşadası.

The main attraction of Sardis must be the Temple of Artemis — Diana to the Romans — the controversial virgin goddess to whom women prayed in childbirth, and who helped slaughter Niobe's children (see above).

Only two columns remain of the 82 that originally supported the temple's portico (roof), but their capitals (capping stones) which show the ornate scrollwork that helps distinguish Ionic architecture are among the best that have survived to modern times. The temple faces west rather than the more conformist east, and by the front steps, facing the sunset, is an altar for receiving sacrifices to Artemis.

Coins The track from the temple back to Sart crosses a small stream, the River Pactolus, source of the alluvial gold on which Lydia's wealth was founded. Nearby is the groundplan of a large area of workshops, perhaps the world's oldest-surviving industrial estate or the earliest Arab-style bazaar. But it was here in these simple ruins that American archaelogists found the equipment on which the Pactolus gold was refined and cast into discs for the ultimate striking of the world's first coinage.

West from here on a scattering of sites are the remains of Sardis's stadium and theatre, the public baths, and a Roman road bordered by a 2nd century AD gymnasium and a 4th century basilica, later converted into a synagogue.

ACCOMMODATION

In Manisa, the Arma Hotel, Doğu Cad 14 (tel 1980); in Salihi (for Sardis), Alkent Tesisler Motel, İzmir-Ankara Yolu (road), Taytanköyü (tel 3462).

ÇEŞME

Çeşme is a resort that's waiting for the outside world to discover it. It has a long quay lining a sheltered bay, but the cruise yachts that make brief calls are based in Bodrum. There's a smart, man-made beach to the north, a mere 20 minutes' walk from the town centre, but few people stretch out on its sands. To the south of town and just five minutes from the castle is a landlocked harbour ideal for small-boat sailing, but there aren't any boats.

Things will inevitably change. Several tour operators are now listing Çeşme's virtues, and the nearby Altın Yunus (Golden Dolphin) Holiday Village with accommodation for almost 600 people is attracting custom to its specialised package holidays. Ironically there are probably more yachts in the Golden Dolphin marina than there are in Çeşme harbour itself.

Çeşme is a beautiful town, its western horizon framed by the peaks of the Greek island of Chios, rising to 1,297 metres — but Çeşme is on the wrong size of Izmir. The authorities have realised the problem and are planning a road that should hug the rugged coast all the way to Kuşadası: that should bring the crowds!

Çeşme is the Turkish word for 'spring,' 'fountain,' and during Ionian times from 1,200BC the area was one of the most important in Asia Minor for its curative waters, offering relief to sufferers of rheumatism in particular.

Fountains The springs are still there today, mainly in the villages of Şifne and Ilıca a few kilometers east, where many of the hotels have the healing waters on tap. There are a few springs which perversely surge up in the sea, allowing swimmers to give a new meaning to 'taking the waters.' In Çeşme itself there are six chubby Ottoman-style fountains where the townspeople collected their spa water in the days before it was piped to their homes, though for many people those days are still with them.

The waters of the Çeşme area are for drinking or for bathing, depending on the temperature. Those which gush out between 19°C and 25°C (67-77°F) are obviously for drinking, while many of the sources up to 52°C (125°F)

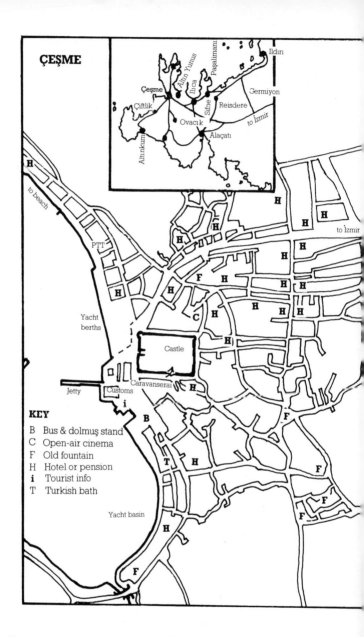

ÇEŞME

Ildırı
Altın Yunus
Ilıca
Paşalimanı
Çeşme
Çiftlik
Sifne
Germiyon
Reisdere
Ovacık
to İzmir
Altınkum
Alaçatı

to beach

H

PTT

Yacht berths

Castle

Yacht basin

Jetty
Customs
Caravanserai

KEY

B Bus & dolmuş stand
C Open-air cinema
F Old fountain
H Hotel or pension
i Tourist info
T Turkish bath

to İzmir

contain high concentrations of common salt and are therefore doubly suitable only for bathing.

Şifne's drinkable spa waters are prescribed for gynaecological problems, diseases of the throat and nose, calcium deficiency, and for sufferers of cerebral palsy.

Erythrai The Ionians, builders of the first thermal baths in the area, also built the city of Erythrai near where the modern village if Ildırı stands, 22 km north-east of Çeşme. Easy access by boat was the ruin of Erythrai after its downfall, as all the available masonry was taken away for use elsewhere and it's only in recent years that archaeologists have begun investigating the site. They've found on the small acropolis the foundations of a theatre and temple, and around it the suggestion of a curtain wall five kilometers long. The 6th and 7th century pottery recovered from the site is now on display in the İzmir Museum of Archaeology.

Castle The 14th century castle which dominates Çeşme town centre was restored in the 16th century by Bayazid II against the threat of attack from the Knights of St John, then at Bodrum Castle.

Çeşme Castle is still in a good state of repair though it's been spoiled internally by the addition of a large concrete floor and a stage, and now there are plans to provide amphitheatre-style seating and a fully-equipped open-air concert platform. The museum of Ottoman armaments in the castle could be improved with the addition of more exhibits.

Caravanserai The intriguing caravanserai immediately to the south of the castle was restored in 1982 and is now a smart hotel-restaurant with attendant boutiques, maintaining the original role of the caravanserais that lined the east-west trade routes across the Anatolian plateau in the days of the Ottoman Empire. The sultans provided these hostelries at around 40km intervals, a convenient day's journey for a laden camel, with the object of supplying free food and lodging for three nights, and free shoeing for men and horses.

Çeşme's caravanserai is of particular importance as it was the gift of Süleiman the Magnificent.

Russia The town had a much less glamorous role in the Russo-Turkish wars in the late 18th century. The Tzar's armies had driven the Turks out of the Crimea and the Balkan states and were advancing through Bulgaria when the Russian fleet sailed into the Aegean, caught the Turkish fleet in Çeşme harbour, and sank it.

The Çeşme Peninsula

One of the best beaches on the peninsula begins at **Ilıca** and stretches the two kilometers into **Şifne.** There are numerous small spas in the two villages with the waters piped to many of the hotels. The Çeşme tourist office claims there is scientific proof that the combination of spa water and ultra-violet radiation is beneficial to health; if that's so, come and luxuriate on the beach at Ilıca.

But the best beach of all — five kilometers of it — is at **Boyalık Koyu** just to the west; it's the home of the Golden Dolphin Holiday Village.

There's no accommodation at all at **Alaçatı**, which makes it another possible camping spot. The village is small but scenic and has a cluster of intriguing windmills. At the head of a deep bay, it has a good beach, and the local craft speciality is handwoven bathing costumes.

Çiftlik Köy (village), nearer Çeşme, has a wide range of accommodation, a grand beach — Pırlanta Plaji, translated as 'Diamond Beach' — and easy access to the sands of Altınkum, the 'Golden Sand.'

Donkey Island To the north of the Golden Dolphin and just off our inset map is Eşek Adası, Donkey Island, populated (as if you haven't already guessed) with wild donkeys.

HOTELS

Akdeniz Hotel, İnkilap Cad
Alakuş Hotel, Ilıca (tel 1308)
Ankara Hotel, Ilıca (tel 1371)
Baykal Hotel, Ilıca (tel 1208)
Çeşme, Ilıca (tel 1240) four-star
Değirmen Hotel, Çiftlik
Erciş Hotel, Ilıca (tel 1233)
Ertan Hotel, Cumhuriyet Mey 12 (tel 6795); town centre Huzur Hotel, Ilıca
Ilıca Palas, Ilıca (tel 1026)
İmren Hotel, İnkilap Cad (tel 1635)
İnkim Hotel, Yaykin Mey (tel 1946)
İstanbulotel, Ilıca (tel 1011)
Kanuni Kervansaray Hotel, town centre (tel 6490)
Küçük Ev, Dalyan (tel 2443)
Mahmudiye Hotel, Ilıca (tel 1359)
Mehtap Hotel, Ilıca (tel 1160)
Rasim Palas Hotel, Ilıca (tel 1010)
Sahil Karabina, Ilıca (tel 1007)
Şark Hotel, Ilıca (tel 1424)
Şifne Hotel, Ilıca (tel 1341)
Şirin Villa Hotel, Ilıca Mah 152 (tel 1021)
Termal Hotel, Ilıca
Turban Çeşme Hotel, Ilıca Mey (tel 1240); four-star
Turban Ilıca Hotel, Dereboyu Mey Boyalık (tel 2128)
Uludag Hotel, Ilıca (tel 1366)
Yeni Karabina Hotel, Ilıca (tel 1105)

MOTELS

Motel Palaz, Ilıca (tel 2128)
Motel Balin, Ilıca (tel 1228)

PENSIONS (A random selection; there are plenty in Çeşme) Acar Pension, Memiş Sok 6

Acar I Pension, Ertürk Sok 36
Afrodit Pension, Davutağa Sok 15
Cesular Pension, İnkilap Cad
Çiftlik Pension, Çiftlik

Durak Pension, Uzun Sok 1
Kale Pension, Keskin Sok (overlooks open-air cinema)
Merkes Pension İnkilap Cad 27
Ruyam Pension, Ilıca
Ünsal Pension, Yalı Cad 26
Uz Pension, Çeşme

HOLIDAY VILLAGE

Altın Yunus Tatil Köyü, Boyalık (Golden Dolphin) (tel 1250)

CAMPING

Altınkum Kamping, Çiftlik
Pirlata Kamping, Çiftlik
Turista Kamping, Çiftlik
Vakıflar Kamping, Ilıca
Ve-Kamp, Ilıca
Tekke-Camping, Çeşme

APARTHOTELS

1st Hotel Park, Ilıca (tel 1266)
2nd Hotel Park, Boyalık

RESTAURANTS (a selection)

Boyalık Pide Salonu, Boyalık; specialises in pide bread
Charlie Restaurant, İnkilap Cad; first-class
Han Pub, Cumhuriyet Mey; classy, nice location
Imbat Restaurant, Ilıca
Pina Restaurant, Ilıca
Kale Pup, by Castle. A true pub though spelled 'pup'
Kervanserai, Çeşme centre; first-class and in historic surroundings
Körfez Restaurant, Kordonboyu; first-class
Park-Otel Restaurant, Ilıca; first-class
Ufuk Restaurant, Hürriyet Cad; mid-range

There are a number of small restaurants along the Hürriyet Cad, most specialising in freshly-caught fish dishes.

Çeşme and the Otel Ertan

ENTERTAINMENTS

The Altın Yunus is the best place for night-life and it's open to non-residents. There are discos at the Hotel Çeşme at Ilıca, and there are two in Boyalık Yolu in town. The Pansiyon Artıf occasionally stages belly-dancing.

TOUR OPERATORS

Allegro, Balkan Holidays, Golden Horn Travel, Metak Holidays, Sunquest. The local firm Ertürk at Cumhuriyet Mey (tel 26147) offers a wide range of services and activities including ticket reservations, water sports, fishing trips, tours of the thermal springs, and trips to Chios and Cyprus on its own boats.

THE ROAD TO EPHESUS

When the Çeşme-Kuşadası road is built it should give easy access to the little village of **Sığacık**, which is something of an anomaly: it's a pretty, typically-Turkish fishing village, yet it has one of the smartest marinas on the Aegean.

Nearby is the site of the Ionian city of Teos, which was once more important than Smyrna. Founded around 900BC the city honoured the Greek god Dionysus, better known to us under his Roman name of Bacchus, god of wine. Appropriately, one of the citizens of Teos was the poet Anacreon who wrote verses about wine, women and song, and who choked to death on a grape pip.

There's little to see of Teos today. Blocks of masonry are littered across the landscape and the only recognisable ruin is the Temple of Dionysus hiding in an olive grove.

71

Colophon and Notion The new road should pass between the Ionian port of Notion and the inland city of Colophon which it served.

The citizens of ancient Colophon didn't welcome visitors and would set their packs of fighting dogs on any travellers whom they didn't trust. Alyatta, father of King Croesus, managed to penetrate their defences around 600BC, and laid waste to the place.

Today, Colophon is still unwelcoming. It's 20 km from the main road along a low-grade lane, and there are only a few low walls to reward the effort.

Claros Claros, around 10 km further along, is the site of the Temple of Apollo which served Colophon, and it's almost impossible to find. French archaeologists discovered it in 1950 but the ruins lie on land so waterlogged that they've almost been buried under alluvium.

It's only 20 km from Claros to Selçuk across country, but the road is so bad you'll need to retrace your steps — and that'll add 100 km to your journey.

SELÇUK

Selçuk's greatest claim to fame is undoubtedly the Temple of Artemis, yet only a tiny minority of the thousands of people who go from Selçuk to Ephesus each summer day are aware that one of the seven wonders of the ancient world stood right here beside the road.

Artemision Only a single stone column rising forlornly from a pond marks the site of the Artemision, the Temple of Artemis, yet in its glory it had 127 columns each almost 20 metres high, a true worldly wonder.

The English architect John Wood came here in 1863 and in 11 years of digging exposed significant portions of Ephesus and found a carving which described the route from the theatre to the temple, along which sacred images were carried. With that clue Wood eventually located the ruins of the Artemision under five metres of silt; his diggings, and those of his successor David Hogarth (who sent many of his findings to the British Musem), created the present pond.

Statue of Artemis The Ephesus Archaeological Museum in Selçuk contains another wonder: the statue of Artemis which is supposed to have fallen from heaven. Some authorities claim that the statue of the mother-goddess of fertility has a bosom consisting of some 25 small breasts, but another argument is that the girdle of egg-like objects is composed of bulls' testes, the seeds of fertility. There are no nipples and as the objects are more obscene than erotic, the latter theory is probably correct.

Selçuk owes its name and its existence to St John the Evangelist, brother of Jesus's mother Mary and a pupil of that other St John, the Baptist. John, for years a fisherman on the Sea of Galilee, stood by the crucifixion cross at Calvary and obeyed Jesus's request to care for his mother.

Gospel John moved to Asia Minor and set up home in this small community near the city of Ephesus, almost certainly bringing his sister Mary. It was here, according to popular belief, that John wrote his Gospel and received the Revelation, and it was here, too, that he was buried: the Virgin Mary was presumably buried at Ephesus as we shall see,

The Roman emperor Justinian I (483-565), best known for his *Codex Justinian*, believing that a third-century tomb marked John's grave, built the Basilica of St John on the nearby hill.

Earthquakes have levelled the church — what you see today is a complete rebuilding job — but the name of *St Jean Theology* endured, for Jean — John — had become one of the patron saints of the Byzantine Empire, and December 27 is still celebrated in his honour.

The Ottomans, however, corrupted St Jean Theology into Ayothologo and eventually into Ayasoluk, which was the town's name until the Atatürk revolution when it became Selçuk. The hill is still known by the old name.

But if you're looking for a twist in the tale, try this: the Seljuks, originating in the eastern Anatolian town now known as Silifke, came here, rebuilt the citadel on top of Ayasoluk hill, and added a Seljuk mosque which is still here. They also built the Isa Bey Camii (mosque) at the base of the hill, which is now a minor tourist attraction.

Camels On a completely different cultural plane, Selçuk holds a camel-wrestling festival every January in which males are urged to force their opponents into submission. You'll probably see a camel or two on the road to Ephesus, but you'll not be able to hire one for the three-kilometre journey; for that you'll need a dolmuş or a pair of good legs.

ACCOMMODATION

There's a Tusan Motel near the turning for Ephesus, and there are several pensions in town: the Akbulut on 2 Spor Sahası, the Kirhan on Turgutreis Cad, the Mengi also on 2 Spor Sahası, and the Sentop on 3 Spor Sahası. *Spor Sahası* is an usual name for a road: it means 'sports field.'

EPHESUS

You wouldn't consider going to Cairo and not seeing the Pyramids. Nor should you consider coming to south-west Turkey and not visting Ephesus.

Ephesus, Efes in Turkish, is not just a heap of stones; it's not just the site of one of the seven wonders of the ancient world; nor is it the historical and religious connections. Ephesus is the largest and best-preserved city of its age anywhere in the world and a walk along its main streets is a truly unforgettable experience — you can always go back to the beaches tomorrow.

The site is vast and starts on the edge of Selçuk with the Temple of Artemis, the Greek goddess who was the patron of women in childbirth and who was associated with Cybele, alias Rhea, whose parents were the heavens and the earth. Cybele became the Phrygian goddess of fertility and, as Diana, the Roman goddess of love.

The first record of her being worshipped was around 6,800BC at Çatal Hüyük, south-east of Konya and arguably the oldest city in the world; by the time her cult has reached the Aegean, she was firmly identified as Artemis.

Herostratus The Temple of Artemis was 107 metres by 55, the columns rose 17.6 m, and it was the largest building of ancient times built completely in marble. But it wasn't just one temple: seven times it was destroyed, and six times rebuilt, on one occasion on a foundation of coal covered with leather. The eccentric Herostratus set fire to the temple in 356BC in what has proved to be a successful attempt to have his name remembered in perpetuity — historians are quick to note that the event occurred on the night Alexander the Great was born — and the subsequent rebuilding incorporated several improvements.

At one stage in its history the temple was a bank, with deposit and loan facilities; it was also a refuge against persecution as were many Christian churches in the Middle Ages. King Mithradites extended the sacred area, the refuge, to the range of an arrow shot from the temple steps, and Mark Anthony doubled it.

Destruction The temple's final destruction was in 262AD when a band of marauding Goths, who had sailed down the Dniestr River into the Black Sea, sacked Ephesus in passing. Ephesus was rebuilt, but the Temple of Artemis never rose again.

Gymnasium Proceed from the temple towards Ephesus proper, if you're

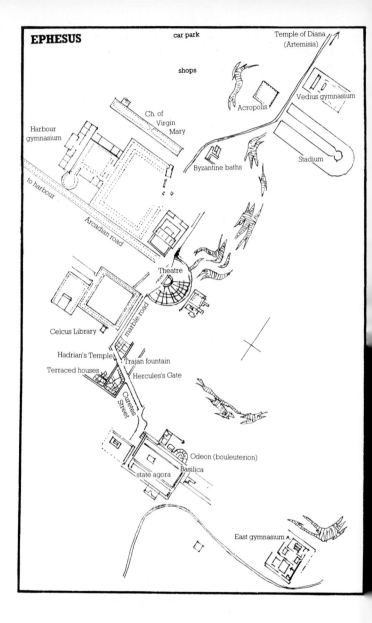

EPHESUS

car park

shops

Temple of Diana
(Artemisia)

Acropolis

Vedius gymnasium

Ch. of
Virgin
Mary

Harbour
gymnasium

Byzantine baths

Stadium

to harbour

Arcadian road

Theatre

marble road

Celcus Library

Hadrian's Temple

Trajan fountain

Terraced houses

Hercules's Gate

Curetes
Street

Odeon (bouleuterion)

Basilica

state agora

East gymnasium

on foot leaving any luggage at the gift shop near the Tusan Motel: you won't be allowed on site if you're equipped for carrying off archaeological treasures.

The first ancient building you'll see is the gaunt ruin of the Gymnasium of Vedius on your left. Built by the Vedius family of Ephesus, the structure was dedicated to Artemis; it contains an exercise room — our interpretation of 'gymnasium' — and lavatories, and excavation is continuing in the basement.

Nearby is the stadium, 230 metres by 30 metres, where gladiators and wild animals slaughtered captive Christians, but when Christianity became the Ephesian religion the people destroyed the stadium, quite literally leaving no stone unturned.

Seven Sleepers A side road leads to the Cave of the Seven Sleepers, where some early Christian youths hid after refusing to sacrifice animals to Artemis. They slept, not for a night, but for 200 years, and found Christianity had become the established religion in Ephesus. Some theorists believe that this is the site where the Virgin Mary is buried.

Walking on, you pass the site of the Byzantine baths and begin to suspect that Ephesus may be larger than expected. Then you see the large car and coach park (cars 100TL) and public toilets (also 100TL) and the avenue of souvenir shops leading to the modern gate into the ancient city of Ephesus.

Virgin Mary Don't go there yet. Turn to your right, look for two Corinthian columns flanked by two stone and brick piers, and you'll have found the first church to be dedicated to the Virgin Mary. The 2nd BC century building, 260 by 30 metres, was the meeting place for the Third Ecumenical Council in 431AD, when the principles of Christianity were decreed. The council also created the first written record that the mother of Jesus was buried here at Ephesus, though nobody knows exactly where.

Now you may enter the city. As you walk in under the welcome shade of a cluster of pines you have the first glimpse of a theatre away on your left as you pass the site of the Verulanus sports area on your right. Beyond the area was the harbour gymnasium which, 2,000 years ago, extended almost to the water's edge.

Even at the peak of Ephesus's prosperity, the River Kaystros (Küçük Menderes or 'Little Meander') began silting the harbour. Attalos III of Pergamon tried to dredge a channel and Emperor Hadrian wanted to divert the river, but eventually the silt succeeded and Ephesus's decline began. Today the sea is almost 5km away, and still receding.

Arcadian Avenue Coming out of the coppice you find yourself suddenly stepping onto the marble flagstones of Arcadian Avenue, more soberly known as Harbour Street. Around 30 complete columns lining the road give it a magisterial atmosphere and as you turn left you come into full view of the vast theatre.

Theatre Compare Ephesus's theatre with the one at the Pergamon Asclepion: *that* wrapped just 90° around the orchestra, the circular area in front of the stage, and could seat 2,500 in its 23 rows. Ephesus's theatre has 57 rows which sweep 125° around the 34-metre-diameter orchestra, and could accommodate 24,000 with no exaggeration. (The Romans extended the orchestra by 5 metres from its Ionian original.)

Climb to the topmost row of seats and try to imagine the scene 2,000 years ago, with the all-male actors playing to a full house, and with merchants and slaves carrying bales and barrels from the harbour along Arcadian Avenue into the city.

Hadrian's Temple at Ephesus

Turning right at the top of the avenue you enter Marble Road which leads you past the agora (market place) on your right, and a brothel on your left; a female head, foot, and symbolised heart carved into the pavement mark the entrance to the premises.

Celcus Library But already you are aware of the immense film-set of a building at the end of the street. This is the Celsus Library and its restored two-storey façade is arguably the most impressive building in Ephesus, even outclassing the theatre. It was begun in 114AD by Tiberius Julius Aquila as a mausoleum for his father, Tiberius Julius Celsus Polemaeanus, governor of the province of Asia around 106AD, and it could hold 12,000 scrolls.

The Goths, attacking in 262, destroyed all but the façade, which was brought down by an earthquake in the tenth century, and rebuilt early in the twentieth.

The road turns to the left, passes the site of the Heracles Gate, and becomes Curetes Street. A curete was a Jupiter-worshipping inhabitant of Crete though the word later applied to Ephesian priests...and perhaps to our own curates?

A walk along Curetes Street is like a walk through a vast open-air museum and takes you through the heart of what was once a thriving city. There are the baths where the Roman élite, and their poor servants, could luxuriate. Further along are the latrines which give the word 'public' another meaning, and there's a second brothel.

Temple of Hadrian The Temple of Hadrian on the left is one of the most impressive buildings now on the street. Four Corinthian columns support a heavily-ornamented semicircular arch, behind which stands most of the ground-floor façade of the temple, with a plaster copy of the original frieze which is in the Ephesus Museum in Selçuk. The frieze shows Androclos chasing the boar which ultimately told him where to establish the city, and with him are several of his supporting Amazons.

Hadrian's Temple was destroyed in one of the 4th century earth tremors and it's believed that in rebuilding the Romans took this frieze from another ruin.

City Walls Continuing along Curetes Street and passing the state agora, a market place measuring 160 by 50 metres, you come to the city walls, built by Lysimachos in the 3rd BC century and still in a good state of preservation (see Pergamon for more about Lysimachos). Beyond the wall is the Virgin Mary Road; turn left and you eventually find yourself by the Temple of Artemis, your tour completed.

House of the Virgin Mary But if you turn right and continue for around 7 kilometers you can relive an extraordinary psychic detective story. Katherina Emmerich, a bedridden German who had never been to Turkey, had several visions showing her where Jesus's mother had lived her final years in Ephesus, and put them in her book, *The Life of the Blessed Virgin Mary*, published late in the 19th century. A Lazarist priest from Izmir followed the indicated trail, found a house which fitted Kathernia's description exactly, and learned that the local Orthodox Greeks traditionally held mass there on 15 August, the anniversary of Mary's death.

The house, whose foundations probably date from the 1st century, was restored in 1951 and 16 years later Pope Paul VI visited it. Katherina also described the Virgin Mary's tomb, located a kilometer from the house, but that remains one of the mysteries of Ephesus.

THE RISE AND FALL OF EPHESUS

Amazons The Amazons, as we all know, were a tribe whose women warriors sliced off their right breasts so they wouldn't foul their bowstrings. They draped clothing across the scar but kept the left breasts exposed. Most people have heard that the Amazons despised men, except for one night of orgy each year, and the resulting male infants were killed at birth.

What is therefore astonishing is that their leader Androclos, a mere male (and in no way connected with the slave Androcles who removed a thorn from a lion's foot), is credited with leading the Amazons down the Aegean coast and founding the city of Ephesus.

But let us go back to Çatal Hüyük near Konya around 8,700 years ago, where began the belief in a mother-goddess, originator of all living things. By the time the Ionians had absorbed this goddess she had assumed a variety of names, the local one being Artemis Ephesia.

Androclos After the fall of Troy, Androclos, son of King Kondros of Athens, led a band of Amazons south through Aeolus and Ionia, seeking a site for his new city. An oracle had told him that a fish and a boar would indicate the exact spot, and when a fish he was frying leaped (or slid) out of the pan, causing a bush fire that set a wild boar into flight, Androclos knew he had arrived. He built the first Temple of Artemis Ephesia on the spot, and so the city had its name.

Earliest relics, now in the Ephesus Museum in Selçuk, include bowls dated to 1,400BC, by which time Ephesus must have been in existence, though totally unlike the city we can see today.

To complicate matters, an Ephesian poet of the 7th BC century stated that the Amazon who *captured* Ephesus, inferring the Amazons were not there at the foundation, was named Smyrna. Later, said the poet, Ephesians travelled north and built the city of Smyrna (İzmir), though other records claim the city's first name was Myrina.

Croesus Androclos died in battle against the Carians and in the 7th BC century the Cimmerians from the Crimea attacked Ephesus, destroying the Temple of Artemis. The rebuilt city rose to great power but in 560BC King Croesus attacked. The Ephesians stretched a rope from the rebuilding Temple of Artemis to the city, and prayed to Artemis for protection.

Of course, it didn't work, but Croesus completed the temple and gave a column cap bearing his name: it's now in the British Museum. Croesus fell victim to Cyrus (Chiros) of Persia who created the satrapy (province) of Ionia, in which Ephesus prospered as a cultural and commercial centre. But the Ephesians resented the ever-increasing taxes they had to pay and in 500BC they revolted, but were put down six years later.

Lysimachus Alexander the Great conquered all of western Asia Minor in 334BC and under his successor Lysimachus, Ephesus again prospered, this time within a protective city wall. Family feuding allowed the Egyptians and the Seleucids from Syria to rule briefly, but when Attalus III of Pergamon died in 133BC bequeathing all his lands to Rome, Ephesus was included.

Asia In 88BC taxes were again so high that the Ephesians revolted; King Mithradites VI of Pontus came to the city and ordered the execution of every Roman within its walls, so that 80,000 people were slaughtered in one day. If that figure can be believed, it gives an indication of the size of the city.

Rome retaliated, Augustus transferred the capital of Asia from Pergamon to Ephesus, and the city became one of the top five in the province, but its fate was already evident as the harbour gradually silted. In 262AD the Goths, who sailed down the Dniestr River to the Aegean, sacked the city. Ephesus was rebuilt, but this time the Temple of Artemis was left in ruins: Christianity had arrived.

Paul, John and Mary St Paul, expelled from Jerusalem around 40AD, is known to have come to Ephesus in 53; he established the first church in the city and began preaching the new religion. Christianity became the rage but not without some dissent, as Acts 19 records:

[11] And God wrought special miracles by the hands of Paul:

[17] And this was known to all the Jews and Greeks also dwelling at Ephesus; and fear fell on them all, and the name of the Lord Jesus was magnified.

[20] So mightily grew the word of God and prevailed.

[23] And the same time there arose no small stir about that way.

[24] For a certain man named Demetrius, a silversmith, which made silver shrines for Diana, brought no small gain unto the craftsmen;

[25] Whom he called together with the workmen of like occupation, and said, Sirs, ye know that by this craft we have our wealth.

[26] Moreover ye see and hear, that not alone at Ephesus, but almost throughout all Asia, this Paul hath...turned away much people...[27] also that the temple of the great goddess Diana should be despised, and her magnificence should be destroyed, whom all Asia and the world worshippeth.

[28] And when they heard these sayings, they were full of wrath, and cried out, saying, Great is Diana of the Ephesians...

St Paul was nearly killed. He fled to Macedonia and ultimately went to Rome for his martyrdom. Meanwhile, St John the Evangelist established himself carefully as the head of the Christian church in Asia. An anti-christian revolt in Smyrna led to his being taken to Rome and exiled to Patmos, but he returned in old age to Ephesus where he wrote his Gospel and received his Revelations.

Ghost town Ephesus was long into its decline when the Arabs first attacked in 768, but the Ephesians managed to reinforce their basilica on the Ayasoluk hill by Selçuk. When the Ottomans under Çaka Bey took Selçuk in 1304 and built the Isa Bey Mosque, Ephesus was already a ghost city. It stayed that way until 1869 when John Wood began digging and found the Temple of Artemis. David Hogarth continued in 1904, and Austrian archaeologists took over in '05.

Up to 1905 all finds from Ephesus were sent to the British Museum, and from that year until 1923 they went to Austria. One glimpse of the treasures in the Ephesus Museum, not to mention the many other archaeological museums in Turkey, is enough to explain the Turkish Government's tough stand on the export of antiquities.

PAMUKKALE

One hundred and eighty kilometers due east of Ephesus along the Büyükmenderes Valley lies yet another ancient city, Hierapolis, but this time the main attraction is the limestone terraces of Pamukkale.

View them from several miles away on the valley floor and you appreciate the name of *pamuk kale*, 'cotton castle.' Come closer and you can see water cascading down the white cliffs and forming basins ten or even 100 metres long, seemingly supported on columns of stalactites.

Death trap The Pamukkale terraces were here before man first set foot in Anatolia, their waters gushing forth at a steady 35°C from a cave that was once thought to be the entrance to Hell. It's now called Cin Deliği, the Devil's Hole, and the excess of carbon dioxide in its atmosphere makes it a death trap for anything venturing inside.

Early priests who walked into the Mouth of Hell would manage to come out alive either because they held their breath or because they knew of pockets of oxygen, but small animals and birds they took in always succumbed to suffocation.

The Phrygians realised the waters had healing properties, and under Roman and Byzantine rule the nearby city of Hierapolis thrived as a thermal resort, with emperors Hadrian and Constantine among its visitors. The fall of Byzantium took Hierapolis into a terminal decline and the area was ignored until excavation began in 1887.

Cotton Castle But nobody bothered about Cotton Castle until the 1960s when the first of the hotels and motels went up. Now there's a thriving health-farm atmosphere about the place with people seeking cures for rheumatic, neurological and circulatory disorders.

As the waters cool with exposure to the air, the carbon dioxide is released, which not only accounts for the death trap at Devil's Hole, but helps dilate the capillaries of people taking the waters. And as the cooling waters evaporate they deposit calcium carbonate, limestone, either on the

The calcified terraces of Pamukkale

HIERAPOLIS

Eumenes II of Pergamon established Hierapolis around 180BC, but did he call it after Hiera, the wife of Telephos, the legendary founder of Pergamon, or should we take it literally as 'holy city,' which is how the Greek translates?

Either way, nothing of that original community remains as the earthquake of 17AD, which did so much damage across the Aegean, levelled Hierapolis. The Romans, who had inherited the Kingdom of Pergamon on the death of Attalos III in 133BC, rebuilt during the first century after Christ, and it's the structures dating from that era whose ruins we see today.

Emperor Constantine made Hierapolis the capital of Phrygia and saw it prosper. With the spread of Christianity, many of the Jewish population converted to the new faith and Hierapolis became in fact as well as in name, the holy city of the area, with a surfeit of temples.

It even became home to a Christian saint, Philip, one of the twelve apostles, who was probably martyred here around 80AD. If the date is accurate, he must have lived to a great age for that period of history.

rims of the basins or on the terraces.

If you want to see Pamukkale at its best, come soon. Tourists are allowed to wander at will across the terraces, which is fine if you want a dip in one of the basins — bring your swimming gear — but is disastrous on much of the hillside where the rock which has taken years to form is destroyed underfoot in seconds.

Hierapolis today

The Roman city was built on the grid pattern and as the main street was more than two kilometers long, seeing the sights involves either a lot of walking or hiring one of the several taxis that cruise the area.

Theatre The second-century Roman theatre, with about 10,000 seats in 45 tiers, is without question the most spectacular of the relics and is still being restored. The proscenium, which looks far too modern for comfort, has a frieze with scenes showing Apollo and Artemis.

St Philip Behind the theatre is the ruin of the large, square 5th-century martyrium of St Philip; it can scarcely be called a mausoleum since we don't know if it's on the site of the saint's grave.

Necropolis North of the city and outside its Byzantine walls lies the necropolis, the 'city of the dead,' a cemetery with more than 1,000 tumuli, sarcophagi and tombs, many showing evidence of seismic disturbance and quite a few having been defaced in the 11th century by the invading Seljuks whose Moslem beliefs forbade acceptance of sculpting of the human anatomy.

Museum The second-century Roman baths near the car and coach park now hold the museum (open daily, 0900-1200, 1330-1700) where once the Emperor Hadrian wandered through the caldarium and tepidarium to the frigidarium.

AMENITIES

The three-star Tusan Motel is top of the market, followed by the Hierapolis Hotel. Middle-range accommodation is at the Turizm Motel

Coach operators have their own ticket offices in most bus stations

where you can swim in what was once Hierapolis's sacred pool, the Belteş Hotel, and several pensions. Most have thermal water on tap and most insist on half-board, yet they provide Pamukkale's restaurants, which makes a mockery of compulsory half-board. You can camp at the smaller Mistur, and at the Belediye Tesisleri where you can also eat cheaply. At the foot of the hill there's the Konak Sade which provides bed and board.

Pamukkale has a tourist information office, a small PTT, and there are plenty of souvenir shops.

Access? Many people come on organised coach tours from the coast which guarantee a seat both ways but rob you of flexibility of movement. On public transport come to Denizli by bus and complete the journey by dolmuş, which will also allow you to see Laodiceia. Aphrodisias isn't far away over the mountains but the best way to reach it from here is via Nazili, half way back to Selçuk. There are three trains a day each way between Denizli and İzmir, and they're all slower than the buses.

You can choose to base yourself at **Denizli** for a night or two in which case it's handy to know that the tourist office is in the railway station which is in the town centre opposite the bus station — and the PTT's only a street away in İstasyon Cad.

Denizli has several reasonable hotels, including the Altuntur on Kaymakçı Cad, the Etemağa and the Sarıkaya on the aforementioned İstasyon Cad, and the Halley on Cumhuriyet Cad 100 metres away. Denizli has 15,000 people, but there's no inducement for you to make it 15,001.

LAODICEIA

Laodiceia is not too far from Denizli but there's not much to see. The city was rebuilt in the 3rd BC century by Antiochus II of Syria on the ruins of the original Diospolis. Cicero lived here for a few years; Mithradites, King of Pontus, sacked the place when he slaughtered the Romans in Ephesus; and earthquakes later finished the destruction. There was a brief revival under the Byzantines but the 'quake of 494 again laid the city to waste.

Excavation began in 1961 but the site, some way from the road near Eskihisar, offers scant traces of two theatres and a 350-metre-long stadium, with much of the other masonry forming the hardcore of the railway...built by the British. Laodiceia's main claim in the Christian community is as the site of one of the seven churches of the Apocalypse mentioned in Revelations 3:14.

AK HAN CARAVANSERAI

The Ak Han, or 'white inn,' on the main road a kilometer east of the Pamukkale turning, rewards a brief diversion. It was one of the chain of caravanserais built across Turkey in the 13th century (see Çeşme), and takes its name from the white marble of its eastern façade.

The remains of a gate lead to the 110 square-metre courtyard from which it's possible to climb to roof level, and from where the Sultan's soldiers watched over arriving and departing camel and horse caravans.

APHRODISIAS

Aphrodite was the Greek goddess of love, and the excavation of Aphrodisias has been a labour of love for the Turkish professor Kenan Erim who began coming over from New York University in the summer of 1961.

As a result, there's plenty to see here, notably the Temple of Aphrodite herself, though few of the columns remain standing. The stadium is one of the best-preserved from the Roman era and could seat around 30,000 spectators, and there's a small odeon or odeum, a theatre dedicated to musical performances.

The first human habitation here was around 5,000 years ago, but the city now on show was built in the 6th BC century. Although it was dedicated to Aphrodite from the beginning, her temple was probably begun in the last century before Christ, and it soon developed into a school for sculptors, as shown by the many unfinished carvings found on site.

The Romans, who worshipped Aphrodite as Venus, knew a thing or two about sensuality, and when the citizens showed loyalty to their new masters, Caesar responded by granting Aphrodite's temple the same right of asylum that Artemis's Temple enjoyed in Ephesus, and he also exempted the city from taxation.

Venus de Milo We can therefore picture the Roman aristocracy coming on pilgrimage to this early tax-haven and devoting themselves to the worship of love...with all that that may entail. No wonder Aphrodisias prospered! The goddess herself may have risen from the sea off Cyprus as her name has associations with *aphros*, the Greek for 'sea foam' — or was she the daughter of Zeus, the Roman Jupiter?

She was married to Hephaestus but she sampled the favours of Adonis, Dionysus and Hermes, as well as Aries (Mars) who, as the son of Zeus, was her own half-brother. Among her children was Hermaphrodite whom we shall meet in Bodrum, but if you want to sample her beauty for yourself look at her statue found on the Greek island of Milos, for Aphrodite is better known to us as the Venus de Milo.

But back to Aphrodisias. The on-site museum, which opened in 1979, has many statues from the city, including some of Aphrodite. The theatre here is in a poor state of repair but the 2nd century odeon provides an unusual alternative.

The Baths of Hadrian give a good insight into how the Romans performed their toilet, surprisingly for here with separate pools for men and women which wasn't always the Roman custom.

Near the main temple is a ruin called the Bishop's Palace, hinting at the great change that occurred here when Christianity arrived. The temple was altered structurally to become a church, the town was renamed Stavropolis, 'city of the cross,' and the Bishop of Caria probably lived here — in the bishop's palace?

Tamburlane In the 5th century the church was expanded at the expense of the original temple, and a 7th century earthquake hastened the destruction of Aphrodite's monument, then Tamburlane came in 1402 and destroyed what was left. Eventually a small Turkish village grew up on the site, perpetuating the province of Caria in its own name, Geyre. But when serious archaeology began in modern times it was Geyre's turn to be demolished, and rebuilt two kilometers away.

Geyre and Aphrodisias are 38 km from the main road in the Menderes Valley but if you come by dolmuş from Nazilli you'll add another 18 km. It means you can just about see Pamukkale, Hierapolis and Aphrodisias in one day by public transport, but it'll be a long haul.

KUŞADASI

Kuşadası has a distinct advantage over its rivals Bodrum, Marmaris and Çeşme in that it has a good beach — wide, long and clean — 20 metres from the main promenade. Its port is busy with big ships, including the Turkish Maritime Lines ferries and the Wednesday morning visit of the *Orient Express*, and its marina is even busier with smaller ships. There's also a

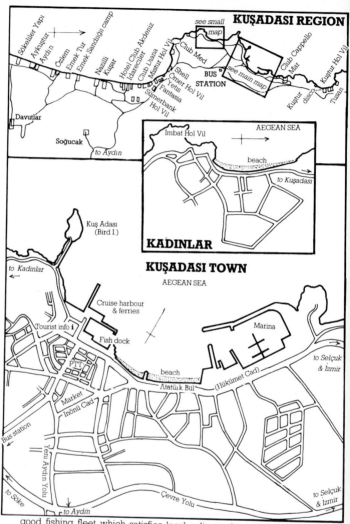

good fishing fleet which satisfies local culinary demand throughout the summer. And it has its own Greek island connection; in this case, to Samos.

It's not surprising, then, to learn that Kuşadası is the smartest resort on the Aegean, and arguably in all of Turkey, but it's still a *very* long way behind Nice or St Tropez.

Kuşadası lacks the town-centre castle that its rivals boast, though it can offer instead the ancient watchtower, now serving as the police station, and the Genoese fortress — it's not big enough to be called a castle — on the island in the bay.

It also lacks something else. Somewhere down the years since tourism and the cruise liners arrived, it has lost much of its Turkishness, although it has avoided the disaster of anaesthetised anonymity which has befallen the majority of Spanish resorts.

But it has the best-signposted *hamam* of all the resorts. The sign, pointing down a backstreet near the watchtower, even reads in English: turkish bath.

Holiday Villages There are several holiday villages in the immediate area, notably Club Mediterranée which occupies a headland three miles south of town, and there's a sàtellite village, Kadınlar Denizi, locally called Kadıkıoy for short, which is totally tourist-orientated though its beach isn't as good as the one in town.

Every July Kuşadası hosts the Turkish Pop Music Festival, and it's the ideal place for a holiday if you want to combine lazing on the beach with some moderately-energetic sightseeing, or if you're looking for a comfortable base from which to explore Ephesus, Pamukkale, or the archaeological sights to the south. Otherwise you'll soon be bored.

The name, by the way, comes from *kuş ada,* meaning 'bird island,' though the island itself, now accessible along a causeway, is called Güvercin Ada, 'pigeon island.' Don't worry about the -*sı* bit.

HOTELS

Akman Hotel, Istiklal Cad, 13 (tel 1501)

Akdeniz Hotel, Karaova Mevkii (place, square) (tel 1521); three-star, 330 rooms

Aydın Hotel, Akıncılar Cad 18 (tel 4034)

Aytaş Hotel, Sarımsaklı Mev (tel 257)

Berk Hotel, Orta Çamlık 23 (tel 1501)

Efe Hotel, Güvercin Ada Cad (tel 3660); three-star

Imbat Hotel, Kadınlar Denizi (tel 2000); four-star, 547 rooms and the town's best; Apr — Oct

Kismet Hotel, Akyar Mev (tel 2005); three-star; Apr — Oct

Martı Hotel, Kadınlar Denizi (tel 3650); three-star

Murat Reis Hotel, Altın Kum Mev (tel 1680)

Ortunç Hotel, Alibey (tel 120)

Qzçelok,, Liman Karşısı (tel 4490); three-star

Sevo Hotel, Sarımsaklı Mev (tel 166)

Tusan Hotel, 31'ler Mev (tel 4495); three-star

PENSIONS

The local tourist office lists 56 pensions, and there are probably as many that are unlisted. Almost all are in the town.

MOTELS

Çam Motel, Ortaçamlık 12 (tel 1515)

Küçük Başkent Motel, Sarımsaklı Mev (tel 116)

HOLIDAY VILLAGES

Club Akdeniz, Neşem Köyü (tel 1521); in British brochures; courtesy bus to town

Club Diana, Yeşil Site (tel 3550)

Club Kervansaray, May — Oct; C17th caravanserai converted 1974; was run by Club Med

Club Mediterranée, (tel 1125); almost a town in itself

Imbat Tatil Köyü, (holiday village) Kadınlar Denizi

Kuştur Tatil Köyü (popular with British)

Ömer Tatil Köyü

Sunset Tatil Köyü

RESTAURANTS

The Çatı Restaurant on Tayyare Cad (Barbaros Cad) is a mid-range rooftop establishment offering a meal with a view. Down by the fish harbour there's a small square with three open-air restaurants taking up two sides. The Cam calls itself a cafe-bar but offers a good range of snacks, while the Diba and the Toros, both claiming to be restaurants, share the space under the arches with such intimacy that it's easy to patronise the wrong one. Not that there's much to choose between them as they're both good quality, mid-range restaurants specialising in fish.

If there's any difference in the menu it's confined to the number of languages in which it's presented: Turkish, German, French and English at the Diba, and just French and Turkish at the Toros.

Elsewhere in town it's impossible to walk for two minutes without finding a *restoran* or *lokanta*; they're just far too numerous to list here.

ENTERTAINMENTS

The holiday villages are the main source of nightlife in the area, and most will accept outsiders at a fee. Otherwise, entertainment is reduced to the disco on Güvercin Ada, 'Pigeon Island.'

TOUR OPERATORS

Aegean Turkish Holidays, Balkan Tours, Cambrian, Celebrity Holidays, Golden Horn Travel, Intasun, Lamington Travel, Lancaster, Metak Holidays, Regent Holidays, Steepwest Holidays, Sunmed, Sunquest, Timsway, Touropa, UK Express, Wings.

The Akdeniz Travel and Shipping Agency on the Kordon Promenade is a useful contact for making bookings for tours or excursions within Turkey, or for ferries.

SOUTH OF KUŞADASI

At Söke, the traffic from Kuşadası joins the main coast road for the journey south towards Bodrum and very soon enters a plain 20 km wide. Two thousand years ago this was the estuary of the Menderes River extending inland towards Aydın and allowing the ancient city ports of Priene, Milet and Heracleia to prosper. Over the centuries the Menderes has deposited so many millions of tons of silt that it has filled the estuary and allowed itself to develop its characteristic meanders. Milet is still close to the river but is 10 km upstream, with the shoreline receding by six metres every year. Priene is 15 km away from water of any kind, and Heracleia is already 30 km inland at the head of Bafa Lake.

All three sites are accessible by dolmuş and if this is your mode of travel you may consider an overnight stop at Altınkum, or you could take in the trio in a day's coach trip from Kuşadası.

PRIENE

Priene is on the western edge of the village of Güllübahçe and is perhaps the most rewarding of the triumvirate. Founded by the Ionians 1,000 years before Christ, Priene is typically Greek rather than Roman, and its grid-system street plan is compact, snuggling into a dramatic setting at the foot of the rugged Mount Samsun.

Temple of Athena Dominating the city is the Temple of Athena, the most impressive building here, restored in 1868 by English patronage but partially demolished by a 'quake in 1955. When Alexander the Great came here in 334 BC he found the citizens rebuilding Priene on this new site as the original one had already succumbed to the Menderes's silt; Alexander funded the temple rebuilding in return for having it dedicated to him, and the dedication stone is now in the British Museum.

This rebuilt Priene was already suffering from silting when the Romans arrived and put heavy taxes on the city, thus adding economic decline to natural catastrophe. Priene was abandoned and is today the best-preserved Ancient Greek city in the world — and among the secrets it has revealed is the near-total absence of lavatories and bathrooms in the private houses with nothing at all in the public sector to compensate. Were the Greeks dirtier than the Romans?

Other ruins worthy of seeing include the gymnasium, which holds a row of washbasins plumbed for cold water, the stadium, and Turkey's best-preserved Hellenistic theatre with some impressive front-row seats which look like thrones but which were reserved for the priesthood.

Temple of Demeter On the slope above the theatre stands the Temple of Demeter with its sacrificial pit intact, allowing us to imagine the lifeblood of Demeter's victims trickling across these gaunt stones.

A winter's tale Demeter, the Greek goddess of agriculture, was distraught when her daughter Persephone (Proserpine) was abducted by her uncle Hades (Pluto), god of the underworld. Demeter at once ordered that crops should not mature until Persephone was returned safe, which created an obvious threat to the existence of mortal man. So the gods did a deal allowing Persephone to come back to her mother for six months and stay with her uncle for the other six. In other words, the creation of summer and winter.

By hire car or dolmuş, head west for Atburgazı, then south for Balat and Miletos.

MILETOS (Milet)

The Minoans from Crete probably founded this city in 1400 or 1300 BC, but when the Ionians landed two centuries later they slaughtered every man and forcibly married the widows, as they hadn't brought any of their own womenfolk along. Their new wives dutifully bore them children but refused to sit at table with their new husbands.

Despite that minor problem, Miletos prospered and by 700 BC was the chief port of the Greek world, and the descendants of the reluctant wives had established more than 1,000 satellite colonies along the coast from here to the Black Sea.

Miletos's Greek theatre could seat 5,000, but the Romans trebled its capacity and reserved seats in the lower rows for their nobility; some of the inscriptions to this effect are still visible.

This theatre, carved into the side of a small hill, is the best preserved and most impressive relic, the next being the Roman baths at the base of the other hillock. The area between is boggy, reminiscent of the mosquito menace which accompanied the silting and helped bring about the city's demise — but the wet ground produces lush grass and you may find more cows than humans on the site.

Dolmuş or car will take you south again to Akköy (white village) and on to Didim.

DIDYMA (Didim)

Didyma was never a city. It was the site of the great Temple of Apollo which measured 110 by 50 metres and was 500 years in the building, never to be completed.

It was begun around 300 BC and based on the Temple of Artemis at Ephesus, although it was smaller. But it has withstood the ravages of time and earthquake far better and is a spectacle worthy of the arduous detour. There were 120 columns in the temple, of which 103 remain standing though few of them are intact.

Oracles In its prime the temple was famous, or perhaps even notorious, for the female oracles who practised here. Apollo had several colonies of oracles, the best known being at Delphi at the base of Mount Parnassos in Greece, but Didyma enjoyed a good reputation. In order to foretell the future the oracles fasted for three days then inhaled the sulphurous fumes from a nearby spring until they fell into a torpor and began mumbling their prophesies. At this point the priests intervened and interpreted the babbling for their clients — so what was the point of the earlier charade?

Maybe there was some occasional truth in the babel, for the young Trajan was told he'd become emperor. When he did, he showed his gratitude by building a sacred way from Didyma to Miletos.

The Goths' raid of 262 AD gave Didyma its first taste of fear and the oracles, who presumably hadn't foreseen this disaster, quickly converted the temple into a fortress, some of which remains. Christianity was the final threat and Emperor Theodosius decreed in 385 that severe penalties would await anybody who tried to read the future. Maybe he should have paid more heed to the First Book of Corinthians, Chapter 14?

Head of Medusa Sir Charles Newton sent the first consignment of Didyma sculptings to the British Museum in 1858, but serious excavation began much later. Some of Trajan's Sacred Way has been found, as well as some Roman baths and the priests' lodgings, but the most impressive single artefact on site is the oversized stone head of Medusa, one of the three Gorgons (monsters) of Greek mythology who had writhing serpents instead of hair.

Monster? Medusa, the Didyma Gorgon, looks pensively beautiful. Probably she's congratulating herself that she was too heavy for Sir Charles to ship her off to London.

ALTINKUM

Four kilometers from Didyma is the small village resort of Altınkum where many Turks have their holiday homes. It now features in the Sunmed brochures on the strength of its excellent beach right in the heart of the village, though its nightlife is rudimentary.

Altınkum is a perfect stopover for a day or two of lotus-eating leisure, and a convenient night halt on a tour of the ancient cities. It's also great if you're looking for a stay-put package holiday as public transport into the village is not up to Turkish standards.

ACCOMMODATION

Didim Motel (March-November); 25 other hotels and pensions feature in the Sunmed brochure so ask around, but be prepared for full bookings in high summer.

BODRUM

Bodrum is the most popular holiday resort in Turkey, if we are to judge by the number of tour operators featuring it in their brochures. You could therefore be forgiven for believing Bodrum to be another Benidorm with tower-block hotels lining the shore and foreign tourists outnumbering the locals by ten to one. Happily this is not so, nor will it ever be.

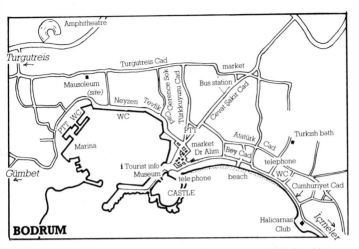

BODRUM

Bodrum has less than 10,000 inhabitants who're never overwhelmed by their visitors, and the town has maintained its character with not a high-rise in sight and with very few buildings of ultra-modern design — and the local authorities intend to see it stays that way.

The explanation is that Bodrum is like Çeşme in that its visitors are scattered thinly around the town and in the villages that lie on the peninsula. Bodrum's satellites are Gümbet, Bitez, Akyarlar, Turgutreis, Gümüşlük, Yalıkavak, Türkbükü, Ortakent, Torba, and the Torba Holiday Village. And the reason is the same: that's where the best beaches are. Bodrum itself has a poor beach fronting onto Cumhuriyet Caddesi (Republic Street) but the town is the natural focal point for the area: here are the shops, the Halikarnas night club, the marina and the castle, all within easy access by dolmuş, taxi or even by boat.

Go to Bodrum town if you're looking for a holiday afloat or intend doing some sightseeing, but if you want a truly restful holiday centred on the beach and the countryside within walking distance, then go to one of the villages. You'll be mixing with the locals and seeing something of the Turkish way of life, albeit diluted, and you'll be eating in a *lokanta* — but for after-dark activity you'll need to journey into Bodrum or the Turba Holiday Village. Just bear in mind that travel in rural Turkey is considerably slower than in rural Europe.

Mausoleum You may read in holiday brochures glowing accounts of Bodrum's picturesque charm and suspect it's an exaggeration. It's not. The beautiful small bay sweeps around the Castle of St Peter on its rocky promontory, and at the back of the town there's an amphitheatre which looks out over the sea towards Kara Ada, 'Black Island.' And on Turgutreis Cad you may find a hole in the ground, all that remains of the burial chamber of King Mausolus, which not only gave us the word 'mausoleum' but was one of the seven wonders of the ancient world: the others, for interest, were the Temple of Artemis (Diana) which we've seen at nearby Selçuk, the Pyramids of Giza, the Pharos at Alexandria, the Colossus of Rhodes, Zeus's statue at Olympia, and the Hanging Gardens of Babylon.

Bodrum's history begins with the region's conquest by the Dorian tribe

89

Charter yachts at Bodrum

who lived either in Macedonia or the Peloponnese, according to which authority you prefer. However, around 1,100BC they settled in Asia Minor and built a stone castle on the rocky island in what is now Bodrum Bay.

The town followed, known in those early days as Zephysium, and from the start its inhabitants had to defend themselves against the Carians to the east, the tribe whom Homer called 'barbarians' in his *Iliad*.

Zephysium fell to Persian invaders in 546BC and became Halicarnassos. It was here in 484BC that Herodotus, the 'father of history,' was born and his writings form the basis of the first properly-recorded account of the city.

Herodotus wrote in glowing terms about Artemisia I, the mortal woman who became ruler of Halicarnassos in 480BC, not to be confused with the mythological Artemis. Describing her bravery as she commanded a warship in an attack on Greece, Herodotus wrote that "Men have shown themselves women, and women, men."

Artemisia's son Psyndalis succeeded her, also ruling Kos and several other islands, but by 377BC the Persians were back to reinforce their superiority. They divided Asia Minor into regions, each ruled by a vassal *satrap* (governor), with Halicarnassos falling to the Carian satrap Mausolus (c376-c353BC) who moved his capital here from Mylasa (now Milas, where the Bodrum road joins the main coast road).

Mausolus had great plans for his new capital. He forcibly brought in the people of six towns on the peninsula — their ruins are still visible — and taxed them heavily for the privilege of being compelled to built the theatre on the hillside, and the city walls.

Mausoleum On his death, his wife Artemisia II, who was also his elder sister, followed Mausolus's instructions and built him a tomb which stood around 140 feet tall, crowned with a statue of Mausolus himself in a chariot drawn by four horses.

The world's prototype mausoleum was destroyed in the 14th century, probably by earthquake, and its masonry used in other buildings. The British archaeologist Sir Charles Newton excavated the site in 1856 and among the treasures he found was a statue of Mausolus and Artemis which he sent to the British Museum: no wonder the Turks now ban the export of all ancient relics.

The people of Rhodes, hearing that a woman was again ruling Halicarnassos and the Kingdom of Caria, sent a fleet to capture the port. This second Artemisia, who was almost as heroic as her namesake, heard of their coming and hid her fleet in a secret harbour supposedly built beneath Mausolus's palace. She waited until the invaders had entered the town before launching her ships, seizing the Rhodian vessels and allowing her own troops to capture the demoralised attackers. Artemisia then sailed the Rhodian fleet back to Rhodes and sacked that city.

Hermaphrodite The defeated Dorians lived for a while on moderately easy terms wih their Carian masters, and peoples from both tribes patronised a tavern established at the spring of Salmakis, now lost under modern Bodrum. Legend endowed the spring with soporific qualities, making strong men become effeminate, and the most notable victim was the son of Aphrodite, the Goddess of Beauty.

Salmakis, the female nymph of the fountain, fell in love with the youth as he bathed and begged the gods to allow her to live with him, sharing his body. The wish was granted and the world had its first bisexual human, Hermaphrodite.

Alexander Alexander the Great (356-323BC), King of Macedonia, led his Greek armies across the Dardanelles in 334BC, at the age of 22, and reached Halicarnassos the next year.

This was where Memnon, vassal of the Persian King Darius, and Queen Orontabatis, the Satrap of Caria, decided to make their last stand. It failed. Alexander broke through Mausolus's city walls and sacked Halicarnassos, though he spared its people. He went on to conquer the remainder of Asia Minor and much of the known world, while defeated and destroyed Halicarnassos sank into obscurity and became a mere boatyard for Ptolemy II of Egypt.

Byzantium The Romans came in 190BC but the region slumbered on, eventually becoming part of the Byzantine Empire with Byzantium, later Constantinople, as its capital. When Christianity came, the people of Halicarnassos accepted it and found themselves in the Archbishopric of Aphrodisias.

Bodrum's story became part of the country's history as the Seljuks conquered the state of Byzantium, letting the wandering Turks settle in the Denizli-Afyon area and so bringing Islam to Anatolia.

Meanwhile, the Christian world had been fighting a losing battle in the Crusades to the Holy Land. In 1291 the Order of St John of Jerusalem was driven from that city to Cyprus, and in 1310 they pulled back to Rhodes.

Crusader knights Bayazid I (Beyazıt in Turkish) absorbed Halicarnassos into the Ottoman Empire in 1392 only to lose everything in 1402 to Tamburlane who abandoned the territory in search of fresh lands to conquer. The Knights of St John had also lost their stronghold of Smyrna (now Izmir) and demanded restitution: surprisingly, Bayazid gave them Halicarnassos, which they renamed Mesy.

Their first action was to rebuild the castle, using the masonry from the ruined Mausoleum. In their occupation of Mesy, which lasted 121 years, they virtually rebuilt the fortress, by then joined to the mainland and standing at the tip of a peninsula. As the Order of St John consisted of the landless second sons of the landed gentry from most of Europe, the various towers of the Castle of St Peter were dedicated to the order's *langues*: Italian, French, German and English.

On the broader front, Bayazid II was the Ottoman Sultan during a period of relative peace and had time to realise his brother Çem was plotting his downfall.

Çem came to the Castle of St Peter and asked the knights of the Order of St John for protection in return for help. If the Grand Master, the order's elected ruler, would overthrow Bayazid and instal Çem, then he, Çem, would guarantee peace between Turk and Christian.

It was an impossible request. How could the order, which held nothing more than Rhodes and Bodrum, invade a sub-continent? Not that they even intended trying: they had accepted Bodrum from Bayazid and they now agreed to hold his enemy Çem as prisoner, though the promise of payment undoubtedly helped. The knights eventually shipped Çem to Italy where he died in 1495, still a prisoner.

Süleiman But in 1520 Bayazid's grandson Süleiman inherited the Ottoman Sultanate and the campaign against Christianity began again. On Christmas Eve, 1522, after a six-month siege, the Order of St John capitulated to Süleiman, soon to be styled 'the Magnificent.' The sultan magnanimously allowed them to leave and after wandering the Mediterranean for eight years they made their final home in Malta.

Bodrum had stepped aside from world history and slumbered on for a further 248 years until the Russian navy shelled it in 1770 during the Russo-Turkish wars. In the closing days of the Ottoman dynasty, Italy managed to snatch a foothold in the south-east of Asia Minor and hold Bodrum for three years, losing it only after Kemal Atatürk came to power and all but reversed the course of Turkish history since the Seljuc invasion.

Bodrum Castle today

The Castle of St Peter is the most impressive landmark of modern Bodrum, even outclassing Mausolus's theatre. Entry is from Kale Sokağı (Tower Street or Castle Street) overlooking the harbour, from 0830-1200 and 1300-1750 (a slight variation on standard museum hours), with last admissions half an hour before closing.

This is the best-preserved Crusader castle in the world, its walls incorporating chunks of masonry from the Mausoleum, one of the seven wonders of the ancient world, and it holds several exhibits that are unique to this planet.

The approach gives no hint of these surprises in store: on the left, outside the main gate, is a long chamber often used as an art gallery while inside the iron gate is the knights' chapel, now a mosque, and an open-air museum with large chunks of masonry from King Mausolus's tomb.

Visitors can explore most of the rambling castle at will but there are several locked rooms which you may enter only with a guide.

Glass Museum There are several museums in the building, each with its exhibits labelled in Turkish and English. The Cam ('jam' — it means 'glass') Museum shows the story of glass from its chance creation on an Aegean beach 4,000 years ago. Exhibits range from 1,500BC to 1,100AD, including the world's oldest known glass, rescued from the Ulu Burun wreck (q.v.). Other exhibits come from the 4th century BC wreck at Yassıada island near

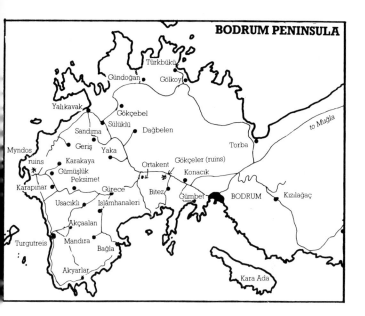

BODRUM PENINSULA

Turgutreis, and from the ancient city of Kaunus (q.v.). Even if you think of glass merely as something to hold your beer, this museum is worth a visit.

Underwater The world's oldest known piece of glass came from the world's oldest known shipwreck, which is the theme of the Museum of Underwater Archaeology.

In the summer of 1982 Mehmet Çakir, a sponge diver working off Ulu Burun near Kaş (it means 'Great Headland' but in another context could also mean 'big nose'), found sheets of metal cast in the shape of pegged-out goatskins. Archaeologists from a Texas university, the National Geographic Society, and Bodrum Museum, began excavating the wreck of a 50-foot ship which was lying between 140 and 170 feet down. They found six tons of copper ingots plus bronze, tin, scrap gold, and blue glass (see the Glass Museum), all presumably intended for resmelting at destination, which might have been Egypt.

After several summers of work the archaeologists have managed to date the wreck to the late 14th century before Christ — around 3,200 years old, and the oldest yet found.

But this vessel was of major importance even when it was afloat. Its cargo held enough metal to forge the weapons for a small army and the vessel was probably on the circular trading route Cyprus-Rhodes-Crete-Egypt-Ashquelon-Tyre-Cyprus, carrying treasures to the pharoah of Egypt.

Excavation continues, but among the latest finds is a fingernail-sized gold tablet inscribed to Nefertiti and the world's earliest-known diptych, a two-page wooden book which held hieroglyphs scratched onto beeswax.

Coin hall And if that's not enough, the castle also has a display of some of the world's earliest coins, reminding us that the Lydians under their King Croesus invented coinage back in the 7th centry BC.

93

Knights' towers Of the four towers built by the Order of St John, the French is the most interesting as it holds a display of medieval armour, reproduction cloaks from the grand masters of the order and, incongruously, a model of the English man-of-war *Sovereign of the Seas*.

The arms of Edward Plantagenet are carved in the outer wall of the English Tower, also rather incongruously as the House of Plantagenet expired before the order arrived in Bodrum. But enough of history: there's a wonderful view of the town from up here.

The Bodrum Peninsula

Ada Boğazı: 'island throat' in Turkish, it's the narrow strait separating the tiny island from the mainland. Clear water and a sandy bottom make it ideal diving territory.

Akyarlar: a small fishing village within easy reach of several bays of differing character. Before the Atatürk revolution in 1923, Greeks had their summer homes here and a few still stand. The modern version has also arrived.

Bağla Koyu: difficult to reach by land and so favoured by seaborne visitors.

Bardakcı: western suburb of Bodrum and legendary site of the first hermaphrodite.

Bitez: quiet and picturesque, ideal for swimming, sunbathing, windsurfing and lazing. Immediately inland lie acres of tangerine groves which fruit in winter. Nearby are the best-preserved ruins on the peninsula, part of the city now called Gökçeler. Mausolus was responsible for its demise.

Gümbet: formerly a camping site, now becoming a resort in its own right, it has the best beach in the area. Yacht charters start from here, and there are several windsurfing schools. Two locally-famed graves are here: the Turk author Cevat Şakir Kabbağaçlı, the 'fisherman of Halicarnassus' who helped popularise Bodrum; and folk hero Salirsah who continued fighting after losing his head in battle. Resort is also known as Kümbet.

Gümüşlük: built near the ancient city of Myndos which fell to ruin after Mausolus removed its people to Halicarnassos. Area is now preserved, with no new building and no scuba diving: too many vulnerable undersea trophies.

Karaincir: or the 'black fig,' a tranquil village with a good beach and a ruined castle just inland.

Ortakent: a straggly village, inland having the Mustafa Paşa tower-house, built in 1601, and on the coast having a quiet beach which also serves as the road.

Torba: handy for Bodrum but on the north coast. Snuggles beautifully into the hills.

Turgutreis: birthplace of the man of this name, better known in the west as the corsair Dragut. He joined Süleiman the Magnificent in the Great Siege of Malta and was killed there. Splendid harbour, good beach, glorious sunsets, and boats for hire.

Türkbükü: a quiet village with scope for camping al fresco.

Yalıkavak: a small village on a large bay, it caters for yachtsmen and overwinters a number of catamarans. Turkey's largest supplier of sponges.

HOTELS

Alize Hotel, Kumbahçe Mahallesi Üçuyular Cad 11 (tel 1401)

Astek Hotel, Turgutreis (tel 1112)

Ayaz Hotel, Gümbet (tel 1174, 2956)

Baba Hotel, Gümbet (tel 2307)

Bahçeli Ağar Hotel, Eskiçeşme Mat Yat Limanı (tel 1648)

Barbaros Hotel, Cumhuriyet Cad 8 (tel 2545)

Baraz Hotel, Cumhuriyet Cad 62 (tel 1857, 1714)
Cinar Hotel, Cumhuriyet Cad 34 (tel 2638)
Durak Hotel, Kumbahçe Mahallesi Rasathane Sok 22 (tel 1564)
Ege Hotel, Çarşı Sok (tel 1307)
Gala Hotel, Neyzen Tevfik Cad, Yat Limanı (tel 2216)
Gözegir Hotel, Cumhuriyet Cad (tel 2541)
Gözen Hotel, Cumhuriyet Cad 18 (tel 1602)
Gurup Hotel, Çarşı Içi Belediye Meydanı (tel 1140)
Halikarnas Hotel, Cumhuriyet Cad 128 (tel 1073); Apr — Sep Haltur Hotel, Paşatarlası Mevkii (tel 2597)
Kardeşler Hotel, Akyarlar
Kalyon Hotel, Cumhuriyet Cad (tel 1030)
Karya Hotel, Cumhuriyet Cad 121 (tel 1535)
Kortan Hotel, Turgutreis (tel 1237)
Mercan Hotel, Comhuriyet Cad 88 (tel 1111)
Mervem Hotel, Atatürk Cad 103 (tel 1546); Apr — Sep

Mola Hotel, Neyzen Tevfik Cad 33 (tel 1328)
Monaliza Hotel, Turgutreis (tel 1361)
Mutlum Hotel, Turgutreis (tel 1142)
Murat Villa, Kumbahçe Mahallesi Azmakbaşı 3 (tel 1710)
Mylasa Hotel, Cumhuriyet Cad 34 (run by Australian family) (tel 1846)
Park Palas Hotel, Gümbet (tel 2294)
Rahat Hotel, Turgutreis (tel 1501)
Regal Hotel, Bitez Yalısı Kabakum (tel 1058); May — Sep; the top-rated hotel in the Bodrum area
Salmakis Hotel, Cumhuriyet Cad 10 (tel 1090)
Sami Hotel, Gümbet (tel 1043, 1662)
Taraça Hotel, Eski Çeşme Mah, Gümbet (tel 1721)
Villa Bergamut, Kumbahçe Mahallesi Meteoroloji Yanı (tel 1719)

APART HOTELS
Papirüs Apartotel, Yat Limanı (tel 1387)
Akyar Turizm Villas, Akyarlar (tel 1242)

PENSIONS
There are far too many pensions to list; these are just a few from Bodrum town centre:

Aşkın Pension, Kumbahçe Mahallesi Uslu Sok, 6
Avcı Pension, Kumbahçe Mahallesi Üçkuyular
Balıkçinin Pension, Cumhuriyet Cad
Heredot Pension, Neyzen Tevfik Cad 116

Mandalin Pension, Türkkuyusu Mah
Mauzolos Pension, Turgutreis Cad
Neşe Pension, Cumhuriyet Cad
Özdoğan Pension, Sanatokulu Cad
Pay Pension, Kumbahçe Mahallesi Üçkuyular Cad
Titiz Türkkuyusu Cad
Uslu Pension, Cumhuriyet Cad

MOTELS
Akşit Motel, Türkbükü
Akyarlar Motel, Akyarlar (tel 11)
Alaaddin Motel, Ortakent (tel 2)
Altınkaya Motel, Ortakent (tel 30)
Anıl Motel, Gümbet (tel 2628)
Ankara Motel, Bitez (tel 1024)
Asarlık Motel, Gümbet (tel 1150)
Ayaz Motel, Gümbet (tel 1174)
Bardakçı Motel, Bardakçı Koyu (tel 2535)
Bargilya Motel, Güvercinlik (tel 2)
Başkent Motel, Gölköy (tel 32)

Dalgıç Motel, Yalıkavak (tel 3)
Deniz Mocamp Türbükü
Deniz Motel, Güvercinlik (tel 83)
Dost Motel, Yalıkavak (tel 30)
Eda Motel, Türkbürkü (services for yachts)
Efem Motel, Ortakent (tel 13)
Ege Motel, Gümbet (tel 1407)
Farilya Motel, Gündoğan (tel 390)
Flamingo Motel, Atatürk Cad
Gezi Motel, Gümbet (tel 1447)
Gölköy Motel, Gölköy (tel 35)
Gümüşlük Motel, Gümüşlük (tel 7)

Harem Motel, Ortakent (tel 8)
Kadıkalesi Motel, Kadıkalesi
Kaktüs Motel, Ortakent (tel 10)
Kaktüs Çiçeği Motel, Gölköy (tel 20)
Kartal Motel, Gümbet (tel 1436)
Kivanç Motel, Gümbet (tel 1612)

Regal Motel, Bitez (tel 1058)
Şah Motel, Bitez (tel 1003)
Turin Motel, Bitez (tel 1222)
Umut Motel, Ttatürk Cad 35 (tel 1164)
Vardar Motel, Güvercinlik (tel 12)

HOLIDAY VILLAGES
Torba Holiday Village, Torba (tel 2343)
T.M.T. Holiday Village, Akçebük Mevkii, Torba (tel 1440, 1207-8, 1222-3)

CAMPING SITES
Ayaz Kamping, Gümbet (tel 1174)
Baba Kamping, Gümbet (tel 2307)
Uçar Kamping, Omurcadere Sok

12 (tel 3357) (cheapest accommodation in Bodrum town)
Yalı Kamping, Yalıkavak

RESTAURANTS (a selection)
Amphora, Neyzen Tevfik Cad 164. Seafood a speciality; credit cards accepted.
Balik, Çarşı Içi Turkish and French cuisine; meat and fish specialities.
Balikçi, Gümüşlük. Seafood specials.
Batı Gümüşlük. Bamboo décor.
Bolulu, Atatürk Meydanı, Turgutreis. Turkish cuisine.
Çavuşun Yeri, Geriş Yalısı, Yalıkavak. Seafood; rooms available.
Chinese, Yat Limanı. Chinese, naturally.
Çimentepe, Geriş Köyü Yalıkavak. Sea food on the seafront.
Fora, Hilmi Uran Meydanı 20. Tables on seafront; open for breakfast.

Karafaki, Bitez. Good pull-in for yachtsmen.
Körfez, Dr Alim Bey Cad. Tables actually on the beach.
Kortan, Cumhuriyet Cad. Tables overlook the sea.
Maça Kizi, Torba Tatil Köyü, Torba. On private beach; free boat ride from Torba village.
Mandarin Pizza, Cumhuriyet Cad 111. Italian, despite its name.
Mindos, Gümüşlük. Seafood specials; rooms available.
Plaj, Torba Tatil Köyü, Torba. Seafood — and a free boat ride to the restaurant.
Teras, Gümüşlük. More seafood on the seafront.
Yalı, Dr Alim Bey Cad 44 Also on seafront.

TOUR OPERATORS
Aegean Turkish, Arrowsmith, Balkan Tours, Beach Villas, Bladon Lines, Cambrian, Celebrity Holidays, CV Travel, Falcon Sailing, Golden Horn Travel, Intasun, Lancaster, Mark Warner, Metak, Regent, Steepwest, Sunmed, Sunquest, Timsway, Wings.
Local operator: Karya-Tour (Mavi-tur S.A.), Yachting and travel agency, Dr Alim Bey Cad 6 (tel 1759, 1914)

ENTERTAINMENTS
TORBA HOLIDAY VILLAGE, Torba (tel 2343)
The holiday village is a complete holiday centre in itself, offering 350 rooms each with toilet and shower, a wide range of sports and evening entertainments including an amusement arcade and disco.

HALIKARNAS DISCO, Cumhuriyet Cad (tel 1073)
This is among the top three disco-night clubs in Turkey with open-air

Dining on the seafront at Fethiye

entertainment. In high summer the laser beams shine far out to sea. Admission, 10,000TL, which includes the first drink.

There are several other discos in the town and the surrounding villages but none worthy of singling out. Average entry fee is 2,000TL, which includes the first drink.

FERRIES

Fahri Kaptan I and *II* offer ferry services on the Bodrum-Datça and the Bodrum-Kos run from Neyzen Tevfik Cad 190 (tel 2870); the *Bodrum Express* sails daily to Körmen and Kos from Neyzen Tevfik Cad 70; while *Büyük Ortak Karyalı I* operates a daily return service to Datça and another to Kos. The *Meander* also operates a daily service to Kos.

A Greek-owned ferry also operates the daily summer-only service from Kos on the 1600-out, 0830-return basis.

In addition, there are smaller boats operating a kind of water-bus service to Gümbet, Akyarlar, Turgutreis and Yalıkavak; you'll find them along the Neyzen Tevfik Cadessi.

Kleopatra Island is a favourite destination. It's at the head of the Gulf of Gökova and has the reputation of having been a secret hideout for Cleopatra and Mark Anthony, and that Cleo brought in galleyloads of white sand from Egypt. The place is also known as Castle Island from the ruins of an Ionian castle and theatre, and nearby there's Snake Island: I wonder why that's so called? In Turkish they're the Şehir or Sedir Adaları.

CAR AND MOPED HIRE

Avis, Europcar and Budget are in town, but see the comments on car hire on page 49 . The proprietors of the Mylasa Hotel have a small fleet of mopeds for hire at their premises at a daily cost of 11,000TL including insurance, but excluding petrol and crash helmet: it's not a legal requirement in Turkey for moped riders to protect their head.

SHOPPING

Bodrum has a wide range of souvenir shops, including one which sells miniature leather face-masks. There's also the Baraz Leather Shop, which has a branch at 32 Studley Gardens, Whitley Bay, Newcastle.

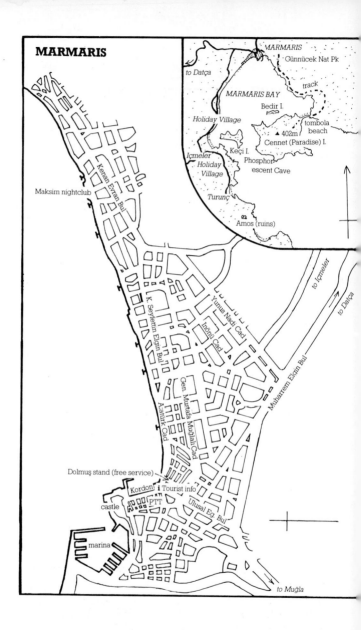

MARMARIS

Maksim nightclub

Kenan Evren Bul

K. Seyfettin Elgin Bul

Dolmuş stand (free service)

castle

marina

Kordon

Tourist info

PTT

Gen. Mustafa Muğlalı Cad.

Atatürk Cad.

İnönü Cad.

Yunus Nadi Cad.

Ulusal Eg. Bul

Muhittem Elgin Bul

to İçmeler

to Datça

to Muğla

MARMARIS

Günnücek Nat Pk

track

MARMARIS BAY

Bedir I.

Holiday Village

to Datça

Keçi I.

İçmeler Holiday Village

Turunç

tombola beach

Cennet (Paradise) I.

▲ 402m

Phosphorescent Cave

Amos (ruins)

THE MEDITERRANEAN
Marmaris to İskenderun

YOU NEED SPEND ONLY AN HOUR in Marmaris to appreciate its attraction. It has the most picturesque harbour anywhere in Turkey, with the rugged, wooded and aptly-named Paradise Island — Cennet Adası — rising to 402 m across the almost-landlocked bay.

The beach begins right here in the town centre and spreads south-westward along the half-kilometer of promenade, at times 50 m wide.

There's an ancient castle, admittedly not as picturesque as the one in Bodrum but almost as historic as it was built by Süleiman the Magnificent in preparation for the Siege of Rhodes.

Yet in the mid 1970s Marmaris was a virtually unknown fishing village and even in the late 1980s with a worldwide reputation, its population is still less than 10,000.

Free buses Visitors arriving by bus may be daunted to find the *otogar* is some way from the town centre, but there's a frequent minibus service which ferries passengers to the seafront — *free* — and drops them outside the Pamukkale coach company's office at the end of a smart *bulvarı*. As Marmaris is notorious for not putting name-plates on its streets, let's use this minibus stand as a reference point.

You're on the main promenade, one of the few in Turkey where parking is already banned, but equally one of the few along which the municipality runs free tractor-trains during the summer, taking visitors from town centre to the hotels and holiday villages around the south-west shore of the bay.

Opposite, on an extension to the promenade, is the town's high-season funfair — it was a mechanical bucking bronco when I was last in Marmaris — and after dark, here is where the first of the many fancy-dress ice-cream sellers set up stall.

Old town Turn left, west, along Kordon Caddesi for the business quarter where you find most of the banks and some of the smarter restaurants. Ahead, beyond the Atatürk Statue, are the tourist office, the customs office, and the first of the fortifications that Süleiman built rather hurriedly in 1522 as the base for his six-month siege of the Order of St John of Jerusalem then in occupation of Rhodes; Süleiman accepted the order's surrender on Christmas Eve of that year.

Bazaar Inside the fortress today lies a touch of old Turkey where narrow streets wander around rickety houses, the entire area converted in the daylight hours to a bazaar where you can shop for a wide range of souvenirs and perhaps even sample some of the plentiful Marmaris honey produced in the pine forests inland.

Marina Beyond the fortress are the stern-on berths for the biggest yachts that visit the town, their size diminishing as you approach the compact but busy marina still only ten minutes' walk from the shopping area.

This is one of the smartest marinas in the country with a clientèle that is beginning to rival the guest list at Cannes. Pop stars, film stars, Saudi sheikhs and Texas tycoons — Marmaris is their chosen Mecca. Some base their luxury yachts here all year round while others use it only in the sailing season.

SOUTH-WEST TURKEY

and features the sort of floor show you'd expect when it costs you 10,000TL just to get in; the night club and disco take over at 2300 and run until 0400 for a modest 4,000TL, plus drinks and the wads of banknotes that male customers thrust down the belly-dancer's bra.

Maksim's sets the tone for Marmaris's night life which is the liveliest on this southern coast. Several of the smart hotels feature their own disco but hundreds of people are content merely to dine at leisure in the seafront restaurants and watch the world go by until two in the morning. It's that sort

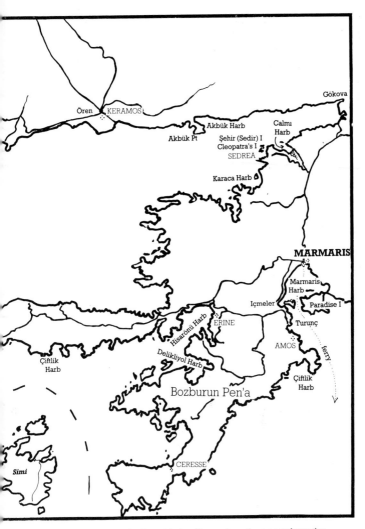

Night club Back now to the Pamukkale office and continue east down the promenade with the beach opening out on your left. Once past the smart public lavatory you notice that everything else is smart: the hotels, the restaurants, and particularly the rather glitzy building with the name Maksim emblazoned high. Come here at night and you'll see a neon version of the name flashing far out across the bay.

Maksim's is the smartest night-club on the Turkish Mediterranean and a worthy rival to Bodrum's Halicarnas. The restaurant opens from 2000 to 2300

Night life in Marmaris: belly dancer at Maksim's; ice-cream seller; dining out.

of town.

Marmaris afloat Marmaris entered history under the name of Physcus in the ancient province of Doria and for centuries the town and its two fingerlike peninsulas, Reşadiye (on which Datçha stands) and Bozburun, were ruled from Rhodes; the knights hospitaller who came to Rhodes in 1309 after their expulsion from the Holy Land, also ruled Kos and Bodrum.

The town has maintained its traditional association with Rhodes in the ferry services linking it to the island, but Marmaris today has a wide range of boating activities to interest its visitors. Stroll along Kordon Caddesi as night falls and watch the charter boats — gulets, they're properly called — slipping into their moorings. Now is the time to sample the market and make your plans for the next day's adventures afloat, be they a simple trip around the harbour or the start of a fully-equipped 'Blue Cruise' along the coast. You'll be in good company: Admiral Nelson anchored his entire fleet in the bay in 1798 as he sought for Napoleon's ships in the prelude to the Battle of the Nile.

Paradise Island Cennet Adası, Paradise Island, is an obvious destination for a short cruise costing a token 3,000TL. While it's possible to hike around the bay or go in a four-wheel-drive vehicle, crossing to Cennet on the tombola beach, the only way to see the blue lagoon, the phosphorescent cave and the green sea, is by boat.

Ancient cities A slightly longer cruise into the outer bay and down the coast of the Bozburun ('Grey Headland' or 'Nose') Peninsula will show you yet more ancient cities, none of them accessible by road. Just beyond Cennet Adası is the small city of Amos, its temple and theatre snuggling inside the well-preserved walls. A further 25 km along the 'Grey Nose' is Ceresse where several Byzantine churches cluster on an isthmus barely 500 metres wide, and on the craggy headland at the southernmost tip of the peninsula, Loryma Castle commands the western approaches to Rhodes.

The rugged coastline south-west of Marmaris holds at least 15 other cities, with 18 on the road to Fethiye and Kaş. But don't tear your hair in despair for most of them are no more than names on a map.

Longer cruises More adventurous all-day cruises can take you to the ancient city of Kaunus up the Dalyan River near Dalaman, and that's an expedition well worth doing. Among boats available for this trip are the *Engür Kaptan* which carries 50 passengers on Mondays, Wednesdays and Fridays, transferring to a smaller boat at the mouth of the Dalyan for the cruise up to Kaunus, and with lunch at a riverside restaurant. On Tuesdays and Thursdays, *Venus* corners the market; fares in 1987 were in the 12,000 to 13,000TL per person range.

You want something more? Then you can go with *Kleopatarayatı* to Kleopatra Island, calling in at Knidos on the tip of the Reşadiye Peninsula beyond Datça.

Underwater This stretch of coast is undeniably among the most beautiful in the Mediterranean basin but all you need do is put your head beneath the water to discover a whole new world of beauty of another kind. It's not up to Red Sea standards, but there are exotic fish, colourful corals, and the occasional moray eel as long as a man is tall.

The Octopus Diving School promises to give a non-swimming novice the basic skills of sub-aqua diving in a week's course for 500DM but if you prefer to take life more leisurely you can go diving for the day under supervision, or just hire a snorkel for 1DM. The company is also involved in all aspects of commercial diving.

Around the bay A mile east of town lies the Günnücek Mîlli Parkı (National Park), which is nothing more than a beauty-spot. West, the tarmac road passes the Marmaris and the Marti holiday villages on its way to the mineral springs of Göleyne and the beach in the tiny bay at Turunç, at the end of the road.

HOTELS

Alinda Hotel, İçmeler (tel 4773)
Atlantik Hotel, Atatürk Cad 11 (tel 1218)
Berkit Hotel, İçmeler (tel 1423)
Efendi Hotel, İçmeler (tel 1057)
Elif Hotel, İçmeler (tel 4491)
Flamingo Hotel, Kemer Mah 23, Siteler (tel 1852)
Halıcı Hotel, Çam Sok 1 (tel 1683)
Hawaii Hotel, Cıldır Mev, Uzunyaltı (tel 4003, 4009) three-star
Karadeniz Hotel, Atatürk Cad 46 (tel 2837)
Kontes Hotel, İçmeler (tel 1203)
Lidya Hotel, Siteler Mah 130, Uzunyaltı (tel 130) three-star
Marbas Hotel, İçmeler (tel 2904) three-star
Marbela Hotel, Uzunyaltı (tel 1049)
Marmaris Hotel, Atatürk Cad 30 (tel 1308)
Mavideniz Hotel, Turunç (tel 1421)

Murathan Hotel, Kenan Evren Bul (tel 1859)
Ocaktan Hotel, Uzunyaltı (tel 2560)
Orkide Hotel, Siteler Mah, Uzunyaltı (tel 2580) three-star Otel 47, Atatürk Cad 10 (tel 1700), restaurant at front overlooks harbour
Oylum Hotel, İçmeler (tel 2916)
Paradise Hotel, Armutalan, Boynuzbükü Mev (tel 1599)
Poseidon Hotel, Dergah Mev, Uzunyalı (tel 1840)
Reisoğlu Hotel, Kemeraltı Mah 19 (tel 2058)
Rodos Hotel, Uzunyaltı (tel 4986)
Sonnen Hotel, Uzunyaltı (tel 3829)
Yavuz Hotel, Atatürk Cad türk Cad 10 (tel 2937) three-star
Yunus Hotel, Kemeraltı Mah, Uzunyalı (tel 1799)
Yüzbaşıı Hotel, Turban holiday village (tel 2762)
Zarif Hotel, Fevzipaşa Cad (tel 4306)

BUDGET HOTELS

The local council has licensed at least 45 hotels and motels, of which this is a selection:
Acar Hotel, Uzunyaltı (tel 1204)
Altın Orfe Hotel, İçmeler (tel 1293)
Bozburun Hotel, Bozburun (no phone)

Elhambra Hotel, Turban village (tel 3146)
Haley Hotel, İçmeler (tel 1258)
Istanbul Hotel, Uzunyaltı (tel 1136)
Kaptan Hotel, Yat Limanı (tel 5121)
Panorama Hotel, Uzunyaltı (tel 2683)

FLOATING HOTEL

Yüzer Hotel, Cennet Adası. *Contact the tourist office, İskele Meydanı 39, Marmaris (tel 1035)*

PENSIONS

There are far too many to list individually but you will find scores of them one or two streets back from the promenade, and if you come by bus you'll probably be accosted in the *otogar*. If you can locate these particular streets you'll find almost every property is a pension: Hamdi Yüzak Sok, Mustafa Çoban Sok, Kadri Yançın Sok and the lower numbers of Uzunyalı Cad.

In addition, there are 20 pensions in the tiny village of Turunç and two or three in İçmeler.

MOTELS
These motels are all from the local council's approved list, which means they're not up to national rating. Call them budget motels.

Akvaryum Motel, Bozburun (tel 1332)

Anfora Motel, Uzunyaltı (tel 1924)

Demir Motel, Uzunyaltı (tel 1352)

Malipo Motel, Uzunyaltı (tel 1721)

Maris Motel, Kumlubük (tel 1220)

Sema Motel, İskele Mey (tel 1595)

HOLIDAY VILLAGES
Marti, İçmeler, (tel 4901) open all year; 580 beds. Turban Marmaris, halfway to İçmeler (tel 1843); May to October inclusive; 520 beds. *Both specialise in water sports*

CAMPING

Afrodit, Uzunyaltı (tel 4393); 16 chalets, 10 tents

Altın Sahil (tel 1244); 50 tents, 20 caravans

Apollo, Uzunyaltı (tel 1710); 26 chalets, 3 tents

As, Uzunyaltı (tel 2070); 18 tents 20 caravans

Ataköy, Cennet Adası (Paradise Island); no phone, and bring your own tent.

Bahar, Siteler Cad (tel 2321) 20 tents, 66 caravans

Berk, Uzunyaltı (tel 4171); 35 tents, 30 caravans

Çubucaj, Datça yolu (road) (tel 1008); 450 tents

Dost, Uzunyaltı, no phone and bring own tent

Durmaz, Uzunyaltı (tel 3509); 18 tents

Güney, Uzunyaltı (tel 2369); 30 tents, 10 caravans

Havuzbaşı, İçmeler (tel 1151); 8 tents .

Karya, İçmeler (tel 6125); 150 tents

Okaliptus, Datça yolu (road); 20 tents

WEATHER INFORMATION
Marmaris Meteoroloji İstasyonu, Atatürk Cad (tel 1036)

RESTAURANTS
The Bigma and the nearby Taşlik on the promenade are good middle-range establishments while nearer Maksım are the Tilla and the Yüksel, both slightly more up-market. There are several popular restaurants on Kordon Cadd, where tables extend 10 metres onto the roadway at night, but for bargains try one street inland.

Maksim must be among the top spots in town, but it's pricey if you're merely looking for somewhere to eat.

The national tourist office lists the Bamboo and the Tilla on Atatürk Cad (tels 1339 and 1088) and the Mangal on Kemeraltı Sok. And there's the Yemyeşil Lokantası on Paradise Island. The local authority lists 33 in town and around the bay: there's no shortage.

ENTERTAINMENT
Maksim, restaurant & floor show, 8-11pm; night club & disco, 11pm-4am, with belly dancing after 1am. Joy Disco in İçmeler. Holiday villages provide their own entertainment, and several larger hotels offer variations on the music theme. Open-air cinema behind Maksim, showing Turkish-language films; conventional cinema near the Kale İçi fortress.

TOUR OPERATORS
Allegro Holidays, Arrowsmith Holidays, Celebrity Holidays, Falcon Holidays, Golden Horn Travel, Panorama, Regent Holidays, Steepwest,

Sunmed, Sunstart.

LOCAL CONTACTS

Günlük Tours, (opposite High School,) Marmaris (tel 3620)
Hek Tours, Yat Limanı 57, Marmaris (tel 3471)
Octopus Diving School (Daliş Merkezi), Rıhtım Sok, Ayyıldız Apt, Pasajı, Marmaris (tel 3612)
boating contacts:
Kaptan Aşık, Selimiye Köy (village), Muğla (tel (code) 6121 1437) *Venus* cruises: Sefa Uzun (tel Marmaris 1740)
Engür Kaptan cruises: Cihan Ekşi (tel Marmaris 1569)
Yeşil Marmaris Travel Agency, Kordon Cadd 37 (tel 6121)

WEST FROM MARMARİS: DATÇA and KNIDOS

The road to Datça has much in common with a helter-skelter. No matter whether you're driving or going by bus, you'll remember this super-scenic road for a long time, but if you find it too nerve-shattering you can always go on to Bodrum or Marmaris by the car ferry which calls in daily.

Datça itself is a small place with an interesting little lake whose sulphurous waters are fine for swimming although there's also a good beach. The village is the original site of Knidos, Knidas or Cnidos, spell it how you wish.

HOTELS

There are three, all in the İskele Mahallesi, the 'quayside quarter.' The Dore (tel 3536) is open May to October, the Fuda Yalı (tel 1042) is year-round, and the Mare (tel 1211) is open April to November. There's a **holiday village** at Club Datça in the same quarter (tel 1170).

KNIDOS

The city moved from its original site in Datça to the tip of this spectacular peninsula and in the 5th BC century led the world in art, particularly sculpture. Its statue of a nude Aphrodite was so beautiful that it drew admirers from Rome, and Pliny claimed it to be the world's finest sculpting.

As well as its Temple to Aphrodite, the city had its Sanctuary to Demeter on the hillside, above which was Knidos's larger theatre, now in ruins; the smaller one is better preserved and close to the modern main road.

Knidos clings to the cliffs almost at the tip of the headland and drew much of its prosperity from the ships that sheltered in its compact harbour while waiting for a favourable wind. Today all you can see of the city are parts of the walls, the base of Aphrodite's temple, the smaller theatre and, some way inland, the remains of the necropolis.

Access by road is difficult, even allowing for the journey to Datça, and although there is a dolmuş you'd travel quicker by hire car. By far the better way to come is by boat from Marmaris or Bodrum — or even from Datça. There's a small modern village with several restaurants specialising, not surprisingly, in fish.

EAST FROM MARMARİS: KAUNUS

On the face of it, Kaunus or Caunos, on the road eastwards to Fethiye, is just another of those ruined cities. It has a small theatre in fair repair, some of its 4th BC century walls built by the Carian King Mausolus, a scattering of stones from the hilltop fortress, and that's it. The average visitor will have seen his fill in 15 minutes.

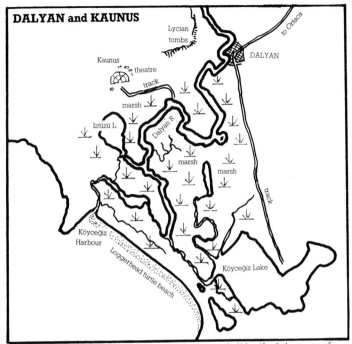

DALYAN and KAUNUS

Lycian tombs

to Ortaca

DALYAN

Kaunus

theatre

track

marsh

Iztüzü L.

Dalyan R.

marsh

marsh

track

Köyceğiz Harbour

Loggerhead turtle beach

Köyceğiz Lake

Yet a visit to Kaunus could be a highspot in your holiday if only because of the effort of getting there. There are two ways: by boat from Marmaris as already mentioned, and by boat from the tiny village of Dalyan. Let's look at that option.

In your own transport leave the main road at Akçakavak, but if you're looking for a dolmuş go to Ortaca (52 km east of Gökova, where the Marmaris branch road joins the main coast highway). From either turn-off, head for Dalyan village on the left (east) bank of the Dalyan River where you'll find about 30 fishing boats engaged in ferrying visitors to Kaunus which is on the right (west) bank and some way downstream.

Rock tombs For 8,000TL you hire the boat for two hours, regardless of the number of passengers. The journey downriver takes half an hour, weaving through reedbeds in which kingfishers nest, and gives a good view of the tombs cut into the near-vertical rock face on the mountain opposite Dalyan. This method of burial marks Kaunus as being under Lycian influence for part of its history.

From the mooring there's a further 15-minute walk to the ruins, with the relief of a wayside shed where you can buy drinks.

And when you climb to the back row of the Kaunus theatre you have a grand view across the flat lands where the city's port once stood. Silting, followed by malaria, killed this community as it did so many others.

Loggerhead turtle If you were to continue downstream, or if you came from Marmaris by sea, you would see one of the longest and widest beaches in Turkey fronting the marshy Dalyan delta. This beach, and one on a   107 nearby Greek island, are the only breeding-places in the Mediterranean of the endangered and much-publicised loggerhead turtle, whose offspring swim upriver to mature in the nutritious waters of the delta. For the sake of those offspring, don't dig in the sand nor camp on the beach during the breeding season.

Dalyan has the **Göl Motel** (tel (code) 6116.1062) which is also a restaurant, and the Mehmet Menteş restaurant serves good fish dishes. There are several pensions and there's also the chance to try a mud bath in a building beside the river.

FETHİYE and ÖLÜ DENIZ

Fethiye is a new town on old foundations. Its origins are unknown but the community of Telebehi was certainly here 500 years before Christ. Yet in 1957 there was little left of the town after a particularly severe earthquake.

A bustling place of around 16,000 people catering for the growing tourist trade most of the year, it's also a commercial port which ships out chromium ore from the nearby mountains. It's deeply involved in agriculture, the acres of plastic 'glasshouses' in the neighbourhood yielding tomatoes and runner beans in winter and the thousands of hives producing pine-flavoured honey during the summer.

Telmessos Fethiye (fet-ee-ah) is an interesting place in its own right with a smart beach on the northern edge of town and, hanging on the slopes to the south, the earthquake-shattered ruins of a medieval castle that the Knights of St John are supposed to have built on what is the site of the acropolis of the Lycian city of Telmessos. There was a Roman theatre down by the harbour but the 'quake of 1856 destroyed it and the nearby Temple of Apollo.

Kaunus: the theatre and the loggerhead turtle lake

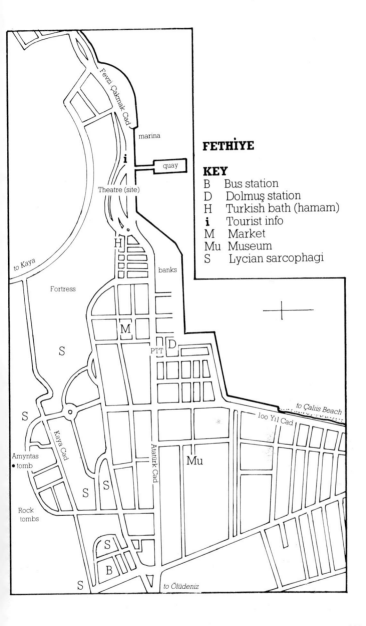

FETHİYE

KEY

B   Bus station
D   Dolmuş station
H   Turkish bath (hamam)
i   Tourist info
M   Market
Mu   Museum
S   Lycian sarcophagi

marina

quay

Theatre (site)

to Kaya

Fortress

banks

M

S

PIT

D

to Çalış Beach

S

100 Yıl Cad

Amyntas
• tomb

Kaya Cad

Atatürk Cad

Mu

Rock
tombs

S   S

S

B

S

to Ölüdeniz

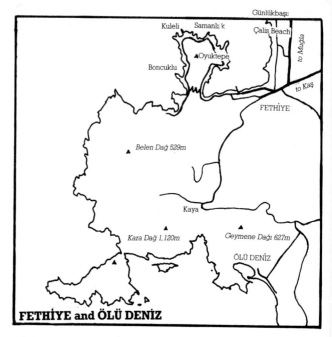

FETHİYE and ÖLÜ DENİZ

Only the sarcophagi and the rock tombs remain of that Telmessos of long ago. The most important sarcophagus, and probably the best in the province of Lycia, is outside the municipal offices by the seafront, while others are scattered around the town which grows up around them after each earth tremor.

Rock tombs The rock tombs, similar to those at Dalyan, are striking monuments in the vertical cliffs on the southern fringe of town, the most impressive being for King Amyntas who ruled Telmessos in the 4th century before Christ. There's an eerie similarity between these rock tombs and those of Abu Simbel in Egypt.

Ölü Deniz

Fethiye is also a dormitory town for exploring the surrounding country, notably the higly-publicised beauty spot of Ölü Deniz, which is photographed on much of the country's tourist literature.

Ölü Deniz means 'dead sea' but it's not dead in the sense of being excessively salt. Imagine a deep cove with wooded hills rising steeply from the water's edge. Now imagine a sandbar across the mouth, preventing so much as a ripple from disturbing the tranquility. That's Ölü Deniz, except that it isn't sand, it's a fine white shingle.

The bar forms an idyllic beach on the seaward side with a string of conifers for shade, and you can sunbathe here in April (average air temperature 21°C (70°F), average sea temperature 18°C (65°F)) and admire the snow on the Taurus Mountains a few miles inland.

Ghost town Three miles from Ölü Deniz on the road to Fethiye is the derelict village of Kaya ('rock'), where 3,500 Greeks lived until Kemal Atatürk's revolution liberated İzmir. In the nationwide swap of Greeks for Turks which followed, Kaya was abandoned and the 1957 'quake has helped accelerate the dereliction.

Beaches

The chunky peninsula which shelters Fethiye harbour is called Oyuk Tepe, 'hollow hill,' where several small bays, each with a beach, provide attractive picnic areas with a background of trees for shade. A coastal road gives easy dolmuş access to beaches with names such as Boncuklu, Karaağaç ('black tree') and Samanlık ('granary'). Beyond the peninsula are the beaches of Kalemye and İçmesu, and the secluded Turunç (a specie of orange) reached only by boat.

North of town lies the Çalış ('industrious') beach leading to the beachside village of Kargı ('javelin') which has a small plantation of liquidambar trees.

Liquid amber The liquidambar or sweet gum tree, a native of the Caribbean, oozes a fragrant perfume and it's found in Turkey only along this stretch of coast with the village of Günlük, 20 km north of Fethiye, having the greatest number.

HOTELS

Dedeoğlu Hotel, İskele Mey, (tel 4010); two-star

Meri Hotel, Ölü Deniz (tel 1); two-star; package tourists, expensive for independent travellers

Mutlu Hotel, Sahil Yolu (road), Çalış (tel 1013); April-November

Kaya Hotel, between market and town hall; budget range

Kordon Hotel, Atatürk Cad 8 (tel 1834); mid-range

Likya Hotel, Karagözler Mah (tel 1169); April-October; pricey but has smart gardens

Oğuz Hotel, town centre (tel 1035); budget range, recommended

Seketur Hotel, Çalış (tel 1705);April-September

Sema Hotel, Çarşı Cad (tel 1015); mid-range

Yıldız Hotel, Çarşı Cad; mid-range

PENSIONS

The tourist office at Iskele Meydanı (at the head of the quay, tel 1527) lists three nationally-approved pensions: Dostlar Pension, Dolgu Sahası (tel 1775); Pınara Pension, Kesikkapı Mahalle (district), Dolgu Sahası (tel 1874) (May-Oct); Üçler Pension, Karagözler Mah (tel 2931) (Apr-Oct).

But since the attraction of Ölü Deniz and the growth of camping, demand has slackened for pensions in Fethiye and you can stroll in the backstreets near the rock tombs and take your pick.

CAMPING

There's a wide range of camping places, the classiest being perhaps the Deniz Camp at Ölü Deniz (tel 1430), but you'll almost certainly be able to rent a tent for the night at any of the camps around Ölü Deniz, at Oyuk Tepe the 'hollow hill,' or amid the liquidambar at Günlük. If you bring your own tent there's virtually unlimited scope for camping, but not on the Dead Sea sandbar, if you please.

RESTAURANTS

My preference is Çim's Restaurant, a blue and white building five minutes' stroll from the sea front up an unnamed backstreet. The food is good and the price, which is reasonable, includes Turkish and English music and often a display of belly dancing.

Nearby are the Antik and Günes restaurants which are good, but their tables are set on unsurfaced backstreets which is no good on a breezy evening. The Kordon Restaurant near the tourist office offers fish and chips with a glass of wine, a sign of things to come!

ÖLÜ DENİZ SHOP

Tokgöž, near the beach and on the road in from Fethiye, is a mini-supermarket, boutique, bar, café, restaurant, and rent-a-tent establishment all in one.

TOUR OPERATORS to Ölü Deniz *only*

CV Travel, Celebrity Holidays, First Resort Holidays, Sunmed.

The Kekova Travel Agency next to Çim's Restaurant, Fethiye, arranges cruises around the harbour and to Bodrum. It can also put you in touch with Big Tur **rent-a-moped.**

EAST FROM FETHİYE

The coastal scenery has been improving in grandeur and sparkle all the way from Kuşadası, but the 273 km from Fethiye to Antalya offer the most beautiful large-scale coastal scenery you're likely to see, for few travellers yet venture beyond Alanya. A generation ago you wouldn't have come here at all, as there was no road for much of the way.

Think of all the tour operators' descriptions: pine-clad mountains cascading to an emerald sea; secluded beaches snuggling into their tiny coves. It's true, but it's also fair to warn that the road is lonely, with no petrol pumps, no villages (they're on side-roads), and little traffic. There are numerous parking areas for admiring the view but it's strangely unphotogenic as it's mostly water.

More ancient cities

East of Fethiye are several ancient cities of Lycia in various stages of restoration. In the anticipation that you've seen enough archaeology, here they are in order of accessibility and interest:

Xanthos, 1 km from coast road; interesting.
Patara, 6 km from coast road on easy dirt road; birthplace of Santa Claus (Father Christmas) and interesting.
Letoon, 4 km from coast road on easy road; interesting.
Pinara, 4 km from coast road up bad track; interesting tombs.
Tlos, 15 km from Kemer village on minor road; interesting history.
Cadianda, 20 km from Fethiye in minor road; moderate interest.
Sidyma, 12 km from coast road up bad track; unimpressive.
Let's take them in sequence from Fethiye.

Cadianda

Cadianda is half an hour's walk from Üzümlü which is 20 km up a track that wanders into the mountains north of Fethiye. The site is mainly sarcophagi from the 5th century BC, and an acropolis (hilltop fort) with ruins of a temple, a bath and a stadium.

Lycian rock tombs: these are at Fethiye

Tlos

You need your own transport or a willing taxi-driver to reach this site, 11 km along a minor road east of Kemer (25 km from Fethiye) and then 4 km up a rutty track. This is one of the oldest cities of Lycia with records going back to the 14th century BC, and in continuous occupation until the 19th century AD.

The eastern walls are Lycian but the large Ottoman buildings in the acropolis were the palace of Kanlı Ali Ağa the 19th century ruler, and the winter hideout of his smuggler brother. The panorama is magnificent and both men would have had fair warning of the approach of undesirables.

Most of the ruins are outside the walls and include a bath, gymnasium, and a Byzantine chapel. There's an impressive Roman tower in good condition, and a theatre buried in scrub.

The most important of the rock tombs is dedicated to Bellerophon, son of King Glaucus of Corinth, who was sent to slay the Chimera, the fire-breathing monster with lion's head, horse's body and snake's tail, which lived in these mountains. Bellerophon went on the winged horse Pegasus and struck Chimera with his lead-tipped spear; the monster's breath melted the lead and Chimera died of poisoning.

Pinara

Pinara is reasonably close to the main road but the track is steep and rutty, impossible for a low-slung car. At road's end is Minare, a village untouched by tourism, but journey's end is still half an hour's hike away.

The location is impressive: a butte-like round hill with vertical sides 600 metres high. There are faint remains of the original 5th century BC Pinara on top and slightly better impressions of the much larger and more recent — but still ancient — city at the bottom, including Lycian-style rock tombs and a theatre, now much overgrown.

The rock wall is even more impressive: there are hundreds of small, rectangular tombs cut into the upper face as tunnels and which could only have been done by workers hanging from ropes.

Sidyma

Sidyma is for the Lycian fanatic. The second half of the track is badly potholed, followed by a stony trail unsuitable for wheels. A modern but

113

medieval-looking village sits amid the ruins and has desecrated them. The Roman theatre is unimpressive and the only interest is in the tunnel-tombs.

Xanthos

By contrast, the city of Xanthos, which dates back to at least 1,200BC, is worth a visit even if the break in your journey costs you your seat on the bus and you have to wave down the next one. Xanthos is only a kilometer from the main road village of Kınık.

Xanthos was the greatest city of Lycia and sent soldiers to the trojan war; later it received Alexander the Great and Antiochus, the King of Syria.

Death by fire In 546BC the attacking Persians herded the Xanthian women, children and slaves into a tower and burned it. The Xanthian men who survived were so infuriated they attacked against overwhelming odds and were wiped out. The city was repopulated from the few survivors in the countryside and in 42BC almost the same thing happened again. Brutus besieged the city, demanding taxes for his dispute against Mark Antony, but the menfolk set fire to the place, threw their women and children into the flames then killed themselves. Brutus, realising what was happening, offered a reward for each Xanthian rescued and his troops saved 150.

The city recovered yet again and under Hadrian became Lycia's capital but it faded into insignificance after the Arab attacks in the 7th century and was rediscovered in 1838 by Sir Charles Fellows, without whose efforts the British Museum's archaeological department would be much smaller: 70 cases of masonry were pirated from the site in 1842 aboard HMS *Beacon* while the officer in charge, Lieutenant Spratt, RN, went prospecting in Tlos and met the smuggler brother of Kanlı Ali Ağa.

Nereid Entering Xanthos under the Arch of Vespasian you should be able to turn right and see the Nereid Monument, allegedly the grandest tomb to come out of Xanthos. Trouble is, it's already gone — to the British Museum.

Sirens By the car park, 400 m on, is the theatre, about half of which remains. Beyond it stand two strange first-century columns which originally had tombs on top, 6 metres in the air. Bas-relief carvings on the sides showing women with birdlike wings carrying children prompted the theory that these were the Harpies, the mythological kidnappers, but they are now believed to be the Sirens who carried the newly dead off to Heaven.

Spratt carried the originals off to London so what you see here in Turkey are plaster replicas.

Five hundred metres across the city site are the first of the tombs cut into the vertical rock face, and a stiff climb to the top takes you to the larger necropolis with a collection of sarcophagi that never made the journey to London.

Letoon

Leto was the mother of Apollo, the god of light, and of Artemis of Ephesian renown, both fathered by Zeus; and Letoon is Leto's holy city. The main interest amid these ruins at the end of an easy tarmac road is the remains of the temples to Leto and her children, standing now in shallow pools abounding with frogs. The theatre, over a slight rise, is the only other building of general appeal.

An intriguing legend recalls that the goddess Hera, whom we may recall was Zeus's sister and wife, prevented Leto giving birth to her two children. She wandered the world until she reached the province of Termilis, named from Termessos, and she bore her children at Patara.

Frogs Shepherds disturbed her while she was washing the babes and forced her to abandon them, but a wolf led her back to them. In gratitude she renamed the region Lycia from the word *lykos,* 'wolf' — and when she became a deity she punished the shepherds by turning them into frogs.

A three-faceted stone found in Letoon and carrying the same inscription in Lycian, Greek and Aramaïc, a Semitic language similar to Hebrew, has helped scholars decipher more of Lycian than the word for wolf.

Patara

At the end of a reasonable dirt road, Patara city has the joint attraction of a long, wide and lonely beach 100 metres away over the dunes, and there's a small on-site restaurant.

Father Christmas Founded in the 5th century BC as the port for Xanthos, Patara has several claims to fame. In mythology the birthplace of the gods Apollo and Artemis it is in reality the place where Saint Nicholas was born. He became the bishop of nearby Myra (Myrrh) where he was buried. Nicholas, the patron saint of children, of travellers by land and sea though not of flying reindeer, and of Russia, Saint Nicholas became the legendary character Santa Claus.

St Paul sailed from Patara on his final journey to Rome and martyrdom, Hannibal called here, and Hadrian gave the town an enormous granary which is still standing, minus its roof.

The port fell to the Egyptian Ptolemy II who renamed it Arsinoë from his wives (the first Arsinoë was Lysimachus's daughter, the second Arsinoë was Lysimachus's widow and Ptolemy's own sister), but the name never stuck.

Triumphal arch You enter Patara today by the double triumphal arch built in 100AD by the Governor of Rome, according to an inscription still legible. The track leads down towards the beach, passing the ruins of a basilica and the modest remains of the baths of Vespasian. Away on the right is the theatre of 147AD, still in fair condition but showing evidence of Patara's continual battle with windblown sand. Strangely, the 300-metre-long pit at the back of the theatre has escaped burial.

Mystery pit Patara was famous in antiquity for its Temple of Apollo, the ground plan of which is barely visible, and for its oracle of which no trace remains. People have guessed that this pit may have held the sacred oracle, or that it was used for sacrifices — there's a suitable pillar in the centre — or again that it was a freshwater reservoir. But where did this water come from and why isn't it there now?

However, it's time to forget history. Clamber over the last sand dune and admire a beautiful Mediterranean beach with scarcely anybody on it. How long will *that* endure?

KALKAN

Seven or eight km beyond Patara is Kalkan, a small village with a growing marina which is popular with flotilla sailors and private yacht charter parties. The Hotel Pirat runs the disco, and Pasha's Inn (10 Sok, 8 (i.e. number 8 on Street No 10), tel Kalkan 77, open May-Oct) has the only good beach, the handiwork of the pasha himself, but there's some publicly-available shingle. The best sand is at **Kaputaş,** 8 km on the road to Kaş. Public transport is limited and the roads out of town have several hairpin bends. Not really the place for a long holiday though some tour operators may disagree.

KAŞ

Kaş is medium-small, but growing as tourism begins to sample the attractions of a picturesque sun-trap village at the base of a major mountain range.

The coast road almost plunges down the mountain into Kaş, but it provides a good view of the village, dominated by its new jetty and bus station and the minarets of its largest mosque. There is a poor beach in town, but a better stretch of sand awaits in the next bay.

Across the sheltered south-facing harbour stands Kastellorizon (Megisti), the most easterly of the Greek islands and, at two miles, the one closest to Turkish territory; some of the offshore rocks are also Greek. And if you look carefully at the large mosque to the west you may see evidence that it was built as a church for the Greek population who inhabited Kaş until the Atatürk revolution.

Antiphellus Looking back at the rugged Taurus Mountains with the peak of Tuzla rising to 1,366 m in the foreground, you may notice more of those Lycian rock tombs cut into the vertical hillside on the edge of town. To the west, beyond the mosque, is a modest but well-preserved Roman theatre which, with the Doric tomb on the hillside a little way above, is all you're likely to see of the original 4th century BC city of Antiphellus, the port for the city of Phellus which has yet to be found. Kaş was called Andifli until a century ago.

The tomb is worth the effort of walking up to it as it was hewn in situ from one massive piece of rock.

Away from it all The modern Kaş is isolated from the outside world — 110 km to Fethiye and 188 to Antalya — and anybody contemplating a holiday here should bear in mind the constraints of travel; there are adequate bus services in both directions but in high summer you'll need to reserve a seat the day before. Most holiday activity would originate in the small marina or the harbour.

Kastellorizon There's no scheduled ferry service to the Greek island of Kastellorizon, which has neither customs nor immigation officers, so your visit must be unofficial and confined to a day trip. Another boat excursion takes you eastwards, past the headland of Ulu Burun where lies the world's oldest known shipwreck (see Bodrum), to three more Lycian cities.

Ancient cities The first is **Aperlae** whose underwater streets were discovered in the 1960s by an American yacht skipper. **Teimiussa** has a scattering of sarcophagi near the modern village of Kale, while opposite the island of Kekov is **Simena** whose theatre, carved from the solid rock, has only seven rows of seats. The latter two cities are now accessible by a reasonable road.

ACCOMMODATION and RESTAURANTS

Ali Baba Motel, Hastane Cad (tel 126); mid-range
Mimosa Hotel, Elmalı Cad (tel 1272); two star.

There are plenty of pensions in the village, and if you ask at the tourist office (Cumhuriyet Mey 6, tel 1238) you'll receive details of private homes that take in guests — useful if you're learning Turkish! Camping sites are along Hastane Caddesi (Hospital Street).

The Shady Restaurant near the tourist office is probably the best place to eat but the Eriş is a fair alternative, though there are others.

TO FATHER CHRISTMAS LAND
Demre

Tomato-growing Demre is not the kind of village you'd choose to explore, yet in a sidestreet it has the much-restored 5th century Church of St Nicholas, named from the man who was born in Patara and who rose to become Bishop of nearby Myra. While in high office Nicholas took pity on the three daughters of a man who had hit hard times, and he dropped a bag of coins down the chimney to save the wedding of each of the girls.

Santa Claus The Christian Church, allocating every day to at least one saint, chose December 6 for. Nicholas, and as Christianty spread into the colder lands of northern Europe the legend of Saint Nicholas, Santa Claus, merged with that of the once-pagan Father Christmas and with some Dickensian licence to give us the cloaked and bearded old man who comes down chimneys at dead of night and leaves gifts.

The real Santa Claus died around 342 and was buried at Myra, but Italian sailors robbed his grave in 1087 and took most of his remains to Bari, near Brindisi, where they are today. His other bones are in a museum in Antalya and there is now a festival for St Nicholas at the Demre church every December 6-8.

Myra

Two kilometers inland up a gravel road, Myra is well worth a visit for its Roman theatre and some of the best rock tombs you'll see in all of Lycia. The city was established in the 5th century BC and damaged by a 'quake in 141AD after which the theatre was built. Associations with Santa Claus maintained a strong Christian interest in the city until the 7th century when the Arab world claimed it.

Painted Tomb The tombs are in two distinct areas two kilometers apart but the eastern necropolis, accessible around recently-built plastic greenhouses, is the more striking, with the Painted Tomb the most outstanding of its kind in Lycia. Carved to resemble a house with a pitched roof, the tomb shows people in the porch dressed for indoor activites and those beyond it dressed for outside. The only colurs remaining are red and blue on one of the figures but a century ago British Museum's benefactor Sir Charles Fellows recorded purple and yellow as well.

Trysa

North of Demre, 8 km into the mountains and extremely difficult to find, lie the ruins of the city of Trysa. Austrian archaeologists rediscovered it in modern times, marvelled at a tomb bearing delicate frieze carvings showing scenes from Homer's *Iliad,* and carried this treasure back to Vienna. Ignore Trysa and continue towards Finike.

Finike

Here is a small, dark brown beach spoiled by rubbish from the tiny River Karasu whose name aptly translates as 'black water.' Ducks swim in the black waters, naval boats mingle with the cargo vessels loading tomatoes or oranges, so there's little point in staying. If you have the misfortune to be benighted here the Hotel Sedir (Cumhuriyet Cad 37, tel 256) can offer low-priced comfort to raise your spirits.

THE ROAD TO ANTALYA
New road or old?

The *new* road east from Finike runs beside a pebbly beach, at times greyish, for 10 miles or more before heading into a spur of the mountains and continuing along the coast to Antalya. The *old* road heads due north from Finike to Korkuteli 120 km away, then turns east for the 64 km run to

Antalya. Buses plying the route between Fethiye and Antalya take the faster coast road. There are dolmuş services to Korkuteli but the only inducement for the tourist to take this route is to see two more Lycian cities.

The old road

Limyra The 5th century BC city of Limyra has one of the largest necropolises in Lycia, straddling several ridges above the city itself. Access is poor, as you need to turn off the road 6 km north of Finike and follow a minor road for another 5 km. There are no signs and you need your own transport since Limyra is not worth the expense of a taxi, the only attraction apart from the cemetery being a smallish theatre.

Arycanda Arycanda is just 20 minutes' walk from the road at a turning around 35 km north of Finike. It is signposted, and was in continuous occupation from the 5th century BC until the 19th AD and the ruins are in remarkably good condition considering this human presence. The Roman baths overshadow much of the city site but the theatre, with 20 rows of seats, has an excellent view over the valley which must have been a distraction for the audience.

The new road

Around 27 km from Finike the road crosses a pass in the mountains and enters some of the loneliest coastal countryside in Turkey, but with splendid panoramas of the Taurus ranges rising fold upon fold into the blue mists of the interior. Ahead lies Mount Olympus National Park — Olimpos Beygağları Milli Parkı — but if we turn off the main road and follow the older track down by the shoreline we can visit the ancient city of Olympus itself.

Olympus The city's origins are unknown, the first record being on some coins struck here in the 2nd century BC. Olympus lies right on the shoreline so that you need a snorkel and swimsuit to exlore some of it, and strong clothing to see much of the remainder, including the theatre, as there is little that's been excavated.

Held for a few years by the Cilicians around 85BC, and briefly renamed Hadrianopolis after Hadrian visited it in 129 AD, Olympus was sacked a second time by the Cilicians in the 3rd century and went into decline, reviving briefly under Venetian influence before fading into total obscurity with the coming of the Ottomans.

Chimera From here it's a hard clamber to one of the strangest natural phenomena in Turkey, the perpetual flame of the Chimera in the Sanctuary of Hephaistos, a cave around 800 feet above sea level that has an excellent view of the Gulf of Antalya. Hephaistos, the son of Zeus and Hera, was the Greek god of fire whom the Romans knew as Vulcan.

This small flame was the same Chimera, the fire-breathing dragon, that Bellerophon set out to slay when he rode from Tlos on Pegasus, but there's no need for a lead-tipped lance to extinguish the flame today; you could do it with the clap of a gloved hand. And Bellerophon's success was only a chimera as the flame reignites within seconds.

So is there a workable quantity of natural gas in the neighbourhood? Geologists investigated in 1967 and decided there isn't.

Phaselis This new highway runs straight into Antalya, still 85 km away, but if you have your own transport you can continue along the coastal road a few more miles to Phaselis, a city founded by the Greeks of Rhodes 700 years before Christ. It has a good selection of Lycian sarcophagi, Roman baths, a theatre, and a street that still has its paving slabs.

Kemer The only town along this coast is Kemer, which is entering the tourist market with the **Club Salima**, a holiday village with capacity for 800 guests and built with government help.

ACCOMMODATION

Between Finike and Antalya the choice is strictly limited. Kemer has the out-of-town Olimpos Hotel (tel 1280; three star, open Apr-Oct) and the two-star Kemer Doruk (tel 1125).

In town are the Kilit (tel 1833, Apr-Oct) and the Kemer (İskele Cad, tel 2488, Apr-Oct) in the hotel range, with several pensions.

The only other accommodation is a few pensions at Tekirova near Phaselis, and a scattering of pensions and camping sites on the way in to Antalya, but they're mostly very basic — and the beach is only a narrow strip of grey shingle.

ANTALYA

Antalya is the 13th largest city in Turkey with 260,000 people, but the only part of interest to the traveller is the Kaleiçi and perhaps the new museum. Antalya is a bustling community of smart buildings and straight streets leading to a gleaming new promenade, the Akdeniz Bulvarı, but you'll find few people with a smattering of any language beyond Turkish.

The city-centre tourist office, usually the place to go for information, is very difficult to find as it's down some steps from the seaward edge of the great Atatürk Meydanı (Square) — and it's often closed.

Kaleiçi Atatürk Square provides some good views across the bay to the Taurus Mountains behind Kemer, and of Kaleiçi, the tiny old city, at your feet. Pronounced as two words, *Kale içi*, it means 'within the fortress' and describes the maze of alleys within the old city wall and surrounding the tiny harbour, the Attaleia founded by Attalus II of Pergamon in the 2nd century BC. The port served Antalya from those early days until very recently when the new docks were opened on the south-west approaches to town, leaving Attalus's port to become a marina.

There is some fascinating architecture to be seen in Kaleiçi, much of it in a poor state of repair but all now under a preservation order and scheduled for restoration.

The most impressive building in this quarter is the Fluted Minaret, Yivli Minare, which towers above all else. It was built by Aladdin Keykubat shortly after the Seljuks captured the city from the Byzantines in 1207, and has become the symbol of Antalya. More recently it held the city museum, closing in 1971.

Most of the city walls have disappeared but the impressive triple-arch Hadrian's Gate, commemorating the emperor's visit in 130AD, survives. The Kaleiçi also holds the Karatay Medrese, the theological school from the same period as the Fluted Minaret, which has some good examples of Seljuk stonework.

Museum The new museum, at the western end of Akdeniz Bulv, opened in 1985 mainly featuring statues and needs more exhibits before it will attract the casual visitor.

Düden Waterfalls Ten kilometers south-east of Antalya on the road to the little resort of Lara, the Düden River pours over moderately-high cliffs into the sea to form the Lower Düden Falls. The Upper Falls are 14 km out of town off the road to Burdur and visitors can walk behind their cascading waters.

Beaches Antalya's beaches are poor. The best sand is at Lara, 12 km away to the south-east at the end of a road that goes nowhere else.

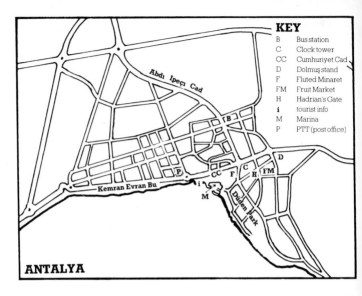

ANTALYA

KEY

B	Bus station
C	Clock tower
CC	Cumhuriyet Cad
D	Dolmuş stand
F	Fluted Minaret
FM	Fruit Market
H	Hadrian's Gate
i	tourist info
M	Marina
P	PTT (post office)

Restaurants and canyons The Antalya area has some unique attractions to offer other than beaches. There's a revolving restaurant atop the hill called Tünektepe, Three kilometres inland from the new port, and 20 km back on the road to Korkuteli (our 'old' road from Finike) is the 110-metre-deep Güver Canyon. But the 14-km long, 400-m-deep Köprülü Canyon is truly spectacular; the trouble is, its 50 km inland up a lonely valley, the last 10 km of which are beyond the end of the bad road. If you still want to go, turn north at Taşağul, 42 km east of town.

Stone Age The oldest known human habitation in Turkey, in use 50,000 years ago, is a cave at Karain, near the Upper Düden Waterfalls — and the site is accessible by road. There's a small museum showing a reconstruction of life in the Stone Age.

Termessos

The Korkuteli road leads to Termessos, an ancient city unlike any that we have seen so far. Around 30 km from Antalya look for a sign pointing south to the *Termessos Milli Parkı*, a further 9 km along a moderately-good track. If you've no transport of your own here's your chance to try hitch-hiking.

The origins of the city are unknown but its founders were not Greeks. They called themselves the Solymi and this was part of the old province of Pisidia. The first mention of Termessos was in 333BC when Alexander the Great besieged it for a day then decided to pass on, for the Solymi were great warriors. Even when Rome ruled the region, Termessos retained its independence.

Your first impression of the city will be of the sheer majesty of its location, 1,500 metres up in spectacular mountain scenery. Your second, as you acclimatise yourself, will be one of scale as you clamber for a kilometer uphill through the crumbling Hadrian's Gate to the gymnasium, standing gaunt, grey and overgrown.

Theatre Ahead lies the theatre, small by Roman standards with a capacity of around 5,000, but magnificent in its setting. Uphill again are the ruins of three temples, one of them dedicated to Artemis: we might guess that another was for Apollo.

Sarcophagi Termessos is impressive, but the real shock comes when you appreciate the size of the cemetery, the necropolis, with hundreds of sarcophagi scattered around the hillside as if some vengeful god threw them from heaven in his fury. Many carry inscriptions with dire warnings against violation, but the hand of later man, plus earthquakes, has brought havoc.

HOTELS

Antalya's hotels are geared more for the luxury and executive market than for tourism.

Atan Hotel, Lara yolu (road) 177 (tel 11192)

Bilgehan Hotel, Kazımözalp Cad 194 (tel 25324)

Büyük Hotel, Cumhuriyet Cad 57(tel 11499)

Lara Hotel, Lara (tel 15299)

Perge Hotel, Karaalı Park Yanı (tel 23600)

Sera Hotel, Lara (tel 28377); five-star, 310 rooms

Start Hotel, Aliçetin Kaya Cad (tel 11280); three-star

Talya Hotel, Fevzi Çamak Cad (tel 15600-9); five-star, 150 rooms

Yalçın Hotel, Hüsnükarakaş Cad, 1253 Sok (tel 14190)

Yayla Hotel, Ali Çetinkaya Cad 12 (tel 11913)

PENSIONS

The Sultan is listed as a pension but it's really a hotel and charges accordingly. It's at Merdivenli Sok 3, Kaleiçi, in the old city, and full of character (tel 22253). The Altun Pension at Kaleiçi Mev 10 (tel 16624) is similarly in a restored Ottoman house.

Budget accommodation is to be found in self-styled hotels which are really pensions, near the bus station on Sarampol Cad, formerly Kazım Özalp Cad. Some of these let you sleep on the roof for 1,000TL.

MOTEL

Antalya Motel, Lara Yolu 84 (tel 14609)

RESTAURANTS

These follow the trend set by the hotels and cater for the business community, Turkish style. The top place is the Talya Hotel's restaurant which also has a night-club, but there are several mid-range establishments at Kaleiçi, within the old city: the Hisar Turistik, the Kafe İskele, the Liman Taverna, the Marina Sandvıç and the Mobidik Kafeterya, and others. For a meal at basic price look along Sarampol Cad near the bus station or in Eski Sebzeciler İçi Sok near the Atatürk-Cumhuriyet cad junction, not far from the dolmuş station.

EAST FROM ANTALYA

The road east from Antalya crosses a totally flat alluvial plain where fields are large enough for mechanised farming, though Turkish cotton is still laboriously harvested by hand, mostly female. Apart from cotton this plain grows grain, citrus fruits, bananas and avocados, while oleander forms some of the hedges. The road itself is uninteresting once it has passed Antalya airport, and the sea is miles away to the south.

Perge But 7km from the city limits you reach Aksu and the turning for Perge, 2 km to the north, and you realise this plain is geologically new and that the Pamphylan city of Perge was much closer to the sea.

The original Perge was built at an unknown time on the hill north of the present city, but nothing remains. The Perge you see made its entry into recorded history when it welcomed Alexander the Great after he bypassed Termessos. The Seleucids ruled Perge and all of coastal Pamphyla until the Romans came in 188BC, and the city sank into oblivion with the arrival of the Seljuks.

The theatre and stadium each had seating for 15,000 spectators. Both lie outside the city and are well preserved, the stadium being the largest in Turkey. The main street is Perge's greatest attraction, its columns reminiscent of Harbour Road at Ephesus. Down the centre of the street is a channel which carried water from the nymphaeum, the theatre specifically for women, at the street's upper end.

Aspendos Thirty kilometers east the former port city of Aspendos lies in the Köprü valley 1 km north of the main road, beyond a 13th century Seljuk bridge that still carries traffic.

Largest theatre? Aspendos was founded around 800BC after the fall of Troy, but these ruins are all from the Roman era and are dominated by the theatre which some authorities claim is the largest in the Roman empire, and by the aqueduct, ruins of which stretch across the country to the north.

A legend claims that two suitors for the daughter of the king of Aspendos built the theatre and the aqueduct to win father's approval. The king, undecided, vowed he'd cut his daughter in half whereon the horrified theatre-builder rejected his claim — and by doing so proved his love and won the princess.

Kemal Atatürk saw this theatre shortly after his revolution and decreed that it be totally restored and brought back into use. Both commands have been kept and the theatre's perfect acoustics are put to the test at the annual Antalya Festival in August.

SIDE (Selemiye)

Side is a surprise. It's the first mass-market resort since Fethiye, and the last but one on this coast. It has all the attractions for a modern package holiday: two wide sandy beaches separated by a headland loaded with history, a rugged mountainous hinterland, and a good mixture of souvenir shops and restaurants.

There is another side to Side (pronounced *see-day*). Development in the early 1960s was uncontrolled and there are some concrete-block monstrosities which are soon to be demolished in the controlled redevelopment of the resort.

Side, still called Selimiye on many maps, is a small village that is filled to capacity at peak season creating an inevitable shortage of rooms for the independent traveller and a lack of competition among the restaurants.

Slavery The headland holds the well-preserved ruins of the Roman city of Side on a site which had been occupied since 600BC. Under the Greeks, 200 years before Christ, the people of Side were pirates who sold their captives into slavery and thus prompted Pompey's anti-pirate raid of 67BC, but under the Byzantines Side was the centre for Christianity in the area and ruled 15 bishoprics. Arab raids began its decline and a 10th century fire finished the city.

The 2nd century theatre, originally with 58 rows of seats and a capacity beween 17,000 and 25,000 according to which authority you support, stands astride this narrow peninsula like a fortress. Beyond it, the Roman baths are now the museum, holding some of the best Roman sculpture which was not spirited away to foreign museums. Beyond again, at the tip of the peninsula, are the temples of Athena and Apollo, built in the 1st century AD.

Mark Antony and Cleopatra chose Side for one of their trysts, and at sunset the old city is once again the meeting-place for lovers from other lands, even if they're humble honeymooners on a Horizon package holiday.

Access Side is 3 km off the main road, but buses and dolmuşes offload in the bus station between the theatre and the museum. Private cars may park here as well as the new village is off limits.

HOTELS
Cennet Hotel, (tel 1167); two-star, Apr-Nov; also has villas
Defne Hotel, (tel 1880); three-star
Karaelmas Hotel, Bingeşik (outlying village) (tel 350)

HOLIDAY VILLAGE Turtel, Selimiye village (tel 2225); Apr-Oct

PENSIONS
There are 30 or so pensions in Side and along the beach to the north-west. In high season start shopping around as early in the day as possible, and furthest from the beach. If no luck, move on.

RESTAURANTS
The hotels provide full board for guests, and many pensions give access to cooking facilities. Otherwise the choice and the menus are limited.

MANAVGAT
Manavgat is 3km east of the turning for Side, and here a sign points to the village of Şelale, another 3 km inland. Just beyond Şelale are the Manavgat Waterfalls, in reality a series of rapids. In front of them is a restaurant serving trout, presumably caught in the Manavgat River, and you'll find the usual assortment of souvenir shops.

The easiest way to get here without your own car is by dolmuş or excursion from Side.

The town also has its own **holiday village,** the Club Aldiana (tel 4260) with its own stretch of beach and accommodation for 640 guests.

ALANYA
The fortress peninsula of Alanya can be seen from miles away, east or west, like a miniature Rock of Gibraltar in the eastern Mediterranean. You arrive to find it's another Side, only better.

Alanya's beaches, on each side of the promontory, stretch into the distance offering ideal conditions for windsurfing and other water sports, the old and the new town are distinct, and the fortress on that headland is like nothing we've yet seen in Turkey: for a start, it's not Roman.

Modern Alanya is fairly compact, for this part of Turkey is surprisingly underpopulated by present standards, and the tourist hotels which look as if they could have spilled over from Spain have yet to detract from the natural beauty of the area.

Cleopatra Old Alanya is where you'll find the charm. As Coracesium it was another pirate and slave stronghold until Pompey destroyed the brigand fleet off this headland in 67BC. Later, Mark Antony gave the town and much of its hinterland, the old province of Cilicia, to Cleopatra so she could use its timber for shipbuilding.

The town faded into early obscurity despite the advantages of its headland, but revived with the coming of the Seljuks in 1221, a reversal of the history of other ancient cities. The Seljuks at this period held all of modern Turkey except west of a line from Fethiye to Zonguldak on the Black Sea, and the south coast from Coracesium eastward. Coracesium, which they renamed Alanya, was therefore a frontier town as well as the port for their capital, Konya.

Aladdin Keykubad I, also known as Aladdin but with no connection with the pantomime character, fortified this headland appropriately for its new role. The walls, still in very good shape, took 12 years to build and run for 7 km. Ancient invaders, like modern visitors, faced a stiff climb to the outer gate and another climb across the outer court to the inner gate, set with double doors at right-angles for extra security.

The flatter inner court was the Ehmedek Kalesi, the residential district of the town, and on its northern side Aladdin built the Süleimaniye Mosque, a caravanserai and a bazaar; the latter two are in poor condition.

Hurled to death On the western edge of the fortress overlooking a precipitous drop, Aladdin built his citadel, containing barracks for his personal bodyguard and cisterns to catch the winter rains for their summer water; there are 100 cisterns in the fortress. And from here Aladdin also had prisoners and adulteresses hurled to their death.

The view from the citadel is splendid, covering the landward and seaward approaches and including the strange finger of rock which projects almost 300 metres out to sea, carrying a monastery and the ruins of a mint.

Caves At the base of the fortress stands Aladdin's Kızılkule, the Red Tower, a five-storey fortification defending the tiny harbour and restored in 1952-3. Around the headland and accessible by boat are, clockwise from the Red Tower, the so-called arched boatyards, five chambers now unique to Turkey in which the Seljuks built their caïques; the Pirates' Cave; and

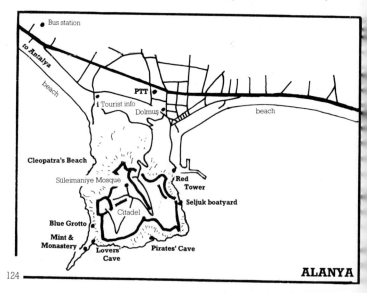

ALANYA

round the rocky finger the Lovers' Cave; the Blue Grotto; and, accessible also by foot, the Grotto of Damlataş, leading to the beach where Cleopatra is believed to have bathed.

Asthma This last cave, opened in 1948 by quarrymen, has a sticky atmosphere with a high humidity and a constant temperature of 23°C (74°F) that asthma sufferers claim to be beneficial. From personal experience I would recommend they also drop cow's milk in any form from their diet.

HOTELS

The majority of package-holiday hotels, most of which are included in my list, are out of town to the east, and package guests may find they need to get on a dolmuş to reach the town centre.

Alaaddin Hotel, Atatürk Cad (tel 2642); Apr-Oct, 108 rooms

Alaiye Hotel, Atatürk Cad (tel 4018)

Alantur Hotel, Çamyolu village (tel 1224); 99 rooms, four-star

Alanya Büyük Hotel, Güllerpınar Mah (quarter) (tel 1138); Apr-Oct

Alara Hotel, Yeşil village (tel 146); Apri-Oct

Atilla Hotel, Güllerpınar Mah (quarter) (tel 2209)

Banana Hotel, Cıkçıklı village (tel 1568); May-Nov

Bayırlı Hotel, İskele Cad 66 (tel 1487)

Çimen Hotel, Güllerpınar Mah (tel 2283); Apr-Nov

Güvenir Hotel, Atatürk Cad 24 (tel 1314)

Güngör Hotel, Atatürk Cad (tel 3142); Apr-Nov .

Kaptan Hotel, İskele Cad 62 (tel 2000); three-star

Kleopatra Hotel, Toptancı Hal Yanı (tel 3980)

Merhaba Hotel, Keykubat Cad (tel 1251); Apr-Oct

Mesut Hotel, Oba village (tel 1339)' Apr-Oct

Özen Hotel, Müftüler Cad 26 (tel 2220)

Panorama Hotel, Keykubat Cad (tel 1181); Apr-Oct

Park Hotel, Hürriyet Mey (tel 1675)

Pehlivan Hotel, Saray Mah, Hacıhamitloğlu Sok 25 (tel 2781)

Riviera Hotel, Güzelyalı Cad (tel 1432)

Sipahi Hotel, Güzel Yalı Cad (tel 2637)

Turteş Hotel, Sarapsu Mev, Konaklı village (tel 1); Apr-Nov

Wien Terbilek Hotel, Keykubat Cad (tel 3617); Apr-Oct

Yeni Hotel International Keykubat Cad 211 (tel 1195); two-star

MOTEL: Cömertoğlu Motel, Okurcular village (tel 72); May-Oct

HOLIDAY VILLAGE: Club Ağuarius (Aquarius), Konaklı Mev (tel 2632); 184 rooms, Apr-mid Nov.

PENSIONS: Pensions and the cheaper hotels are either in the town centre or within half a mile of it to the east. Start looking by the PTT on Atatürk Caddesi and work east or, if it's not high season, head south down İskele Caddesi. There are also several **camping** sites east of town, usually a dolmuş ride away.

TOUR OPERATORS: Allegro, Horizon Holidays, Panorama, Steepwest.

RESTAURANTS: The smaller and therefore cheaper places are on the Gazi Paşa Cad, the seafront, and include the Şirin and the Havuzbaşı; there are others a little way inland beyond the main road.

ENTERTAINMENT: The usual — discos in the town centre or the hotels out east.

ANAMUR'S CRUSADER CASTLE

East of Alanya the Taurus Mountains plunge to the sea in unfettered majesty, creating tiny coves that were the nuclei for early Greek and Roman mini-cities and the hideouts of pirate ships in the decades before Pompey's raid of 67BC.

Since then the march of civilization has taken other routes. Alexander the Great never came to this southern coast. The Seljuks never came, leaving the region ostensibly to the Armenians, who stayed at home in the lowlands around Adana.

The Crusaders did come, but only to build isolated forts on lonely headlands, guarding their routes to the Holy Land. The Ottomans conquered, but for generations they never came. At last, in 1967 the Turks came — and built this lonely but splendidly scenic road which loops and twists its way along the coast, linking Alanya with Silifke, 270 km to the east.

For a few miles east of Alanya there are small villages growing bananas and tomatoes. Beyond Gazipaşa the new road gives better access to the ruins of some of those early cities and castles, but none is of note until you reach Anamur.

Phoenician Anemurium was a Phoenician city-port which reached the height of its prosperity in the 3rd century but which was deserted soon after the Arabs began raiding the coast 400 years later. Ruins visible today include parts of the walls and theatre, much of the baths, and several houses to roof level.

The Seljuks came in 1240 to build a castle on the headland. The Crusaders followed them as tenants, handing over to the kings of Cyprus who pulled out in the mid-15th century as the Ottoman Empire expanded. Eventually the Ottomans took control of the castle and kept it in commission until 1921, which is why the walls and towers are still in near-perfect order.

Southernmost Anamur was Turkey's southernmost community until 1939 when the French, who were the colonial masters of Syria, pulled out of İskenderun and so allowed that to become the southernmost part of Turkey.

SİLİFKE to İSKENDERUN

You are now well off the tourist routes, and it shows. **Silifke**'s Byzantine castle, rebuilt by the Crusaders, is just as nature left it, and the only remnant of the old Seleucia is a Roman theatre. Inland, 38 km along a minor road winding into the mountains, is the Roman city of Diocaesaraea with a theatre and a Temple of Zeus which became a Byzantine church.

Boats and hydrofoils for Cyprus leave from Taşucu, 4 km west of Silifke (see the end of chapter 'Getting There') where you'll also find accommodation.

Mersin, which also has a ferry link with Cyprus, is a modern city, its hotels in the centre inland from the Atatürk Park. **Tarsus,** the birthplace of St Paul or Saul, is also the spot where Mark Antony first met Cleopatra as she came upriver in splendour aboard her galley.

Adana, the fourth largest city of Turkey with 776,000 people and still growing, is industrial, but Hadrian's stone bridge, the Taş Köprü, with 14 of its original 21 arches surviving, is worth seeing.

The name of **İskenderun** is a corruption of Alexander the Great, the city's founder, but the modern port and industrial areas have wiped away all signs of the past. **Antakya,** the ancient Antioch founded by the Seleucids in the 3rd century BC, has a Roman bridge and an out-of-town grotto where St Peter first preached. Both cities fell to the Egyptians in 1831 and were returned in 1939.

ANATOLIA

Hidden Turkey

TURKEY IS MANY COUNTRIES IN ONE. While the Aegean and Mediterranean coasts are becoming the playground of the Western world, there's a vast and lonely interior that seldom sees a foreigner from one year to the next. Anatolia, Anadolu in Turkish, is the heartland of Asia Minor and many of its secrets and treasures are doomed to remain hidden for years to come.

Anatolia is vast, reaching 900 miles, 1,200 km, east to west, rising to 16,916 feet at mystic Mount Ararat, and possessed of a climate and landscape that are often formidable, occasionally frightening, but always fascinating.

Without your own transport so much of the interior is accessible only with great effort; even with a car, or on a motor-coach tour, time and distance limit what can be seen in a conventional holiday.

It's a pity, for here is the homeland and battlefield of peoples whose names are part of the human story: the Mongols, the early Persians, the Hittites, the Ottomans themselves.

On the practical front, the summer climate of western Atatolia — say, west of Sivas — is hot by day (but never as hot as on the coast) and cool by night, sometimes with a warm breeze. East of Sivas on the higher steppes, temperatures are several degrees lower and nights can be chilly. Rain is rare except in a thunderstorm.

In winter, western Atatolia is bleak, with temperatures often plunging well below freezing at dusk. In the east, snow covers the landscape for months at a time, isolating remote villages for weeks. You have to be born of special stock to endure this climate, but peoples who could spend generations on the long march from Mongolia and other parts of Asia, were of that stock.

If you venture — or should I say 'adventure'? — from the coast, you will find Batman as different from Bodrum as Bodrum is from Benidorm.

ADIYAMAN & Nemrut Dağı

In 80BC the Persian-born Mithradites Callinicus found some unclaimed territory on the bank of the Euphrates — Fırat in modern Turkish — and declared it to be the Kingdom of Commagene with himself as its ruler. Commagene was only a small and landlocked country and as it was the age of unrest he made a marriage of political convenience with a Seleucid princess who bore a son, Antiochus.

Temple of Antiochus This son, as King Antiochus I, built an enormous temple the like of which had never been seen. He chose the top of a mountain as its location, commanding a view over almost all of Commagene including two major crossing-points on the Euphrates. The temple contained many statues of himself, his father, his supposed ancestors the gods, and stylised animals including eagles and lions.

The heads were up to two metres high on columns up to 10 m tall, and when it was finished Antiochus ordered tons of small rocks and rubble to be heaped on part of the site, probably where he had arranged to have his own tomb: since that section of the mountaintop hasn't yet been excavated, nobody knows.

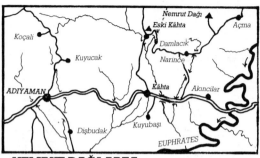

NEMRUT DAĞI AREA

Commagene had a short life. The Romans annexed it in 18AD (but King Antiochus IV recovered it for a short while with the help of his friend Caligula, emperor from 37 to 41AD) and soon the strange temple on the top of Mount Nemrut, Nemrut Dağı, was forgotten. The Hittites, the Urarti, the Assyrians, Persians and Macedonians had already passed this way and in the centuries to come the Byzantines, Seljuks, Mameluks and the Ottomans would rule the area.

But nobody knew about Nemrut Dağı until 1881 when the German geologist Karl Sester discovered the site. He spent only an hour there and the place was ignored for two more years. Then in 1953 excavation began and the giant heads were revealed. The last of them, the Fortune of Commagene, was toppled from her pedestal in 1963 by lightning.

Arsameia Mithradites chose a nearby valley as the site of Arsameia, the capital of Commagene. It's close to the route up to Nemrut Dağı but there's little to see; however, at the village of Kahta, where you turn off for Nemrut Dağı, there's a packhorse bridge which was built in 196BC across a dramatic narrow point of the River Kahta, a tributary of the Euphrates. The museum in Adıyaman contains smaller relics from the mountaintop site.

Access Getting to Nemrut Dağı is not easy. Adıyaman is around 180 km from Malatya and its airport (four flights daily from Ankara and Istanbul) and 65 km from Gölbaşı railway station (trains to here are notoriously slow).

From Adıyaman you have two choices, assuming you don't have a car. Either go by dolmuş to Kahta which is a further 41 km, with another 60 km to Nemrut Dağı itself. You can break this by taking a dolmuş the 25 km to Eski Kahta, the village near Arsameia and walking or hitching the rest of the way.

Or you can join an organised tour in either Adıyaman or Kahta which is obviously by far the easiest way but can also be expensive. There are plans afoot to improve the roads to the north of Nemrut Daï and build a 20 km link to the mountain which should ease the problem of access.

ACCOMMODATION

In Adıyaman are the Antiochus Motel (tel 1240) on the west of town and the Arsemia Motel (tel 2112) on the east. Kahta has the Nemrut Tur Motel on Adıyaman-Kahta Yolu (i.e. on the road linking those two places, tel 863), the Merhaba Hotel (tel 139) the Komegana Pension (Eski Kahta Yolu, tel 92) listed by the Tourist Office, and a few basic pensions in the town centre. Eski Kahta has one pension.

It may be useful to call in at any or all of these places for the latest news on organised tours.

AĞRI and Mount Ararat

Ağrı Dağı is the Turkish for Mount Ararat, and this is one of the few provinces not to take the name of its chief town — but who could ignore Ararat, at 5,165 m (16,946 ft) the highest peak in Turkey?

Mount Ararat The extinct volcano of Ararat rises far higher than the surrounding mountains and is perpetually snow-capped; it's also wrapped in cloud for most of every day making dawn, and occasionally dusk, the only time to see the peak. Ararat took its name from the Urartu, the Bronze Age people of the area, but the Persians know it as the Mountain of Noah, Koh-i-Nor. 'Noor' in Persian means 'light' and the famous Koh-i-Noor diamond has no connection with Turkey's most spectacular peak.

Noah The three major religions of the world are familiar with the story of Noah (in China they talk of Nu-wah), who built an ark to save mankind from the Flood. I'll steer clear of debate on the issue beyond commenting that since the first recorded ascent of the mountain in 1829 nobody has found traces of the ark — and that includes people studying spy satellite photographs.

The ascent Ararat is in a politically sensitive area and the Iranians and Soviets are aware of its potential for surveillance. You *may* climb it, but only with written permission from the government and then only with an official guide. The route is difficult and dangerous, and an 1840 earthquake caused a major landslip which destroyed a village. If you're still keen to make this the adventure of a lifetime the easiest way is to join a trek organised by either Trek Travel at Taksim Mey 10/6, İstanbul or Metro Turism, Cumhuriyet Cad 43, Taksim, İstanbul. Allow three days for the ascent and take the full Alpine gear. If you're not an experienced mountaineer, stay away and just take photographs.

ANKARA

Ankara had 30,000 people when it became the capital of the new Republic of Turkey on 13th October 1923. At the 1985 census it had 2,251,000, putting it comfortably into second place (Izmir, third, had 1,489,000 but Istanbul was unassailable at 5,494,000).

This rapid expansion means that Ankara today presents itself as a modern, European-inspired city of wide, tree-lined boulevards with plenty of parks and other open spaces, but despite that image it has a history going back to the Hatti in the Bronze Age. The Hittites gave it the name *Ankuwash* (English spelling) which the following Phrygians altered to *Ancyra*.

Galatian citadel The Lydians came in the 3rd century BC but were soon defeated by Alexander the Great. In the carve-up that followed Alexander's death, Ancyra fell under Seleucid influence until a band of wandering Gauls settled the area and came to be known as the Galatians — the apostle Paul wrote a letter to them which is now part of the New Testament. The Galatians held this town to be their capital and built its citadel — the Hisar or Kale — on a rocky outcrop, though what you see now is more recent.

Roman The Romans extended their *Ankyra* to the north-west; yes, 'K' *was* used in the Latin alphabet though it soon gave way to 'C.' Ankyra lost its status as chief city to Ephesus and, under the Byzantines, to Constantinople which remained the capital until 1923, sometimes sharing the distinction when the territory was divided as, for instance, when the Seljuks invaded Anatolia in 1073.

Seljuk The Seljuks called this city *Engüriye* (modern Turkish spelling) and in their three centuries of occupation they built a number of mosques, inside and outside the walls of the Hisar.

Ottoman Yıldırım Bayazid led the conquering Ottomans into the city in 1402 and its name changed to *Angora*. The Ottomans stayed for more than 500 years but there was little change in Angora beyond the addition of a few mosques, though a small cluster of ancient Ottoman private houses survives in the Hisar as a fascinating living museum. As the Ottoman sultans' influence declined with the territory they ruled, Angora became a city known only for the excellent sheep-wool it produced, and which is still produced in Anatolia.

Capital city İstanbul was still the capital, and it was there that the last Ottoman sultan, Mehmet VI, watched his country being carved up by the conquering Allies and invaded by the Greeks. His rule ended in 1922 (though Abdül Mecit II held office to 1924 as caliph) when Mustafa Kemal reached İzmir with his revolutionary troops, took the name of Kemal Atatürk, 'father of Turks,' and the following year proclaimed Angora the de facto capital: it had been his provisional capital since 1920.

. With the new role came the new name, *Ankara*. Atatürk never visited İstanbul for years, to establish Ankara's new status, not only to Turks but to the world. Embassies moved from Istanbul to Ankara, Parliament assembled here, then the city fathers built the first good hotel. Culture arrived with the opera house and concert hall, sport was represented with the Hipodrom (horse-racing circuit) and the 19th May Stadium. Ankara had its university, its medical school, its airport, its smart shops, and its role as one of the quieter capital cities of the world.

Atatürk Mausoleum Kemal Ataturk never lived to see it all. He died in November 1938 and his body now rests in the Atatürk Mausoleum, a large limestone building with austere lines that was begun in 1944 and completed in 1953. It stands on a slight rise at the end of Anıt (Memorial) Caddesi south of the railway station, the large coloured-brick plaza in front of it being a natural spot for public celebrations.

Modern Ankara From the mausoleum there's a good view across the city, with the old Hisar standing defiant on its rocky outcrop. We'll start our tour of modern Ankara from the Hisar, its ancient heart.

The **Hisar** or Kale stands on the site of the old Galatian fortress, but the walls are 7th and 9th century Byzantine. Inside is the much-restored 12th century **Alaeddin Mosque** and a cluster of old Ottoman houses which take you back to Medieval times. The **East Tower,** Şark Kulesi, offers a panoramic view of the city.

South of the Hisar and on the same mount is the 13th century **Arslanhane Mosque,** one of the oldest and therefore most revered in the city; beside it is the 14th century Ahi Elvan Mosque and the covered bazaar and Ottoman warehouse which have been restored and combined to form the **Museum of Anatolian Civilization,** the Anadolu Medeniyeteri Müzesi which holds most of the finds from Çatal Höyük plus a predominance of exhibits from the Urarti to the Phrygian era.

Across Hisarparkı Cad and near the **Ulus Meydanı,** 'Nation Square,' are the Roman outdoor relics, the 2nd century **Temple of Augustus** which began life as the Pergamene Temple of Cybele but which was converted to a Christian church in the 5th century. On part of the site and completing the religious pot-pourri is the Hacı Bayram Mosque. The **Column of Julian** in a small park nearby marks the visit of Emperor Julian; across the road are the foundations of the **Roman baths.**

From Ulus, **Atatürk Bulvarı** runs south to the Presidential Mansion at the other end of the city, and is a convenient reference line as well as a transport route by dolmuş. South-west of Ulus, along Cumhuriyet Bul, are two museums of special interest as historical buildings rather than for their exhibits, since their labels are only in Turkish. The nearest is the **War of Salvation Museum,** Kürtülüs Savaşı Müzesi, where Atatürk's Grand National Assembly first met. Next is the **Republic Museum,** Cumhuriyet Müzesi, to where the assembly moved before going to its permanent home further down Atatürk Bul at the junction with İsmet İnönü Bul.

Republic Avenue continues to the **railway** station (the main **bus** station is nearby) where you may find the unusual **Railway Museum** with Atatürk's private railway carriage in a nearby siding. The carriage is not open to the public.

Proceeding down Atatürk Bul and passing the Opera House, the **Ethnography Museum** is on the left, fronting Talatpaşa Bul. It holds a comprehensive range of Turkish arts and crafts exhibits and a reconstruction of Atatürk's private office.

Now entering southern Ankara, you pass the **Kizilay** roundabout and see the first of the smart hotels and shops. At the end of Mesrutiyet Cad, on your left, is **Kocatepe Mosque,** the city's largest. At the far end of Atatürk Bul, near the British Embassy, is the so-called 'Belltower Pavilion,' the **Çankaya Köşkü,** in reality the Presidential Mansion. In the grounds is a small bungalow that was Atatürk's country home, and it's open to the public on Sunday afternoons.

Shopping The main shopping areas in Ankara are around **Kizilay:** Atatürk Bul north and south, Ziya Gökalp Cad east, and Gazi Mustafa Kemal Bul west; **Tunali Cad:** east of the Büyük Ankara Hotel which is further south from Kizilay; and **Ulus:** Hisarparkı Cad and Anafartlar Cad.

Getting around The best way to travel in Ankara is probably by dolmuş up or down Atatürk Bul, as other dolmuş routes are rather complex. Taxis in the city are metered, so the fare is fixed and you can budget accordingly.

Access to the city Ankara is at the centre of a good road network and the large otogar, on Hipodrom Cad between the racecourse and the railway station, has regular buses to everywhere in Turkey that can warrant a pasenger load — and that's virtually everywhere. There are good train services to İstanbul and İzmir, but there are slow ones as well, so be careful. Esenboğa Airport, 35 km north, has internal flights to Adana, Antalya, Dalaman, Diyarbakır, Elazig, Erzurum, Gaziantep, İstanbul (up to 80 a week), İzmir, Malatya, Sivas, Trabzon and Van. The city-centre THY terminal is outside the railway station.

ACCOMMODATION

Ankara's hotels cater for a clientèle of businessmen and diplomats on expenses-paid trips, so it offers the most luxurious and the most expensive rooms in the country. As the average tourist will spent one or two nights here at the most, this list is selective.

Five star: Büyük Ankara Hotel, Atatürk Bul 183 (tel 1344920); 194-room tower block near Parliament with casino, pool, tennis court and nursery. Etap Altınel Hotel, Gazi Mustafa Kemal Bul 151 (tel 2303235); 176 rooms with casino, Turkish bath and other amenities.

Three star: Ankara Dedeman Hotel, Büklüm Sok 1 (tel 1176200); 252 rooms, pool, casino, etc.
Büyük Sürmeli Hotel, Cihan Sok 6 (tel 2305240); 118 rooms
Kent Hotel, Mithatpaşa Cad 4 (tel 1312111); 117 rooms

Some of the others:
Altınışık Hotel, Necatibey Cad 45(tel 2291185)
Best Hotel, Atatürk Bul 195 (tel 1670880)
Canbek Hotel, Soğukkuyu Sok 8 (tel 3243320)
Efes Hotel, Denizciler Cad 12 (tel 3243211)
Ercan Hotel, Denizciler Cad 36 (tel 3104890)

Etam Mola Hotel, Atatürk Bul 80 (tel 1339065)
Hitit Hotel, Hisarpark Cad (tel 3108617)
Keykan Hotel, Fevzi Çakmak Sok 12 (tel 2302195)
Taç Hotel, Çankırı Cad 35, Ulus (tel 3243095)
Turist Hotel, Çankırı Cad 37 (tel 3103980)

Cheaper hotels: Look around the backstreets in the Ulus area for a selection which the average Turk would use, with prices to match this market.

ÇORUM & the Hittite communities

The province of Çorum holds the sites of the two main Hittite cities and their religious sanctuary, but put them on your itinerary only if you're fanatic about ancient history or if you happen to be passing, for there's not a lot to see. The sites are not worth a visit from the casual tourist though they all occupy commanding positions in a landscape that is stark, vast, treeless and seemingly endless, similar to the western Meseta in Spain.

Alaca Höyük Alaca Höyük, at 4,000BC is somewhat younger that Kültepe near Kayseri, but there are only a few stone carvings to see on site.

Hattuşaş Hattuşaş, built around 1,300BC, has more to offer. Here the Hittites built four imperial temples, the largest being dedicated to their storm god. The city walls exended for 5 km, their gates decorated with stone lions or sphinxes.

Excavation began here in earnest in the 1880s and all that is worth removing and can be removed, has gone; one of the lions is in İstanbul and another was last known in Berlin. Much more is in museums in Ankara, with some tempting relics in the local museums on site and in Boğazkale village.

The best way to appreciate Alaca Höyük or Hattuşaş is to tour the museums first, carrying those mental pictures with you to the site, and letting your imagination do the rest. The Hattuşaş foundations are not original, by the way; they've been rebuilt this century.

Yazılıkaya Ten thousand cuneiform tablets were found at Hattuşaş, allowing us to crack the Hittites' language and understand more of their way of life. Across the valley at Yazılıkaya, the 'written rocks,' the Hittites had their sacred shrine, its canyonlike enrance guarded by marching soldiers carved in bas-relief. The Hittites worshipped hundreds of gods, far more than the ancient Greeks, but effigies of only a hunded or so were recovered at Yazılıkaya.

Access The easiest way is to come on an organised tour from Ankara but if you're using public transport strike for Sungurlu on Route 190 from where you'll need a taxi or dolmuş to Boğazkale for Hattuşaş and Yazılıkaya. The taxi could take you to the sites, otherwise allow for a strenuous walk.

As Alaca Höyük is around 20 km from Alaca village, that same taxi is also the most practical way of visiting this site.

ACCOMMODATION

The Hitit Motel on the Ankara-Samson Yolu (road), Sungurlu (tel 1042) or the Turist Hotel at Boğazkale.

DIYARBAKIR

The walled city of Diyarbakır slumbered for centuries until the recent arrival of light industry forced it to expand onto the surrounding steppe. The gaunt black walls, stretching for 6 km around the old city, ravaged only on the side facing the Tigris (Dicle in Turkish), make this an interesting stop in an exploration of remote eastern Anatolia.

Standing at one of the crossroads in history the city has seen more than its share of invasions since its founding around 1,500BC. The Assyrians, the Persians, Alexander the Great, the Seleucids and the Romans occupied it in its formative years, the Byzantines being responsible for the walls and their many surviving fortress towers.

The Seljuks took the city in 1085 and the Ottomans seized it in the early 16th century. Islam grew strong here, and there are many mosques within the old city, but religious tolerance has allowed several churches to survive including an Armenian, a Greek Orthodox, and two dedicated separately to St George and the Virgin Mary.

Race and religion are still important, for the Kurdish community, which is strong in this south-east corner of Turkey, would like to include Diyarbakır in a new Kurdistan stretching into Iran and Iraq.

ACCOMMODATION

Amit Hotel, Gazi Cad, Suakar Sok (tel 12059)
Aslan Hotel, Kıbrıs Cad 23 (tel 13971)
Demir Hotel, İzzetpaşa Cad 8 (tel 12315)
Dicle Hotel, Kıbrıs Cad 3 (tel 23066)
Diyarbakır Büyük Hotel, İnönü Cad 4 (tel 15832)
Saraç Hotel, İzzetpaşa Cad 16 (tel 12365)

ERZURUM

With 250,000 people, Erzurum is Turkey's 14th largest city and the largest east of Gaziantep. It's a conglomerate place, showing evidence of many of the peoples who have occupied it.

Byzantine The Byzantines called this outpost of empire Theodosiopolis from its founder with the less tonguetwisty name of Theodosius, who built a castle here. Little of it survives.

Seljuk Near the castle ruins is the aptly-named Great Mosque, Ulu Cami, completed in 1179 for the Turkish emir of the town in sober style, while the neighbouring School of the Twin Minarets, Çifte Minare Medrese, of 1253 built for the Seljuk Sultan Alaeddin Keykubat II, is more flamboyant. Inside is the tomb of the sultan's wife Huant Hatun, whose mosque is in Kayseri.

Mongol The Mongol influence is here in the early 14th century Yakutiye Medrese with its tiled minaret, but modern military needs have put this building out of bounds to foreigners.

Ottoman The Ottomans built several mosques and in their closing years began military works as the border with Russia grew closer.

Russia Britain and France attacked Turkey at Gallipoli to take pressure off their Russian allies in the northern Caucasus, and while the Allies were losing heavily — the future President Kemal Atatürk was commanding the Turkish troops — Russia invaded from the north-east and in 1916 seized Erzurum. The original railway from here to Sarıkamış in the east was a Russian narrow-gauge track, with Russian standard-gauge, but broad gauge to the rest of us, from there to Leninakan in the USSR.

You need go only a few miles out of town in any direction, turn your back on the works of man, and you can appreciate the atmosphere of Erzurum and indeed of this part of Turkey. The landscape is empty, empty, empty, and gives the impression of limitless space with lazy, treeless hills that could roll around the Caucasus and on, for ever, into the lonely steppes of Mongolia. It's easy to see why the wandering Seljuks and Ottomans settled on the plains of Anatolia: one reason, of course, was that they couldn't go any further west.

Erzurum is still a place for transient peoples. It has an important road junction, it's on a railway which is busy by Turkish standards, and there's an airport with daily flights to and from İstanbul and Ankara.

ACCOMMODATION

Buhara Hotel, Kazımkarabekir Cad (tel 15096)

Büyük Erzurum Hotel, Akirevai Cad 5 (tel 16528); three-star

Çinar Hotel, Ayazpaşa Cad (tel 13580)

Efes Hotel, Tahtacılar Cad 30 (tel 17081)

Oral Hotel, Terminal Cad 3 (tel 19740); 90 rooms

Kral Hotel, Erzincankapı 18 (tel 17783)

Polat Hotel, Kazımkarabekir Cad (tel 11623)

Sefer Hotel, İstasyon Cad (tel 13615)

KARS

The Russian influence is strong in Kars. The Russians took the province in 1878 in the carve-up which followed the Crimean War and their influence is seen in the architecture of some of the public buildings. The Turks regained the territory in 1920 during their War of Independence, and the Communists haven't stopped bearing the grudge.

Kars is a grim fortress town, bleak for most of the year, and if you've reached this far you'll probably want to visit Ani, the city 44 km east which the Mongols abandoned to the elements soon after their invasion of 1239.

Ani Think carefully before going to Ani. It's within the no-man's-land on the *Turkish* side of the Iron Curtain — here marked by a small river — but the *Russians* reserve the right to shoot to kill.

The only tolerance shown is to visitors to the ruins of Ani, provided those visitors don't do *anything* which might annoy the Soviets, and that includes staring at them. Binoculars and cameras are not allowed, you *must* go in a party organized through the tourist office in Kars, and you will have Turkish soldiers escorting you.

Probably Ani isn't worth the effort. The Urarti capital before Van, it has been ruled by Armenians, Byzantines, Seljuks, Kurds and finally the Mongols who left it to decay. The walled city contains ruins of eight churches but you are forever aware of those Russians staring at you down their gunsights. Maybe *glaznost* will ease the situation?

KAYSERİ & Kültepe

The architecture doesn't allow you to forget you're in Seljuk country, and the out-of-town Archaeological Museum will remind you that it's also Hittite country, with the first Hittite capital being at Kültepe, 'ash hill,' around 32 km north-east near the village of Karahöyük, 'black hill.' The ash is a reminder of a fire which destroyed part of the Hittite community and which was still traceable into modern times; it has no connection with any outpourings from Mount Erciyes.

The site is easy to reach if you're prepared for a long walk but it won't repay the effort unless you're doing a PhD on the Hittite civilization. *(For other Hittite remains, see Çorum.)*

There is no record of whether the Hittites settled on the Kayseri site, since the oldest relics are the more recent Hellenistic, but the Romans developed the place, calling it Caesaraea from which the modern name derives. The

Göreme's bizarre rock-dwellings

Byzantine Justinian built the black-walled citadel in the town centre near where the PTT and tourist office now stand.

Black Foal The Seljuks arrived in 1084 and held the city for 159 years, giving it the now-covered bazaar beside the citadel, several mosques and theological schools, and the Karatay Han, the Inn of the Black Foal, on the winding Route 300 about 80 km east of town. The caravanserai, built in 1240 and restored in the 1960s, lies in the village of the same name, though it's sometimes spelled Karadayı. As it's 10 km off the main road, access is difficult without your own car.

Mosques The Seljuk Huant Hatun Mosque of 1228, dedicated to the daughter of Sultan Alaeddin Keykubat I, is conveniently near the citadel, but the more interesting Ulu Cami,the Great Mosque, is 500 m north-west. The Hacı Kılıç Mosque of 1249 lies 1 km to the north, along Istasyon Cad.

Medreses The Çifte Medrese is, as the name implies, two medreses in one, for çifte means 'twin.' One of the two was an early school for anatomy and medecine. The Sahibiye Medrese on the north of Cumhuriyet Meydanı, is a museum. The most impressive of the Ottoman mosques, the Kurşunlu, by Atatürk Park, is unusual in having a lead-roofed dome.

ACCOMMODATION

The 67-room Hattay Hotel at İstanbul Cad 1 (tel 19331) is pricey, the 70-room Turan Hotel at Turan Cad 8 (tel 11968) is more reasonable and has a Turkish bath, and the Terminal Hotel by the bus station on İstasyon Cad (tel 15864) is the most reasonable.

KONYA

Konya is an oasis of commerce in a vast and lonely plain, a major carpet-weaving town and the most Islamic of Turkey's cities, so try to avoid coming here during Ramadan. Most places of interest are conveniently within a comfortable walk of the main square, Hükümet Meydanı, an area which holds several of the mid-range hotels.

Iconium to the Romans, the city was the capital of the Seljuk kingdom in the 12th and 13th centuries when most of the buildings of current interest went up.

Dervish Konya's greatest claim for attention comes through its connection with Celaleddin Rumi, founder of the order of Whirling Dervishes. Rumi was born in Balkh, now in Afghanistan, around 1207 and moved west with his family in advance of the Mongol hordes. He reached Konya in 1228 and studied Islam. After his friend and adviser Mehmet (Mohammed) Tebrizi was murdered, Celaleddin went into meditation and founded the order of Dervishes of which he became the leader, the guide, Mevlana. The order's basic philosophy was admirable for the times, concentrating on equality of the sexes, the pursuit of righteousness, and communion with God.

The dance The Mevlevi, followers of the guide, carried the sect east and south, teaching the semi-hypnotic whirling dance for which they have long been renowned in the west. Each dancer holds his right palm towards heaven to receive a blessing and his left palm down, to pass the blessing on to earth. Pivoting on his left heel with his shroud-like skirt forming a cone, he goes into a mild trance.

After the dance, which is a form of worship, a man who has learned the entire Koran chants passages from it.

The Dervishes were Moslems who welcomed followers from other faiths yet they joined the campaigns of their benefactor Süleiman the Magnificent, notably the invasion of eastern Europe and the siege of Malta, in which they were fanatical enemies of Christianity.

Dervish Festival In the closing days of the Ottoman Empire they were staunch supporters of democracy and monarchism, the former policy hindering their relations with the sultans and the latter with the new president, Atatürk, who stripped them of all power in 1925. Today devoid of political ambition as well, the few remaining Dervishes are officially recognised as a part of Turkey's cultural past because of their unique dance and dress. They travel the world to perform but come back to Konya's bitter cold each winter to mark Celaleddin's death in 1273 with the Dervish Festival from 9 to 17 December.

Dervish Museum The Mevlana Museum and mausoleum in the Mevlana Tekke (monastery), east of Hükümet Meydanı is now the most impressive among the Seljuk buildings of Konya, its blue-green tiles making it a landmark. The museum part contains many Dervish manuscripts and, allegedly, part of Mahomet's beard.

Nearby is the Selimiye Camii (mosque), the rather austere gift of Sultan Selim II who died in 1574. Many of the Seljuk buildings share this austerity in design, but they all show their builders' skills in making doorways inviting.

Mosques Konya's other attractions are west of Hükümet Meydanı around the Alaeddin Park, the acropolis of Iconium. The largest is the Alaeddin Keykubat I Mosque which was started around 1150 and took 70 years to complete. It holds the mortal remains of eight sultans.

Opposite it on the road which encircles the park is the Karatay Medrese, begun as a theological college as the name implies, but now a museum of ceramics.

On the western side of the ring road, the İnce Minare (the slender Minaret) and its medrese form a museum of sculpture in wood and stone. And on the south side a slip road leads to the Sırçalı or glazed Medrese.

South again, by the Archaeological Museum (mostly Seljuk works) is the complex of 13th century charitable buildings by Sahip Ata containing school, hospital and canteen. Sahip Ata was a wealthy vizier who also financed the slender minaret and put Dervish philosophies to work in his home city.

ACCOMMODATION
Başak Palas Hotel, Hükümet Mey 3 (tel 11338); mid range
Dergah Hotel, Mevlana Cad 19 (tel 11197); near Mevlana Mus
Konya Hotel, Mevlana Alanı (tel 21003)
Otogar Hotel, (tel 32557) *this hotel and the next are near the bus station*
Özkaymak Park Hotel, Otogar Karşısı (tel 33770)
Şahin Hotel, Hükümet Alanı 6 (tel 13350)
Selçuk Hotel, Alaeddin Cad, Babalık Sok (tel 11259)
Sema 2 Hotel, Otogar Yanı (tel 32557); has Turkish bath
Yeni Sema Hotel, Yeni Meram yolu (road) (out of town on Meram road) (tel 13279)

There are numerous basic hotels offering a bed and a roof at rock-bottom prices.

NEVŞEHİR: The Göreme Region
Göreme is the best-known of the cave-villages and gives its name to the Göreme National Park and to the area. You could comfortably spend a day on foot exploring the many churches in this small valley but you will have tasted the wine and left the bottle half full. There is much more to see, but it stretches from the Kîzîlîrmak River in the north 50 km to Derinkuyu in the south.

Base camp Most visitors come here on conducted tours from the coastal resorts, so accommodatin is limited. If you're master of your own destiny base yourself either in Ürgüp, a fascinating small town in the heart of the cave communities, or in Nevşehir, the city 20 km to the west where there are ruins of Seljuk and Ottoman castles as a bonus.

Your first call must certainly be the Göreme National Park (open daily 0830-1700) in which lies the village of Avcılar, now renamed Göreme.

Here is the greatest concentration of Byzantine churches, all carved from the soft tufa rock that was deposited in this valley from eruptions of Mount Erciyes in bygone ages and has since been eroded into the cones you see around you, some of them 60 metres tall and many capped with a boulder which has checked erosion.

Churches The churches date from the 5th to the 13th centuries, the later ones being those with the more elaborate frescoes. Elmalı Kilisi, the Church of the Apple, shows scenes from Christ's life; Yılantlı Kilisi, the Church of the Snake, has a clear fresco bearing Constantine the Great; while Çarıklı Kilisi, the Church of the Sandals, has paintings of footprints.

Tokalı Kilisi, the largest church and named from a common buckle, has 13th century paintings showing many saints, among them the patron of England, Portugal, Catalonia and Aragon, and formerly of Cappadocia, St George, who was martyred in 303 by Diocletian.

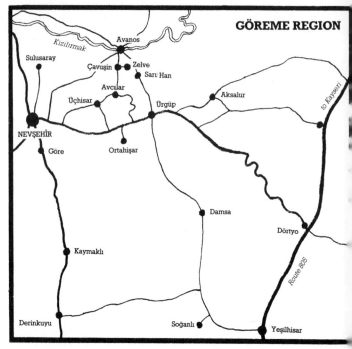

GÖREME REGION

Karanlık Kilisi, being restored, was part of a monastery, and monasticism was prominent in this valley for 1,000 years.

John the Baptist North of Avcılar is Çavuşin, noted for its 5th century Church of St John the Baptist, the oldest church in the region. A side track leads east to Zelve (Zilve), recently abandoned due to the threat of collapse and containing the only mosque to be carved from these soft rocks.

Red pots Avanos, on the bank of the Kızılırmak or Red River, has produced red-clay pottery from ancient times to the present and some of its pottery shops are lodged in caves.

Fairy Chimneys From Avanos a road leads direct to Ürgüp passing the ruins of Sarı Han, the Yellow Caravanserai, of which the doorway is the main feature of interest. Much of the han has been recycled for building the bridge at Avanos. The same road passes the entrance to the Valley of Fairy Chimneys whose name aptly describes the rose-coloured columns of compressed volcanic ash which are seen here at their best.

A second journey from Ürgüp should take you to Ortahisar and Üçhisar, villages of more conventional buildings surrounding honeycombed rock pillars.

Fall-out shelters? Twenty km south of Nevşehir is Kaymaklı, with Derinkuyu a further 10 km away. In these communities you leave the concept of the individual home or church carved from the rock and come to a communal subterranean city, as if its Byzantine creators were digging the world's first nuclear shelter. There are no rock columns here; the earth at your feet is the solid rock and the masons have tunnelled 120 metres down into it, adding air shafts and wells.

During the Arab raids of the 7th century the peoples of these two communities — and of a score of others in the area — were prepared to go to earth for days or weeks, losing their crops and livestock but saving life and liberty. The caves were last used as hideouts from the invader in the 1830s when the Egyptians surged into Asia Minor.

Tours If you're without transport you could ask at the Tourist Office in Ürgüp (Kayseri Cad 37, tel 1059) or in Nevşehir (Osmanlı Cad 37, tel 1137) for the latest news on tours, or band together and hire a taxi for the day.

ACCOMMODATION
Avanos: Venessa Hotel, Orta Mah (tel 1201)
Nevşehir: Fatih Mehmet Hotel, Sebze Pazarı 40 (tel 1810); Mar-Nov Göreme Hotel, Bankalar Cad 16 (tel 1706); Mar-Nov Lale Hotel, Belediye Yanı (tel 1797)
Orsan Kapadpkya Hotel, Kayseri Cad (tel 1035); Mar-Nov
Viva Hotel, Kayseri Cad 45 (tel 1326)
Ortahisar: Paris Motel, Aksaray Mev (tel 1435)
Üçhisar: Kaya Hotel, (tel İstanbul 1461030); three-star, May-Nov
Ürgüp: Buyuk Hotel, Kayseri Cad (tel 1060); three-star
Tepe Hotel, Teslimiye Tepesi (hill) (tel 1154); Mar-Oct
Sinasos Hotel, Mustafapaşa (tel 9)
Boytas Motel, Karayazı Köyü (village) (tel 1259)
Turban Ürgüp Motel (tel 1490); 235 rooms
Pensions are reasonably plentiful in Avanos and Ürgüp.

SİVAS & Divriği
Mustafa Kemal came to Sivas in September 1919 to address the second congress (the first had been at Erzurum after the Russians withdrew at the end of World War I), which led to the Turkish War of Independence and to Kemal's presidency.

Apart from that, the slumbering town's interest lies in its Seljuk buildings, several of them dating from 1271 or thereabouts. The Gök Medrese in Cumhuriyet Cad, built by the wealthy Sahip Ata whom we met in Konya, has blue tiles adding to the intricate Seljuk masonry around the doors and windows. The Çifte Minare Medrese (school of the twin minarets) has little remaining beyond the minarets but the nearby Bürüciye Medrese on Konak Meydanı holds the tiled tomb of its builder, Bürücirdi. The Şifaiye Medrese, built as a medical school in 1271, also holds the tomb of its founder, Sultan Keykavus.

The Great Mosque, Ulu Cami, of 1197, is the oldest major work in town and one of the most impressive.

Divriği The journey to Divriği calls for a major expedition of 180 km over poor roads, the last 100 km of which must be backtracked unless you have a four-wheel-drive vehicle capable of tackling the onward trail over the mountains. Optionally there's a morning train from Sivas calling at Divriği, and a return train in the evening, unless you were to continue up the Euphrates (Fırat) valley to Erzincan.

So what's at Divriği? It's certainly not on the tourist route but a visit here is like a step back into *living* Seljuk history, a picturesque little town where a crumbling castle watches over an ancient hospital and an incredibly ornate Great Mosque built in 1228 and carefully restored. A pity access is so difficult, but if you plan to experience the leisurely travel of Turkish railways, use it as an excuse to visit Divriği. The line up the Euphrates takes you through some splendidly isolated mountain scenery as well as through several tunnels.

ACCOMMODATION

In Sivas: Köşk Hotel, Atatürk Cad 11 (tel 11150); Madımak Hotel, Eski Belediye Sok 4 (tel 18027); both two star, and the one-star Sultan Hotel, Belediye Sok 18 (tel 12986).

VAN

At the back of beyond, you can still find carpet sellers in Van who speak English!

The modern city stands a little way back from Lake Van, leaving the shoreline to the ruins of Tushpa, capital of the Urart kingdom which occupied Kurdish lands in the Bronze Age. World War One battles with Egyptian forces caused more damage than the preceding two millennia and little now remains of Tushpa.

Rock of Van Van's dominant feature, visible for miles, is the Van Kalesi, the Rock of Van, a natural formation topped with a mud-walled castle eroded now into gentle curves but still impressive. The original castle was the work of the Urartians, and there are inscriptions dating from 800BC, but Armenians, Seljuks and Ottomans have added to the defences. The Seljuks carved a 1,000-step stairway down the south side of the rock to Tushpa, but there's better access today from the north.

Lake Van The only other dominant feature is the great Lake of Van, more than 100 km at its longest and highly alkaline, containing enough soda to let you wash your clothes without soap. The soda comes from the extinct volcano of Nemrut Dağı and makes Lake Van similar to those other soda lakes in Africa's Rift Valley; after all, eastern Turkey isn't far from the north end of the Great Rift.

Akdamar Church From Gevaş, on the lake's southern shore, you can hire a boat to the island of Akdamar ('white rock') where Armenian king, Gagil Artzruni, built a church and palace between 915 and 919. The Palace is in ruins but the church interior is in excellent condition and contains bas-relief carvings of scenes from the Old Testament.

Fifty kilometers south-east of Van, in remote and rugged country, the ruins of the Castle of Hoşap cling to precipitous crags overlooking an Ottoman Bridge. The castle had 380 rooms and is worth a detour if you're on the main road to Iran.

The town Van's street plan is simple. Alpaslan Caddesi runs east-west and Cumhuriyet Cad north-south. They meet at the town centre where you'll find the bus station; the tourist office is south of here, the hotels southwest in the backstreets, and the railway stations west along Alpaslan Cad, then north down minor roads. The Şehir İstasyon is the town station; the İskele İstasyon the one at the terminal of the train ferry which crosses Lake Van to Tatvan.

ACCOMMODATION
The three-star 69-room Akdamar at Kazım Karabekir Cad 56 (tel 18100) is the best; others are Beşkardeş Hotel, Cumhuriyet Cad 54 (tel 11116); Büyük Asur Hotel, Cumhuriyet Cad (tel 18792); Büyük Urartu Hotel, Hastane Sok 60 (tel 20660); Çaldıran Hotel, Sıhke Cad (tel 12718); Güzel Paris Hotel, Hükümetkonağı Arkası ('rear of') (tel 13739); the cheapish Kent Hotel, (tel 2404); and the Tekin Hotel, at Küçük Cami Civarı ('near small mosque') (tel 13010).

BLACK SEA

The quiet riviera

TURKEY'S NORTHERN COAST is probably the next part of the country that the tour operators will discover as a contrast to the resorts on the southern coasts. The Black Sea littoral lacks the deeply-indented bays of the Aegean and there are no Graeco-Roman theatres, but for most of its length there is an impressive mountain range temptingly close and, in the far west, there is the lure of İstanbul.

The sea temperature is a few degrees cooler than in the Mediterranean and as the coast faces north — though İğneada and Sinop face south — the summer heat is seldom oppressive. The climate is milder and moister, and in the extreme east there is the chance of rain at almost any time of the year.

As there are so many rivers flowing into the landlocked Black Sea, it is less salty that the Mediterranean, which helps its northern waters around the Crimea and the Sea of Azov to freeze in winter.

Pontus Euxinus The 7,300 foot (2,200 metre) deep Black Sea was called Pontus Euxinus, the hospitable deep,' in ancient times, the 'pontus' epithet gradually being applied to the mountainous Turkish coastline where the Kingdom of Pontus arose around 400BC, absorbing the Arcadia which the colonising men of Milet had founded in the 6th century BC. This Pontus expanded until its King Mithradites VI, born in 131BC, ruled the region from the Crimea to Cappadocia, then conquered all of Roman Asia to the Aegean. His glory was short-lived, the emperor Pompey driving him back into Armenia and on into exile in the Crimea where he was assassinated in 63BC.

The Black Sea is in no sense black, no matter that every European language, and Turkish itself, uses that name. The word describes the seas's moods in winter when Siberian storms make navigation perilous for small boats.

Access by sea In the summer cruising season, from April to October, Turkish Maritime Lines runs a weekly car-ferry-cum-cruise-liner along the coast, sailing from İstanbul on Thursday morning and taking six days for the round trip to Trabzond, calling twice at Sinop, Samsun and Giresun.

It's the most popular as well as the most practical way to see this coast, and you need to book a berth if you plan a high-summer cruise. The winter service is once fortnightly.

Access by air A year-round daily flight from İstanbul (0800; 1745 on Sunday) to Ankara (0935; 1910 on Sunday) goes on to Trabzon, departing at 1145 (2110 on Sunday) for Ankara and İstanbul. At the time of writing Samsun has been dropped from the schedule.

Access by road Turkey's European coast has poor road access until you're on the wooded dunes near the only place of interest, the fishing village of İğneada near the Bulgarian border. From Istanbul to Sinop there is just a minor road not conducive to fast motoring, but from Sinop to Hopa, near the Soviet frontier, the road is good and potentially fast in places.

Access by rail The passenger service to Samsun is notiously slow along the branch line from Sivas.

THE COAST

Kilyos, on the European side of the Bosphorus, is the Black Sea resort closest to İstanbul and naturally draws the city-dwellers in their thousands. It's a modern town with good beaches extending inland to dune country.

Sile, comfortably in Asia, is the weekend resort for the İstanbul elite. It's a lively place clinging to a steep slope topped by the ruins of a castle built by the Genoese, who had several strongholds along this coast in the 13th and 14th centuries; they briefly held the islands of Chios and Lesbos and part of the Crimea.

Sile has good beaches, several caves, and is the base for a textile industry producing shirts and summer garments. Eastward are the little fishing villages of **Kefken,** at the end of a side-road, and **Karasu** (black water) near the mouth of the Sakarya River. Neither place is geared for foreign visitors but there are some appetising fish restaurants.

Akçakoca (ak-cha-ko-ja) is another fishing community blessed with good beaches, caves, and the ruins of a Genoese castle. The provincial capital **Bolu,** some way inland, was the Roman Claudiopolis but its main appeal now is its aptly-named 14th century Great Mosque.

If we continue along the coast we find another ruined castle at **Ereğli,** but this one is Byzantine. **Zonguldak,**, the provincial capital, has a decent beach but the place is predominantly involved in running its iron foundries and port. The road wanders inland before coming coastwards again at **Bartın,** which has a number of Ottoman wooden houses.

Only 16 km away is **Amasra,** a fishing village with a splendid beach and the potential of being a minor resort one of these days. Built on a rocky peninsula almost like the Bird Island at Kuşadası, Amasra has the ruins of a Roman bath-house and temple, a Byzantine citadel commanding the seaward approaches, and a Byzantine church now serving as the Fatih Mosque. The village is quiet and picturesque, which is also true of **Çakraz,** a small boatbuilding community 14 km east.

The coast road from here to Sinop becomes increasingly difficult and serves only a scattering of small villages, some of which have some enticingly empty beaches. The inland road goes via Safranbolu and **Kastamonu,** a town crouching at the foot of a rocky massif capped by a 12th century Byzantine castle.

Sinop is the birthplace of Diogenes, the 3rd century BC philosopher who reputedly lived in a barrel. It's also where Mithradites, the last king of Pontus, held court and from where he briefly ruled his empire, but the town's story goes back to Hittite times around 1,500BC. A Hittite temple was the probable site of the 3rd century BC Roman Temple of Serapis, the god of the underworld. Mithradites restored the temple, and a museum in its grounds houses some impressive Byzantine icons.

Sinop was a major port for the Seljuks, who built several mosques in the 13th century, the most important being the Alaeddin Mosque, completed in 1214, but the Ottomans neglected the town in favour of Samsun.

Bafra, standing at the mouth of the Kızılırmak, the Red River that flows through the Göreme region, is known to Turks for its tobacco and caviare, and there's a 13th century Turkish bath still in use.

The first city of any size along this coast is **Samsun,** which had 280,000 people in the 1985 census, placing it 12th in order of size.

The Genoese destroyed the old city by fire in the 15th century, giving the Ottomans scope to rebuild the place how they liked and to develop its potential as a port. There is, as a result, nothing to see older than the Pazar Camii, a 14th-century mosque which survived the fire, though the archaeological museum has relics from the nearby ancient sites of Amisos and Dündartepe. Neither the sites nor the exhibits are of interest to the casual visitor.

Samsun's importance comes from its position on the coastal plain, the creation of the Kızılırmak and the Yeşilırmak, the Green River. The city has an important agricultural fair each July but has a growing interest in industry.

If you venture into the central park the Atatürk statue will remind you that it was here Mustafa Kemal landed on 19 May 1919 on what was to become his road to the presidency and total Turkish reform. A local road, 19 Mayıs Bul, recalls the date in its name, and it is here at number 2 you'll find the tourist office (tel 11228).

The main street is Kazım Paşa Cad, where you'll find the PTT and several hotels, but in deference to the number of banks it's also known as Bankalar Cad.

The **bus** and **rail** stations are on the east of the city, with a dolmuş service to the town centre.

Around 130 km inland is **Amasya** (not to be confused with Amasra), a Hittite town that became capital of Pontus before Sinop, and where a number of Pontic kings are buried in tombs cut into the rocky sides of the Yeşil river, in similar style to the Lydian tombs of the south.

Ottoman crown princes usually had a spell as governor of the province of Amasya to bring out their qualities of leadership. Kings and princes lived in the same building, the Kızlar Sarayı, the Palace of Maidens, which was also the site of a harem. Sadly, it's now in ruins.

The town has some photogenic Ottoman houses by the river and a scattering of Seljuk mosques of which the Gök Medrese Camii has the most impressive doorway: the Seljuks loved their doors.

The road between Samsun and Trabzon is wonderfully scenic, with green woods and mountain pastures as a distinct contrast to the arid interior. At the little port of **Ünye** the pinewoods tumble down to the beach and provide a perfect location for several camping sites, particularly at nearby Çamlık village.

If you fancy a holiday camping under the pines and spending the day lazing on a quiet beach with mountains to one side and a warm blue sea to the other, and you also want to break fresh territory, you could consider Ünye or **Fatsa**, 20 km to the east. There is no tourist office for the area, there are no package holidays, few people speak anything but Turkish, and getting here from your home is a long haul. But you won't meet your neighbour on the beach.

Ordu, the provincial capital, is a port and fishing community with some interesting old houses, and a decent beach 2 km away at Güzelyalı where there's also an 18th century church. **Bulancak** has a small beach.

Giresun has a tiny offshore island where the warlike man-hating Amazons built a temple to Mars, the god of war who was among the most macho of males. The Romans called this town Cerasus after seizing it from Mithradites, and the Roman general Lucullus took home some cherry trees he found here. As a result, *cerasus* is now the botanical name for the tree and the origin of *cherry, Kirsch, cérise, cereza, ciliegia, cereja, kers,* and the Turkish *kiraz.* By the way, there's a Byzantine castle crumbling away on the clifftop.

Trabzon is historically the most important city on this coast though at 155,000 people it is 22nd in order of size and much smaller than Samsun. Many Europeans still think of it under its Ottoman name of Trebizond, the gateway to the mystic Orient. In pre-Khomeini days it was the northern gateway to Iran for the riches of the west, financed by oil revenues.

Founded as Trapezus in the 7th century BC by the Arcadians, colonists from Milet on the Aegean, it saw considerable development under Hadrian and was the last Byzantine outpost in Asia Minor. Alexis Comemnus created the so-called Comemnus Empire, later to become the Empire of Trebizond but at no time extending beyond the coastline from Samsun to Hopa. The Ottomans seized it in 1461.

The Christians who made this last stand in Asia Minor left a fine legacy of churches in Trabzon, with the 13th century **Aya Sofya,** the Church of the Holy Wisdom, the most impressive. It stands on a hill 3 km west of town, with views out to sea, and some of its recently-found frescoes are a major exhibit in its new role as a museum.

The 9th century Church of St Anna (Küçük Ayvasıl Kililesi) was another, but there's little of it to see as you walk along Maraş Cad, the main east-west road in town.

Some 200 m west of St Anna is the **Kale,**, the citadel, with substantial parts of its walls remaining; inside is the Fatih Camii which was built in the 9th century as a church. The old town has a wealth of wooden houses lining its narrow streets, a medieval fire hazard that has endured into modern times.

South-west of the town is **Atatürk's Villa,** where in 1919 he planned the first stage of the revolution after his landing at Samsun. Czarist Russia had occupied Trabzon in 1916 after pushing the Turks back from the Crimea, but after the October Revolution in St Petersburg and the 1918 Armistice, Bolshevik Russia withdrew to its present frontier. Modern Trabzon centres along Maraş Cad and Taksim, the square at its eastern end. At Taksim you will find the THY office, police, city hall, and the tourist office (tel 35833), with the port to the east and the PTT to the west.

Everybody who comes to Trabzon must surely have the urge to visit the most unusual building along the entire Black Sea coast, the **Monastery of the Virgin Mary,** known locally as Meryem Ana. The trouble is, it's at Sumela, 54 km out of town, there aren't many dolmuşes, and you'll probably have to club together for a taxi.

The monastery is a warren of passages and corridors leading to unexpected courtyards and chapels, the first stage of it completed in 472 as a suitable home for the icon portrait that St Luke painted of the Virgin Mary; the monastery was therefore dedicated to Christ's mother. There have been many extensions, most notably in the 19th century with the addition of the upper floors, but in true monastic style the building has always been difficult to reach and clings to a near-vertical mountainside much like the Monastery of Montserrat in Spain.

When the Greeks invaded Turkey in 1919 they had a dream of creating a new Byzantium in Asia Minor, and might have done so had Kemal Ataturk down in the town of Trebizond not thought differently. If the dream had been realised, this monastery may have been among New Byzantium's treasures, but its occupants abandoned it in despair in 1923 with the expulsion of the Greeks, and it's now an empty, echoing shell with the remaining Byzantine frescoes flaking from the walls. Even St Luke's icon has gone — to Greece.

If the monastery itself gives the impression of not being in Turkey, the road to it is anything but Turkish as it climbs in tight valleys through dense misty woods with rushing streams for company. Turkey? Surely this is the French Pyrenees, or even southern Scandinavia!

144 **Rize** is at the centre of Turkey's tea plantations which cover steep, misty

hillsides and are reminiscent of the hill country of India. The town's Genoese castle is in advanced decay. **Hopa** is the last port on Turkish Maritime Lines's extended summer-only schedule and the end of our route, as the Russian frontier is 25 km away along the coast. The road swings inland to the provincial capital of **Artvin**, whose ruined castle is 16th century. Again you wonder if this is truly Turkey, for Artvin holds an annual bullfighting fiesta.

ACCOMMODATION:

Akçakoca: Sezgin Pension, Tevfik İlleri Cad; May-Oct.

Amasra: Nur Aile Pension, Çamlı Cad, Küçükköy (tel 1015), Apr-Nov.

Amasya: Turban Amasya Hotel, Emniyet Cad (tel 4054), 2-star.

Artvin: Karahan Hotel, İnönü Cad 16 (tel 1800).

Bafra: Bafra Belediye Hotel, Çetinkaya Köprü Yanı (tel 1524)

Bartın: Bar-Tur Motel, Dörtkol Mev, Tuzcular Köyü (tel 1015).

Bolu: Koru Hotel, Ömerler Köyü (tel 2528), 3-star, 128 rooms; Menekşe Hotel, Hürriyet Cad (tel 1522); Yurdaer Hotel, Hürriyet Cad (tel 2903); Çizmeci Motel, Kılıçaslan Köyü (tel 1066); Emniyet Motel Ayrılık Çeşmesi Mev (tel 1290).

Bulancak: Gedik Ali Turist Tesisleri (establishment), Maden Köyü (tel 1081).

Fatsa: Dolunay Motel, Yapraklı Mev (tel 1528).

Giresun: Giresun Hotel, Atatürk Bul 7 (tel 3017)

Hopa: Cihan Hotel, Orta-Hopa Cad 3 (tel 1897); Papila Hotel, Orta-Hopa Cad (tel 1440) (both on seafront).

Kilyos: Kilyos Kale Hotel, Kale Cad 78 (tel 54); Grup Hotel, Kale Cad 21 (tel 031); Turban Kilyos Motel.

Ordu: Turist Hotel, Atatürk Bul 134 (tel 11446), 2-star.

Samsun: Burç Hotel, Kazımpaşa Cad 36 (tel 15480), mid-range; Gökçe Hotel, Kale Mah, Ferah Sok 2 (tel 17952), mid-range; Terminal Hotel, near the Otogar (tel 15519); Turban Samsum Hotel, Sahil Cad (tel 10750), 4-star, 116 rooms, swimming and tennis; Vidinli Hotel, Kazımpaşa Cad 4 (tel 16050); Yafeta Hotel, Cumhuriyet Mey (tel 16565), 3-star.

Sile: Değirmen Hotel, Plaj Yolu 24 (tel 148); Kumbaba Oberj (auberge), (tel 38), May-Oct.

Sinop: Melia Kasım Hotel, Gazi Cad 41 (tel 1625); Köşkburnu Tur Motel, Köşkburnu Mev (tel 1081)

Trabzon: Horon Hotel, Sıra Mağazalar 125 (near Taksim) (tel 11199); Kalfa Hotel, Belediye Karşısı (opposite town hall) (tel 12690), basic; Özgür Hotel, Kıbrıs Şehitler Cad 29 (tel 11319), 2-star; Usta Hotel, Telegrafhane Sok 3 (near Taksim) (tel 12195).

Ünye: Kumsal Hotel, Gölevi Köyü (tel 4490).

Zonguldak: Ay Hotel, Gazipaşa Cad 61, (tel 11310); Otel 67, Fevzipaşa Cad 1 (tel 16767). Çamlı Cad, Küçükköy.

İSTANBUL AND ENVIRONS
Gateway to the Orient

İSTANBUL IS THE WORLD'S ONLY CITY to stretch into two continents. It's a city that has attracted conquerors, thriller writers, film makers, dreamers and adventurers over the centuries, and it's probably the most mystic, magic and maligned city in Europe — for it *is* essentially a European city no matter that half its suburbs are in Asia.

FROM BYZANTIUM TO İSTANBUL

A small fishing village, Semistra, existed on the shores of the Golden Horn around 1,000BC. A century later, the village of Lygos was built on the heights where the Topkapı Palace now stands. But it was Byzas of Megara, a city near Corinth, who founded a community here in 667BC and built the first acropolis and city walls, though the defences were not strong enough to deter King Darius of Persia who stormed the place in 512. The young Byzantium was lost to Greek culture until the Spartans liberated it in 478BC.

The Romans came in 196AD and again Byzantium fell. Its conqueror, Emperor Septimus Severus, destroyed the city then on his son's urging rebuilt it, expanding the site so that the new wall ran due south from where the Galata Bridge now stands.

Hippodrome He built several palaces, none of which survives, but in 203 he created the Hippodrome, an open concourse 400 m long by 120 wide for chariot races and gladiator fights and later to be the scene of two great massacres: in 532 against Justinian when 40,000 rebels were slaughtered;

The Blue Mosque of Sultan Ahmet I in Istanbul

and in 1826 when Mahmut II ordered the execution of 30,000 Janissaries.

Constantinople Emperor Constantine I came here in 324 chasing a rival: he found Byzantium so intriguing and so easy to defend that he made it his capital. On 11 May, 330, at a ceremony in the Hippodrome he declared this city to be his 'New Rome,' but the people preferred to call it Constantine's city, Constantinople.

The emperor increased the size of his city fivefold and gave it another wall, starting at the Golden Horn near the present Atatürk Bridge and swinging far to the west before reaching the Sea of Marmaris. Palaces and churches followed, then Emperor Theodisius ordered the destruction of all pre-Christian temples in the city.

Byzantine Empire Constantinople was already a major city, but Theodosius inadvertently made it greater by splitting the empire in two. The western half, the Roman portion, didn't survive for long, but the Eastern Roman Empire, Byzantium, moved on to greatness and Constantinople was the most important city in the western world.

Under Justinian, emperor from 527 to 565, Byzantium encompassed most of the Mediterranean and the empire stretched from Gibraltar to Aswan, from Nice to Odessa and from the Caucasus to Aqaba. It was the Golden Age, but it was soon to turn to dust.

Fourth Crusade In 1024 the Fourth Crusade paused in Constantinople and decided it would go no further. The Holy Land could wait; the Byzantine capital was rife for plunder. Emperor Basil II fled to Nicaea (İznik) and other citizens went to Trabzon as Christian soldiers tore apart the Christian city that was their major defence against the barbaric hordes in the east. Then in 1071 came the crushing defeat at Manzikert and Byzantium itself was in retreat.

The Latin Confederation occupied weakened Constantinople in 1204 and divided the city and its lands, three-eights going to the Venetians and the remainder to Baldwin of Flanders, who promptly called himself the Emperor of Rumania, the new name for the Byzantine lands in Europe.

It was the beginning of the end; a divided nation lacked the strength to resist the growing menace of Islam and of the Ottoman Empire and gradually Byzantium was reduced to the city of Constantinople and a few lands in central Greece. In 1453, after a short siege, the city fell; Constantine XI was killed and Mehmet the Conqueror — Mehmet Fatih in Turkish — let his troops loot the city for three days.

One of the worst instances on record was of the thousands of refugees crowding into the Church of Haghia Sophia trying to evade slavery, but Fatih denied them sanctuary and declared the place forthwith to be the Mosque of Aya Sofya.

İstanbul He began rebuilding the run-down city, renaming it İstanbul and moving his capital from Edirne. And in 1470 he saw the completion of his mosque, the Fatih Camii, which prompted his viziers to build their own mosques. Constantinople was truly in the Islamic world, where it would stay.

From this point on the story of İstanbul can be told in its mosques, its palaces, and its other monuments. We shall repeat what geography has done and divide the city into three sections: old İstanbul south of the Golden Horn; the newer city to the north; and the Asiatic suburbs across the Bosphorus around old Üsküdar. And where better to begin than in the Palace of Topkapı?

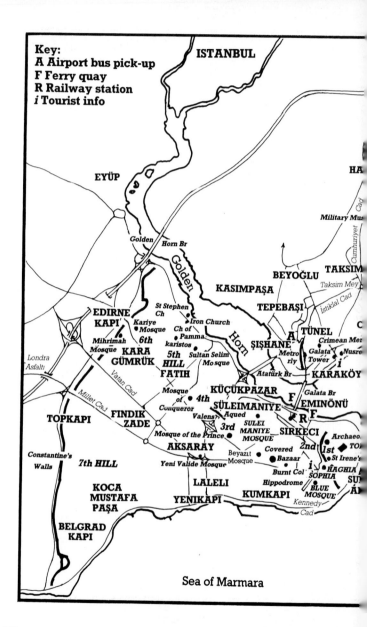

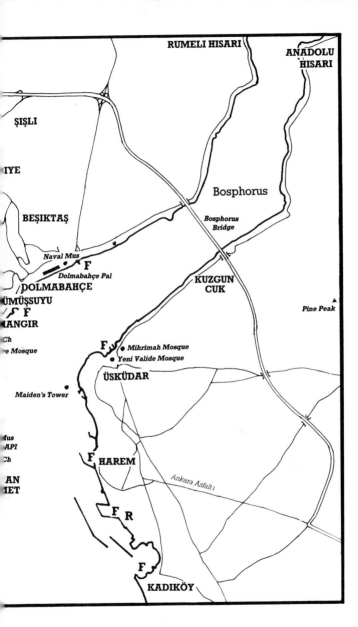

RUMELI HISARI

ANADOLU HISARI

ŞİŞLİ

İYE

Bosphorus

BEŞİKTAŞ

Bosphorus
Bridge

Naval Mus
F
Dolmabahçe Pal

KUZGUN
CUK

DOLMABAHÇE

ÜMÜŞSUYU

F

Pine Peak

ANGIR

Ch

e Mosque

F
Mihrimah Mosque
Yeni Valide Mosque

ÜSKÜDAR

Maiden's Tower

Mus
API

Ch

F HAREM

Ankara Asfaltı

AN
IET

F R

F

KADIKÖY

OLD İSTANBUL: from Topkapı to Top Kapı.

Our tour of the old city starts at the Palace of Topkapı and moves westward, following the approximate route of Divan Yolu and Fevzi Paşa Cad, to the present city walls, built by Constantine II in 641. There are several gates in this impressive fortification but Top Kapı is the most significant as there's a major bus station nearby. How many visitors have arrived at Top Kapı ('cannonball gate') and thought they were at Topkapı Palace!

The confusion of names goes one step further as the Turks never refer to 'old Istanbul' or even 'old city,' which translates as Eskişehir and is way over in Anatolia. Stick to the names of districts, which means we start in Sultanahmet.

TOPKAPI PALACE

Topkapı is much more than a simple palace. It's a walled city in miniature covering 700,000 square metres and in its prime was home to several thousand people with thousands more on Divan days when the sultans held court.

It was completed in 1459 by Mehmet II as his original palace was too small, and it served the Ottoman sultans untill 1839 when Abdül Mecit I moved to Dolmabahçe on the Bosphorus shore. The harem was added after the original, elsewhere in the city, was burned down and Roxelane, the Russian wife of Süleiman the Magnificent, suggested she should live with her husband.

Church of St Irene The Bab-ı-Hümayün, the Imperial Gate in the outer walls, leads into the grounds, the so-called First Court or Court of the Janissaries, with the Church of St Irene, Haghia Eirene, on your left. This is now a concert hall used during the İstanbul International Festival when Mozart's *Seraglio* is among the works performed. 'Seraglio' is an Italian corruption of the Turkish *saray*, 'palace.'

Second Court You enter Topkapı Palace through the impressive Babüs-Selam or Ortakapı, the Gate of Peace Greetings — but not on *Tuesdays* when the entire complex is closed — and find yourself in the Second Court, a large walled garden with the old kitchens lining the right side. As the entire place is a museum these now hold Chinese and Japanese porcelain; Turkish porcelain is in the old soap factory and European porcelain nearby. A small collection of weapons is on the left.

Harem The sultan was the only person allowed to ride through these gates on horseback; even his viziers walked. The sultan was also the only fully-equipped male allowed into the private quarters of the Harem, but today's visitors can take a guided tour of part of the complex for an extra fee.

Most stories you read about harem life are over-glamourised, for life was strictly regimented. There was, and is, a reception room where the sultan entertained his guests — men, of course — with the private rooms being strictly off limits to strangers. Here were the quarters of the Black Eunuch who held high office, the school for the young princes, the quarters for the slaves, the chambers for the concubines, of whom the first to present the sultan with a son could rise to become first lady and the power behind the throne.

Third Court The Third Court is smaller but dominated by the free-standing Imperial Hall or Audience Hall, its wide verandah making it look like an Indian bungalow. This was where the sultans sat in regal splendour as they entertained ambassadors — and what splendour! Around the court

The Audience Chamber, Topkapı Palace

are chambers showing embroidery (in the White Eunuchs' Apartments) and royal gowns (School for Page-boys), and the four-roomed Treasury which is probably the most impressive place you will see in all of Turkey.

Treasury Selim I created the Treasury in what had been Mehmet II's summer palace. The interior of the main room is recognisable as the setting for the Peter Ustinov film *Topkapi* but with subtle differences. The four rooms together hold enough wealth to finance a small country for a year or more and include the 86-carat Spoonmaker's Diamond, the world's seventh largest, which Napoleon's mother used to buy her son from exile; the gold-and-emerald dagger which was the centrepiece of *Topkapi*; an uncut emerald weighing 3.26 kg; and two golden chandeliers each studded with 6,666 brilliants and each weighing 48 kg. Then there is the 250-kg gold-plated Bayram Throne, showpiece among other thrones.

You may have seen the Crown Jewels in London. You might have seen the Inca gold and jewels paraded through Spanish streets in Holy Week. Put them all together and you have an idea of the scale of treasures on display here at Topkapı.

Relics Around the other walls of the Third Court are a collection of clocks and one of relics, which include swords of the first four caliphs, part of a gate in Mecca, some hairs from the beard of the Prophet, and a gazelle-skin parchment bearing his writing.

Fourth Court The Fourth Court is less impressive, but so are the Alps after the Himalayas. It holds the 15th century Chamber of the Head Physician, the elegant Baghdad Pavilion built in 1639 to mark Murat IV's capture of that city, and the 17th century Pavilion of Sultan Ibrahim, the Circumcision Room for the young princes.

151

Archaeological Museum You haven't yet finished with Topkapı for there's a very well endowed Archaeological Museum in the grounds, the farsighted gift of Abdül Hamit II (1876-1909) which holds many of the Ottoman Empire's finds from Anatolia and North Africa. From Turkey's point of view it's a pity that so much went to London and other European capitals instead of coming here where they truly belong.

And yet who could claim that the sarcophagus of Alexander the Great still belongs here in İstanbul? It was 'borrowed' from Sidon which is now in Lebanon. Other exhibits of particular note are finds from Magnesia, Assos, the Mausoleum at Halicarnassos, and a statue of Neptune from the Vedus Gymnasium in Ephesus.

Other museums The Museum of the Ancient Orient has exhibits from Egypt, Nineveh, Mesopotamia, and Turkey's own Urarti and Hittite periods. The Tiled Pavilion, built as a pleasure palace in 1472 for Mehmet II, has lost most of its own tiles but has exhibits of this superb Turkish craft.

HAGHIA SOPHIA (AYA SOFYA)

This great Ottoman-styled mosque was in fact built between 532 and 548 by Emperor Justinian and was the greatest church in Christendom until Christendom was driven out of Constantinople: St Peter's in Rome was built after the fall of Byzantium.

Constantine I built the first church on this site in 325, but fire destroyed it in 404. In 415 Theodosius II built the second version, but riot-induced fire claimed that as well, in 532. Forty days after the blaze Justinian announced plans for version three and he dedicated the completed dome on 26 December 537 with the boast "I have outdone you, Somolon!"

In 557 the dome collapsed. Justinian swallowed his pride and rebuilt, higher but narrower, and he dedicated this new dome on 24 December 563. There was much restoration and alteration over the centuries and Mehmet Fatih must have been bursting with elation 890 years later as he rode on horseback through the sacred Imperial Door and condemned the Christian refugees to slavery. The minarets, of course, are totally Ottoman for Haghia Sophia was a mosque for the next 481 years until Atatürk converted it into a museum in 1934.

The essential beauty of the museum is in its mosaics which tell the story of Byzantium and Constantinople through the eyes of its emperors, and add a religious flavour with portrayals such as Christ sitting beside Constantine IX. A puritanical revolt threatened the mosaics in the 7th century when 'graven images' were considered blasphemous, and again in 1453 when Islam took over. Islam, of course, is even more opposed to idolatry, but Aya Sofya's mosaics were plastered over and so preserved. In the 1950s the American Association for the Preservation of Byzantine Monuments began restoration, which is still going on.

Most mosques have bare interiors — it's that abhorrence of graven images — and Aya Sofya is no exception. But it gives you the opportunity to concentrate on the structure itself, built when the only machinery available was powered by muscle, be it from man or mule. Stand under the middle of the dome and applaud the achievement, and the acoustics will give you another pleasure.

THE BLUE MOSQUE (SULTAN AHMET CAMİİ)

Mosques, as I have said, have bare interiors. Don't, therefore, expect anything from the contents of the Blue Mosque or you'll be disappointed. Even the blue tiling of the interior does little to detract from the feeling of emptiness that comes after seeing Christian cathedrals, for there are no pews, no organ, no reredos, and the pulpit is insignificant. Look at it purely as a building and it'll enchant you.

The Blue Mosque was founded by Sultan Ahmet I — hence the name for this district of İstanbul — as a visual counter to Haghia Sophia and is the only one in the world with six minarets: the Mosque of the Ka'aba in Mecca had six, but a seventh was added. The story is that Ahmet, about to leave for Mecca, told his architect to build 'golden minarets,' but the architect foresaw financial problems and interpreted the word 'golden,' *altın* as 'six,' *altı*, and built them from stone.

The great dome and the six minarets now dominate the İstanbul skyline but have a cold, concrete appearance: it's a pity Mehmet Ağa the architect couldn't have gilded his masterpiece.

Enter the mosque compound from the Hippodrome, noting carefully the chain across the gateway which compelled the sultans to dismount and acknowledge they were entering a house of God and not of mere mortal man. The ablutions fountain is in the centre of the courtyard, where 20 columns support 29 small domes, but visitors such as ourselves are not allowed in the main door which is rightly reserved for worshippers.

If you want to go inside, walk around to the door on the left where for a donation of your choice you may enter, leaving shoes and photographic flash with the custodian. The dome, 23.5 m wide by 43 m high, is impressive, but not as impressive as the dome of Haghia Sophia built a millenium earlier.

STAMBOUL DELIGHTS

The Hippodrome

Septimus Severus's Hippodrome was more than merely a racecourse for charioteers and a duelling-ground for gladiators. It was the sports ground, the council chamber, the parliament and the opinion poll of the Byzantine Empire, as the 100,000 spectators who could gather here supported their teams with a fervour that at times had political and social overtones. Football hooliganism is nothing new; the emperor could lose his throne in the riots which might follow a victory by the wrong team.

The Fourth Crusade had its hooligan element as the Doge of Venice, Enrico Dandolo, stole the bronze statue of four horses from the Hippodrome and sat it over the main doorway to St Mark's Church in Venice. The Crusaders also stole the bronze plaques from Constantine VII's limestone Colossus, that weird-looking rock at the south end of the Hippodrome. The game can be played two ways, of course, for the Egyptian obelisk was part of Theodosius I's spoils from Egypt in 390: it was originally erected by Thutmose III in the 15th century BC in Heliopolis, Cairo.

The Serpent Column of three intertwined snakes was first erected outside the Temple of Apollo in Delphi in 478BC to mark the victory of the 31 cities against Persia in the Battle of Plataea, but Constantine grabbed it in 330 AD or thereabouts. The snakes lost their heads in the early 18th century, but part of one head is now in the Archaeological Museum.

Burnt Column

A kilometre west, where Divan Yolu meets Yeniçeriler Cad, stands the 36-m *Çemberlitaş* or Burnt Column. Constantine I had it erected in 328 to carry his statue but a 12th century storm brought down the emperor and fires are believed to have caused the smokey effect on the stonework.

Covered Bazaar

A hundred metres further, a bus stop draws attention to Çarşıkapı Cad, 153

Bazaar Gate Street, leading to *Kapalı Çarşı*, the Covered Bazaar, acknowledged to be the largest of its kind in the world. Founded by Mehmet Fatih soon after his conquest, it has occupied the same site and the same size ever since, though fire has destroyed it on several occasions, the latest in 1954.

A survey in 1880 said the bazaar had 4,399 shops, 2,195 workshops, 497 stalls, 12 warehouses, 18 fountains, 12 small mosques, one large mosque and a school. The total establishments must be about the same today but we can add restaurants, cafés, banks, a public toilet and shops selling tourist knick-knacks.   Merchants now, as of old, congregate according to trade, thus you have the *Kuyumcu Kapısı*, the Goldsmiths' Gate, leading to İnciciler Sok, Pearl-merchants' Street. The Ottoman merchants built caravanserais around the bazaar so that merchandise from anywhere in the empire could be offloaded straight to the point of sale; some of the caravanserais are still doing business in a modified manner. In the centre of the çarşı is the great domed old bedesten, a warehouse for high value goods where you can shop around for that souvenir of extra merit.

Even outside the covered part of the bazaar you are still in a maze of backstreets lined with small shops, extending some way north towards the Galata Bridge.

Beyazıt Mosque

The large open square ahead was the Forum of Theodosius, created on his orders in 393. It's now Hürriyet Meydanı, Freedom Square, but most Istanbullers still know it by its old name of Beyazıt Meydanı from the Beyazıt Mosque. Built for Sultan Beyazıt II between 1497 and 1505 the mosque is similar to Haghia Sophia, but smaller. It features the unusual design of a large dome supported by two half-domes, with the side rooms each covered by four small domes. Beyazıt's tomb is in the grounds, and the doves (pigeons?) that roost on the mosque roof are said to be offspring of a pair that the sultan owned.

University

On the north side of Beyazıt Mey an enormous Ottoman gateway that formerly opened onto the War Ministry now leads into the İstanbul University. In the grounds is the Beyazıt Tower, a stone structure with 180 steps that replaces the wooden tower of 1828. The original use was for firewatching but it's now used for meteorology, and the tower's lights offer a quick forecast for the morrow: blue for fine, green for rain, yellow for fog and red for snow.

Süleymaniye Mosque

North of the University is the Süleymaniye Mosque, built by Süleiman the Magnificent between 1550 and 1557. It's not the biggest, it's not the best known, but it is the grandest mosque in all Turkey and the most important Ottoman building in İstanbul. It was built on one of the seven hills of old İstanbul (Rome and Lisbon have seven hills, so why not Constantinople?) in the compound of a palace that no longer exists.

The 24 columns of marble or granite of the outer courtyard were plundered from the Hippodrome. The ten balconies of the great dome are supposed to signify that Süleiman was the tenth sultan of the Ottoman Empire, while the four minarets indicate how many sultans had reigned since the relief (as the Turks have it) of İstanbul, but that's stretching credibility a bit: surely not even Süleiman would build another six-minaret mosque?

The interior is clean and simple, the only decoration being some excellent İznik tiles, and some stained-glass windows done by Ibrahim the Drunkard and held in place with a glue of goat hair and egg-white. The dome is 53 m high internally and 27.5 m in diameter, rising from four massive pillars which were purloined from other buildings: one was the Column of Virginity from the Church of the Apostles in the city, another came from a palace near Haghia Sophia, and a third came from Baalbek near Damascus. The fourth was probably from İskenderun.

If you peer up into the main dome you may see some black objects hanging on short cords. They're ostrich eggs used as fly-repellents, and generations ago they were changed each year. The architect Sinan, a former Janissary who designed much of Süleiman's masterpieces, put a small window in the dome to allow for the gathering of condensation from the stonework and of soot from the oil lanterns. According to rumour these were the ingredients for the best ink of the time.

Mosque of the Prince

Some way to the west is the Şehzade Camii, the Mosque of the Prince, which was Sinan's first work for Süleiman. The Sultan ordered the mosque as a memorial to his son, the crown prince Mehmet, who had been killed on Süleiman's orders at the age of 21. Mehmet, and a grand vizier, lie in tombs in the outer courtyard.

The mosque had a medrese and a caravanserai, the latter now serving as lodgings for students.

Valens Aqueduct...

An impressive aqueduct strides across Atatürk Bulvarı to the north of the Mosque of the Prince. It's the only surviving major part of the complex water supply system devised under Byzantine rule and it linked the third and fourth of those seven hills. The section that remains is 800 m long and a maximum of 26 m high. Built by Emperor Valens (364-378), it was one of many aqueducts that the Byzantines and the Ottomans found necessary to bring water from the streams in the Belgrade Forest 10 km to the west. Belgrade Forest? It's now only a moderate-sized wood, but it got its name in 1521 from Süleiman's capture of Belgrade that year.

..and other waterworks The aqueducts fed 'cisterns,' which were in effect either open reservoirs — the Cistern of Aetios is now the Vefa Stadium on Fevzi Paşa Cad near Edirnekapı — or underground chambers such as the **Yerebatan Saray,** the 'Underground Palace' built by Justinian around 532 but no longer in use. It has a capacity of 80,000 cubic metres, it's 140 m by 70 m and the vast roof is supported by 336 columns each 8 m high. Want to visit it? It's on the south side of Yerebatan Cad, which runs north-west from the Hippodrome, and it's open daily. They shot some of the scenes from the Bond film *Greetings from Moscow* in here.

The **Binbirdirek Sarnıcı,** the Cistern of 1,001 Columns, is also near the Hippodrome, but casual admission is not allowed. There are many other cisterns known to be under İstanbul and probably a few that have yet to be rediscovered.

Mosque of the Conqueror (Fatih Camii)

The first mosque built in İstanbul after the Islamic conquest was the enormous Fatih Camii that Mehmet the Conqueror commanded be erected on the fourth hill, north-west of the Aqueduct of Valens and on the site of the destroyed Church of the Apostles. Building began in 1463 and took seven years.

The mosque *complex* was, and still is, the largest in the city and included a library, primary school, eight Koranic schools, a hospice, hospital, caravanserai and Turkish bath. But Mehmet's mosque is no more. It was destroyed by an earthquake in 1766 and what you see now is a smaller version built in baroque style between 1767 and 1771.

Mehmet's *türbe*, tomb, is behind the mosque beside that of his wife Gülbahar who is supposed to have been a French princess.

Mihrimah Mosque

At the north-west end of Fevzi Paşa Cad and close by Hadrian's Gate — Edirnekapı — is the unusual Mihrimah Mosque built in 1555 by the young lady of that name who happened to be the daughter of Süleiman the Magnificent. Almost all major mosques have a cluster of smaller domes around the main one, but Mihrimah has only the single main dome, 37 m high by 20 m in diameter. The architect Sinan set the building on a platform but if that was a precaution against seismic damage, it didn't work. Mihrimah was severely shaken in 1766 and 1894 and had major restoration in 1910 and 1958.

In view of the earthquakes which have shattered Turkey throughout its history, it is astounding why mosques have such tall and slender minarets. The single minaret at this mosque appears extra tall as it has only one balcony for the muezzin.

The City Walls

A two-minute stroll takes you to Edirnekapı, the gate for Edirne or Adrianople, at 77 m above sea level the highest point in the walls that Theodosius II built in 413; they're on the site of Constantine II's defences and are still frequently referred to as 'his' walls. The gate was also known to the Byzantines as Porta Polyandriou, Cemetery Gate, from the large burial grounds outside it, in use from Byzantine times to the present.

To Topkapı

The part of the wall which goes north-east to the Golden Horn is in good condition but the stretch that runs south-west from Edirnekapı to Topkapı is in poor state for this was the section, lying in the valley where Vatan Cad now runs, that the Turks breached on the morning of 29 May 1453.

Topkapı, the Cannon (or Cannonball) Gate, earned its name from the enormous cannon called Urban which the Turks ranged on it during that siege. Urban had a range of 1.6 km, and some of the 550-kg stone balls that it fired against the city wall are on display in the gateway itself.

Outside Topkapı is one of the busiest bus stations in the city and a place to avoid at the morning and evening rush hours. Beside it, the dual-carriageway with the exotic name of Londra Asfaltı — tarmac way to London — leads to the airport, and home.

DOWN THE GOLDEN HORN

Home, for us, must wait awhile. We shall retrace our steps from Edirnekapı to the Galata Bridge, mostly along the shores of the Golden Horn.

Kariye Mosque Turn north-east onto Hoca Çakır Sok, the road beside the wall, and take the third right which leads directly to Kariye Camii, the former Church of St Saviour in Chora and the second most important Byzantine church in Istanbul.

It was built between 1077 and 1081 outside Constantine I's wall but inside the Theodosian defences in what was then open country, which is the meaning of 'Chora.' Major rebuilding between 1315 and 1321 removed all traces of the earlier work and the new church's interior was heavily decorated with mosaics, which is its attraction today as they offer an incredible family tree from Christ back to Adam. They survived Ottoman puritanism by being plastered over, as at Haghia Sophia.

As the Church of St Saviour it was dangerously close to the city wall during the Ottoman siege of 1453 and the parishioners paraded along the front line carrying St Saviour's most important possession, an icon by St Luke of the Virgin Mary who was the church's protrectress. But not this time. When the Turks breached the walls they pillaged St Saviour and the icon disappeared.

Theotokos Pammakaristos Draman Cad and Fethiye Cad lead south-east to the Fethiye Mosque, formerly the Church of Theotokos Pammakaristos, the Joyous Mother of God (open daily except *Wednesday*). The place was built in the 12th century by a member of the Comemnus family and, amazingly, was left in the hands of its Greek priests after Mehmet Fatih took the city in 1453; three years into Turkish rule it became the Greek Orthodox Patriarchate when the Church of the Apostles was abandoned.

Mehmet III converted it into a mosque in 1573 and named it *Fetih*, 'conquest,' from which comes its present name of Fethiye.

From here we have the option either of following the relatively easy road (now called Manyasızade Cad) south-east to the dead-straight Yavuz Selim Cad and turning left to the Selim Mosque and so to the Golden Horn, or navigating north-east through a maze of backstreets to Mörselpaşa Cad, the main road fronting the Golden Horn. If we take this latter route we see a truly surprising sight, the Church of St Stephen of the Bulgars.

St Stephen of the Bulgars The church, and everything in it, is made of cast iron, as is the exarchate opposite. (An exarch is the equivalent of a bishop in the Orthodox Church) Both buildings were cast in Vienna, shipped down the Danube and erected here in 1871. While the moulds were available, an identical church was cast for Vienna itself, but it was a victim of the Second World War. A small community of Bulgarians here in Istanbul uses the church and keeps it in repair, including repainting it regularly.

During the 19th century the European member states of the Ottoman Empire wanted to express their nationalism and the sultan conceded the Bulgars the right to establish their own branch of the Church, but under an exarch rather than a more important patriarch.

Selim Mosque

Siuleiman the Magnigicent completed this mosque which Selim I, 'the Grim,' had begun three years earlier in 1519. Its chief characteristic is its shallow dome, appreciably less than a hemisphere, which gives it a sense of space if not of height. There are some early Iznik tiles in the main room, and to north and south, passages lead to smaller domed rooms which were once the lodgings for travelling Dervishes. Selim's tomb is in the grounds, nowhere near as grim as the man whose body it contains.

To go from here, the Carşamba district, to the Galata Bridge in Eminönü, and our last two mosques in the old city, the option is to use the infrequent ferry from the Fener jetty, or go by bus down Abdülezel Paşa Cad.

The New Mosque (Yeni Camii) of the Sultan's Mother The Yeni Valide Camii, commanding a view along the Galata Bridge, is the last of the imperial mosques to be built in the classical period, and its name is somewhat confusing. *Valide* is Turkish for 'mother' hence a Valide Sultan was the mother of the reigning sultan, the Ottoman equivalent of our Queen Mother. It was Safiye, mother of Mehmet III, who started the mosque in 1597, but when her son died she lost her authority and the work ceased.

Sultan Ahmet was too engrossed in his blue mosque to spare interest in this one, and his successors had other interests so for half a century the place fell into decline and was severely damaged by fire in 1660. That was when the Valide Sultan Turhan Hadice, mother of Mehmet IV, took command of the work and finished the building in 1663. Internally it is much as the other mosques, with a good display of İznik tiles, but its ablutions fountain in the courtyard is reckoned to be the best in the city.

Egyptian Bazaar The Egyptian Bazaar, *Mısır Çarşısı*, also known as the Spice Bazaar, is part of the *külliye*, the complex, associated with the Yeni Valide Camii, though it's several times larger than the mosque itself. The 88 shops in this L-shaped building originally handled spices and medicinal herbs brought from Egypt, plus an assortment of locally-produced ingredients including asses' milk and gunpowder. The rents from the shops helped support the mosque's charitable functions but traders had to stop stocking gunpowder (used with lemon juice to treat haemorrhoids) because it destroyed several shops and cut into the mosque's income.

The **Pandeli Restaurant**, open only at lunchtime, is over the entrance from Eminönü Mey (Square).

The 470-metre double-deck **Galata Bridge,** which was built in 1912 and floats on 22 pontoons, has shops on the lower floor and is a tourist attraction in its own right. It now leads us from Old İstanbul across the Haliç, the polluted Golden Horn which is due to be cleaned up soon, and into modern İstanbul.

BEYOĞLU AND THE NEW CITY

North of the Golden Horn, İstanbul is a different city. This is the quarter — or should one say the 'third' — which has the smart hotels, the consulates, the night life, the tower blocks of offices, the newer Ottoman palaces lining the Bosphorus, and one of the oldest underground railways in Europe.

The Karaköy and Galata area at the south, overlooking the Golden Horn, was where the Byzantine and the Ottoman rulers banished the foreign merchants who needed to live in the city. The Genoese predominated; after all, they had a chain of castles along the Black Sea shore and were ardent traders, and their descendants still run the import and export firms based here.

Underground Railway

The aptly-named Tünel was built in 1875 by French engineers, 12 years after the Metropolitan Railway started its underground services in London. The line is 620 metres long and links the base station on Tersane Cad (the first left from the main Yüksek Kaldırım Cad north of the Galata Bridge) to the top station on Galipdede Cad. The original station buildings have gone, to be replaced by unattractive objects, but the new rubber-tyred trains are smart.

Frequency of trains depends on demand, ranging from two minute to ten minute intervals, and the fare is low.

Galata Tower If the gradient of Yüksek Kaldırım Cad is too steep for you, take the train, but you'll miss the Galata Tower, the largest landmark on this side of the Golden Horn. The Genoese built it as the Tower of Christ in 1348 and over the centuries it has been added to and restored several times, the last in 1975 when it was reroofed. It was originally a vantage point for watching enemies approach; later it was a firewatcher's tower but it is now a tourist attraction by day — the top balcony is 68 m above the road and 140 above the sea — and after dark a restaurant and night club.

Nightspots İstiklal Cad, which runs from the top metro station to Taksim Mey, is the smartest road in İstanbul. The name means 'Street of Independence' and along it or on Meşrutiyet Cad which runs parallel but to the west, you find the British Consulate (Meşrutiyet Cad 34), the Unites States Consulate (Meşrutiyet Cad 104), the Swedish consulate and the Dutch and Russian embassies, the hotels Etap İstanbul, Perepalas, Büyük Londra, Inka and Yenişehir, and several good restaurants.

There are also several churches in the neighbourhood, starting with the Crimean Memorial Church down Kumbaracı Cad (right just before the Russian Embassy), the largest and most ornate church in the city. It was built between 1858 and 1868 by Lord Stratford, the former British Ambassador to the Ottoman Empire. St Mary Draper is on İstiklal Cad beyond the embassy and down a flight of stairs. Built in 1789 to replace the original church of 1678, it holds an icon of the Virgin Mary.

Turn right into a sidestreet by St Mary and you quickly come to the Dutch Chapel on the left. This late 17th century building once had a prison in its basement, and it now serves as the Union Church for an English-speaking congregation.

Atatürk Memorial İstiklal Cad ends at the İstiklal Anıt, the Independence Monument put up in 1928 in the centre of Taksim Meydanı. On one side it shows Atatürk fighting the Greeks; on the other, Atatürk and İsmet İnönü are at the declaration of the republic. This is the central point of new İstanbul and is the prestigious address of the Etap Marmara Hotel and the Opera House.

High living North, Cumhuriyet Cad leads to the smartest part of town and to the Hilton, the Sheraton and the Divan. On the right, by the Hilton Arcade, is the Kervansaray Night Club, arguably the top night spot in Turkey and certainly the place to go for the best in belly dancing and Turkish music.

Military Museum A little further, on the right, the Askeri Müzesi or Military Museum has a range of weaponry from the 12th century to the Korean War where Turkish troops joined the United Nations' force. But the main attraction is undoubtedly the Mehter, the Janissaries' Band, which gives a stirring display of martial music every day except Monday and Tuesday (when the museum is closed) at 1500. Doubtless you can imagine the terror felt in a town that had just fallen to the conquering Janissaries at the height of Ottoman supremacy. Listen to this music, see the band march, imagine you're back in the 17th century, and you'll begin to appreciate living in the 20th century.

Dolmabahçe And now back to Taksim. Go down Gümüşsuyu Cad (Silver Water Street) to the Bosphorus and you'll see the Dolmabahçe Mosque. Pause merely to admire its minarets, the most slender in İstanbul, then hurry on to the vast and breathtakingly opulent Dolmabahçe Palace.

Entry is by the four-tier clock tower between 0900 and 1200, and from 1330 to 1630, any day except Saturday and Monday, but you must take a guided tour.

The site took its name, 'filled-in garden,' from the small harbour that Sultan Ahmet I converted for a small pleasure garden. Selim I built a wooden pavilion here which was burned out in 1814. Abdül Mecit I wanted a European-style palace as Topkapı gave a too-Oriental image to European ambassadors, so in 1843 he commissioned this ostentatious extravaganza at a time when the Ottoman Empire was well into its decline.

Dolmabahçe was the official residence of the sultan for a mere 20 years from its completion in 1856. In 1877 Abdül Hamit II opened the first Turkish Parliament here, but it survived just two months. After the War of Independance Atatürk stayed here on his infrequent visits to Istanbul and he died here at 0905 on 10 November 1938, aged 57.

Among the influential guests who have stayed here are Edward VII of England before his accession, Empress Eugenie, King Emanullah of Afghanistan, King Faisal of Iraq, Franz Josef of Austria, Shah Reza Pahlevi and Kaiser Wilhelm II of Germany. The place has 285 rooms and 43 halls, containing 94 chandeliers and 156 clocks, every one standing at 0905. The furnishings and decoration used 14 tons of gold and 40 tons of silver; see some of it if you can spare the time.

Naval Museum Beyond Dolmabahçe are the Naval, the Fethiye and the Fine Arts museums, but we'll confine ourselves to the Naval Museum (closed Monday and Tuesday) which houses several of the sultans' barges, 30 metres long but just 2 m wide, and the prize exhibit, a copy of the map of the Americas drawn in 1513 by the Turkish cartographer Piri Reis. It shows the eastern seaboard from around Charleston, down through South America to the Antarctic, and gave Erich von Däniken food for thought in his *Chariots of the Gods*. The original map is in safe keeping in Topkapı.

Victory Mosque Come south down the Bosphorus to the Nusretiye Camii, the Victory Mosque, and the nearby mosque of Kılıç Ali Paşa. The Victory Mosque was built between 1822 and 1826 by Mahmut II and its name marks his victory over the Janissaries by his slaughter of 40,000 of them in the Hippodrome.

Kılıç Ali Paşa Mosque was the gift of the admiral of that name in 1580. Kılıç Ali was born in Calabria, kidnapped as a child by Algerian pirates, spent 14 years as a galley slave, then rose to become admiral in Süleiman's navy. He was one of the few Turkish officers to aquit himself well at the Battle of Lepanto in 1571, and when serving as Governor of Algeria, his reward for valour, he bought the relase of a Christian captured at Lepanto: Miguel Cervantes, author of *Don Quijote*.

THE BOSPHORUS AND ITS BRIDGE

'Bosphorus,' which is optionally spelled without its 'h,' derives from the Latin for 'cow ford' in memory of a tiff between Zeus and his wife Hera who was jealous of Io, her husband's mistress. Zeus turned Io into a cow for protection, but Hera sent a bee which stung the cow into swimming across the strait. The Turkish name, by the way, is İstanbul Boğazi, the 'throat of Istanbul' and the brackish surface current flows south at 2 to 3 knots (3 to 4 kph) while at 40 m deep a saltier current flows north.

The waterway is 31 km long, ranging in width from 4.73 km to 660 m, the latter point a little north of the bridge where the European Rumeli Hisarı (castle) and the Asian Anadolu Hisarı (castle) face each other.

Mehmet the Conqueror ordered the European castle in 1452, and 10,000 men built it in four months; the Asian counterpart is the work of Beyazıt I.

The bridge was opened in 1973 and is the only one in the world to link two continents — though that statement denies that Eurasia is one land mass and ignores the tiny bridges across the Panama Canal at the Gatun locks. The Bosphorus Bridge is the work of an Anglo-German consortium, took 3½ years to build and has an impressive span of 1,074 m with a clearance of 64 m above the cow ford. It carries more than 200,000 vehicles a day and will soon have another suspension bridge beside it.

Cruise One of the most interesting ways of seeing İstanbul is from a ferryboat along the Bosphorus: *see page* **163** for *details*. Not only will you appreciate the beauty of this natural channel, an ancient geological fault that also takes in the Dardanelles, but you can have another aspect of the bridge and Dolmabahçe Palace. But there are other sights to see, including the burned-out **Çirağan Palace** of 1864 which is to become a luxury hotel.

The European shore, northward İstinye, where Jason and his Argonauts supposedly built a temple, has floating docks — unless they've already completed their promised move to the Sea of Marmara. **Yeniköy,** the 'new village,' is a smart *old* suburb with several summer embassies, though the German summer embassy was at **Taraba** on land that Abdül Hamit II presented to Wilhelm II. **Sarıyer** is the largest village with a busy fish market. Beyond **Rumeli Feneri** the coast road is closed to all but military traffic.

The Asiatic shore, southward Anadolu Feneri, the 'Anatolian lighthouse' matches the European one opposite, and **Anadolu Kavaği,** the furthest ferry stop, has a 14th century Genoese palace. **Hünkar İskelesi** gave its name to the treaty of 1883 between the Ottomans and the Russians, banning the latter's warships from the Dardanelles, but **Beykoz,** midway down, is where the Anglo-French fleet waited in 1854 before attacking the Crimea.

At **Çubuklu** was the Cloister of the Unsleeping, a monastery built by Alexander the Great in which the monks prayed round the clock. **Çengelköy,** Anchor Village, has an imposing 19th century military college, which leads us to Üsküdar and our last sector of İstanbul.

ÜSKÜDAR AND ASIATIC İSTANBUL

Üsküdar, the Chrysopolis or City of Gold in ancient times, is almost as ancient as the Stamboul part of the city. It has timber-framed houses lining narrow and twisting streets, and several mosques of significance, but cannot begin to compete with European İstanbul for sights of interest.

Two mosques here have identical names with two across the Bosphorus but Üsküdar's Yeni Valide Camii of 1708 to 1710 came between the classical and baroque periods and missed both. It was built by Ahmet III for his mother, the Valide Gülnus Emetullah, 'rose-drinker.'

The İskele Camii is also known as the Mihrimah Camii and was, like its European namesake, built by Süleiman's daughter.

Maiden's Tower The Maiden's Tower, Kız Kulesi, is a 30 m high lighthouse on an islet 180 m from the Asian shore and marks the southern end of the Bosphorus. A customs station was here in 500BC and the Byzantines built a castle from which they stretched a chain across to Europe to block the sea lane. The present tower dates from 1763 and was built to hold the sultan's daughter who, according to prediction, would die from snakebite. She did, too: the snake was smuggled to the island in a basket of fruit.

Çamlıca Çamlıca, the Pine Peak, is a few kilometres east of Üsküdar but repays a visit as it offers a splendid view of the city, particularly in the early morning with the sun still in the east. Access is by bus or dolmuş from İskele Mey to Kısıklı; bus, another dolmuş, or your feet, will take you the remainder of the way. Çamlıca is a popular spot for newlyweds seeing their married life symbolically spread before them, rather like the magic and mystic city of İstanbul.

HOTELS

As İstanbul has such a wide range of hotels I have listed them according to star rating. Most of the top class places are in the Beyoğlu area, the new city north of the Golden Horn, but see the İstanbul map on page 148 for the various districts.

5-star

Büyük Sürmeli Hotel, Saatçibayır Sok, G.Tepe (tel 1721160), 224 rooms, pool, casino

Büyük Trabya Hotel, Kefeliköy Cad, Tarabya (tel 1621000), 261 rooms, pool, casino

Divan Hotel, Cumhuriyet Cad, Şişli (tel 1314100), 96 rooms

Etap Marmara Hotel, Taksim Mey, Taksim (tel 1514696), 424 rooms, pool, casino

Hilton Hotel, Cumhuriyet Cad, Harbiye (tel 1314646), 410 rooms, pool, casino

Sheraton Hotel, Taksim Parkı, Taksim (tel 1312121), 437 rooms, pool

4-star

Çinar Hotel, Fener Mev, Yeşilköy (tel 5732910), pool, casino

Etap İstanbul Hotel, Meşrutiyet Cad, Tepebaşı (tel 1514646), pool

Fuar Hotel, Namık Kemal Cad, Aksaray (tel 5259732), casino

İstanbul Dedeman Hotel, Yıldızposta Cad, Esentepe (tel 1728800) casino

Maça Hotel, Eytem Cad 35, Teşvikiye (tel 1401053), casino

Olcay Hotel, Millet Cad 187, Topkapı (tel 5853220), pool, on main road

Perepalas Hotel, Meşrutiyet Cad 98, Tepebaşı (tel 1514560) (built for the *Cie Internationale des Wagon-Lits*)

3-star

Akgün Hotel, Ordu Cad, Hazdenadar Sok 6 (tel 5120260)

Dilson Hotel, Sıraselviler Cad 49, Taksim (tel 1432032)

Dragos Hotel, Sahil Yolu 12, Cevizli-Maltepe (tel 3520503), May-Oct

Harem Hotel, Ambar Sok, Selimiye, Üsküdar (tel 3332025)

Kalyon Hotel, Sahil Yolu, Sultanahmet (tel 5201303)

Kaya Hotel, Millet Cad 86, Fındıkzade (tel 5214783)

Keban Hotel, Sıraselviler Cad 51, Taksim (tel 1433310)

Kennedy Hotel, Sıraselviler Cad 79, Taksim (tel 1434090)

Topkapı Hotel, Oğuzhan Cad 20 Fındıkzade (tel 5254240)

Washington Hotel, Gençtürk Cad 12, Laleli (tel 5205990)

Zürih Hotel, Vidinli Tevfik Paşa Cad, Laleli (tel 5122350)

2-star

There are plenty of two-star hotels, the majority clustering in Laleli in the old city and Taksim in the new European quarter. This is a selection.

Astor Hotel, Laleli Cad 12, Aksaray (tel 5224423)

Bern Hotel, Millet Cad, Aksaray (tel 5232462)

Büyük Hamit Hotel, Gençtürk Cad 72, Laleli (tel 5121708)

Büyük Keban Hotel, Gençtürk Cad 47 Laleli (tel 5120020)

Büyük Londra Hotel, Meşrutiyet Cad 117 Tepebaşı

Cidde Hotel, Aksaray Cad 10, Laleli (tel 5224211)

Davos Hotel, Gençtürk Cad, Laleli (tel 5270424)

Diana Hotel, Fetihbey Cad, Ağayofuşu, Laleli (tel 5280760)

Doru Hotel, Gençtürk Cad 44, Laleli (tel 5276928)

Ebru Hotel, Mustafa Kemal Paşa Cad 29, Aksaray (tel 5867557)

Gezi Hotel, Mete Cad 42, Taksim (tel 1452167)

Hakan Hotel, Gençtürk Cad 9 Laleli (tel5122370) Hanzade Hotel, Şelimpaşa Sok, Laleli (tel 5277373)

İnka Hotel, Meşrutiyet Cad 225, Tepebaşı (tel 1431728)

İnter Hotel, Büyük Haydarefendi Sok, Beyazıt (tel 5114086)

Levent Hotel, Şair Haşmet Sok, Laleli (tel 5118897)

Malkoç Hotel, Mesihpaşa Cad 41, Laleli (tel 5223638)

Monaco Hotel, Fitnet Sok 28, Laleli (tel 5112401)

Ons Hotel, Kocaragıp Cad, Aksaray (tel 5121683)

Opera Hotel, İnönü Cad 38, Taksim (tel 1435527)

Oriental Hotel, Cihangir Cad 60, Taksim (tel 1451067)

Şahinler Hotel, Koska Cad 10, Laleli (tel 5207556)

Star Hotel, Sağlık Sok 11, Taksim (tel 1450050)

Toro Hotel, Koska Cad 24, Laleli (tel 5280273)

One-star There is a plethora of one-star hotels in the Laleli, Aksaray and Taksim areas. Laleli is by far the more convenient for the interests of the old city and, rate for rate, is cheaper than the classy Taksim.

RESTAURANTS

You need never go hungry in Istanbul. The provision of food to the working class is a major industry, and the quality and quantity is little different from that provided in a top-class restaurant, the only differences being in the surroundings and the service.

If you want to sample the best service available, try any of the smart hotels. If you fancy something less pricey but still want to be made to feel like a millionaire, try any of the restaurants on Soğukçeşme Sok, outside the Topkapı Palace walls and to the left of the main gate. The whole street looks as if it's just in from New Orleans.

The Konyalı Restaurant in the Fourth Court of Topkapı Palace is good without being expensive, as is the Pandeli over the Egyptian Bazaar.

For a bargain blowout you have the pick of the town. Taksim is one of the best places to start looking, despite its being in the classy area. Laleli, down near the Sea of Marmara, is a popular district for locals as well as for students from the university, and you can find a number of cheap tourist lokantas in the Grand Bazaar and on Divan Yolu in Sultanahmet. For a range of drinks and cocktails try the Sultan Pub opposite the tourist office in Sultanahmet.

The Sirkeci district by the European rail terminus has a good choice, and you can even have a meal of fresh fish on the lower deck of the Galata Bridge itself.

GETTING AROUND

Bus İstanbul is an overcrowded city as you will learn if you find yourself caught in the frantic crawl to work every morning. The bus service is the cheapest form of land travel but is slow and many buses fill up at the start of the journey, particularly around 0730 and 1700. The main bus stations are at **Taksim, Eminönü, Beyazıt, Üsküdar and Kadiköy.** NOTE THAT BUSES FOR THE AIRPORT leave from the THY terminal in Şişhane, near the top terminal of the Tünel metro in the modern city.

Dolmuş Dolmuş travel is much more practical, and as these minibuses operate on shorter routes there's less chance of getting lost. The main dolmuş termini are at **Taksim, Karaköy, Eminönü, Sirkeci, Beyazıt, Üsküdar and Kadiköy.**

Ferries Ferries are the cheapest way of travelling and provide some of the best views, with the chance of taking some good photographs. Most ferry termini are in Eminönü near the Sirkeci rail station. Imagine yourself walking from the Galata Bridge eastwards, these are the quays and their routes, in sequence:

4 Up the Bosphorus, zigzagging from Europe to Asia all the way; 5-hour return trip.

3 Üsküdar and Çengelköy.

2 Üsküdar.

1 Kadiköy, Bostancı (Asian coast south).

A Car ferries to Harem (Asia).

5 Slow boats to Adalar, the Princes' Islands.

West of the Galata Bridge on this shore is **6,** for a service zigzagging up the Golden Horn to Eyüp.

North of the bridge and to the east are **7** and **8** for Kadiköy and Haydarpaşa (Asia, south of Üsküdar) respectively. Haydarpaşa is the Asiatic rail terminal.

At Kabataş near the Dolmabahçe Palace is **B,** for fast boats to the Princes' Islands and Yalova, on the other side of the Sea of Marmara.

AROUND İSTANBUL

The Princes' Islands, Kızıl Adalar

They're known in Turkish as the Red Islands, or just simply 'the Islands' as there aren't any others. There are four inhabited isles in the group of nine, with the 5.4 sq km of **Büyük Ada,** Big Island, not surprisingly the most important. Two hills, each with a monastery, dominate the community; to the north on İsa Tepe is the Monastery of Christ while Yüce Tepe has the Greek Monastery of St George.

That overworked word 'charming' rests well with Big Island, particularly since private cars aren't allowed and all transport is by horse carriage. There's no fresh water on any of the isles, but Big Island manages the Splendid Hotel (tel 3315167) and the Villa Rıfat Pension-Hotel (tel 3516068).

Heybeli, the 'Saddle-Bag Island' of 2.3 sq km, takes its name from its shape, though it was formerly Copper Island from the mine here. The Turkish Naval Academy has been here since 1944, in the old Greek Orthodox orphanage.

The other inhabited isles are the wooded **Burgaz** of 1.5 sq km and the

Çanakkale, the car ferry from Europe arrives

164

denuded **Kınalı** of 1.3. Of the remainder, **Sedef** has occasional summer residents, **Yassı** has the ruins of Sir Henry Bulwer's palace: he was ambassador in the 1850s. And in 1910 thousands of stray dogs were offloaded on **Sivri**. I wonder why?

İZNİK

The ferry to Yalova is a convenient way of reaching İznik, the ancient Nicaea, built on a splendid grid pattern with Atatürk Cad running due north and south and Kılıçaslan Cad due east-west, crossing in the centre of the old walled city.

Nicene Creed How apt if you visit İznik at Easter! The First Ecumenical Council of the Church met on 19 June, 325, at Nicaea to decide, among other important issues, the date of Easter Sunday. The delegates fixed it as the first Sunday after the first full moon after 21 March (which still holds true) and included it in their Nicene Creed.

The Seventh Council, meeting in 787 in the Sancta Sophia Church by the city-centre crossroads, settled the issue of iconoclasm: while it was blasphemy to 'bow down before graven images,' icons were to be regarded as works of art and so spared the wrath of early puritans.

The first settlement here was around 1,000BC, but it was Lysimachus, local successor to Alexander the Great, who established the city and named it Nikaea from his wife. The Byzantines built the walls, which survive in a remarkably good state of repair. When the Fourth Crusaders pillaged Constantinople in 1024, Emperor Basil II escaped to Nicaea with his retinue.

Theodor Lascaris stayed in Nicaea when the retinue returned to Constantinople, and in the two centuries that followed his descendants created the Empire of Nicaea which by 1230 occupied all of Asia Minor west of the Marmaris — Zonguldak axis, less the Bosphorus shore. The Latins clung on to Constantinople and parts of Greece but were in terminal decay, as a Nicaean commander found on 25 July 1261: Constantinople was all but deserted.

The Nicaeans moved back, but the Byzantines had already noted this power vacuum and soon re-established themelves, absorbing both the Latins and the Nicaeans. But in 1331 the Ottomans moved in and Nicaea became part of Islam.

Iznik tiles Selim the Grim seized the Persian city of Tabriz in 1514 and forcibly resettled its craftsmen in Iznik. The many ceramic artists among them soon created the tile industry for which Iznik became famed in the coming two centuries; a visit to the mosques of Istanbul shows the extraordinary quality achieved.

Iznik today The Church of Sancta Sophia has seen many changes; the Justinian church was destroyed by earthquake in 1065 and the rebuilt structure had Byzantine mosaics. The Ottomans converted it into a mosque, which was severely damaged by fire in the early 16th century, but the replacement which is what you see now, incorporated Iznik's own tiles. Parts of a Justinian mosaic of Jesus and Mary have survived almost 1500 years of troubles.

Soup kitchen Near the interesting eastern gate, Levkekapı, a soup kitchen dating from 1388 now serves as the town museum. As you'd expect, it has a good display of Iznik tiles as well as Ottoman weapons.

HOTELS

The Motel Burcum (tel 11) and the Iznik Motel (tel 41) on the lakeside, offer mid-range accommodation, with the Hotel Babacan (Kılıçaslan Cad

104, tel 211) near Sancta Sophia a suitable bargain-basement stopover.

BURSA

Bursa is Turkey's fifth largest city with 614,000 people in 1985. It's a major university city, the centre of the Turkish motor industry with the assembly of Fiats, Renaults and the building of the country's own Anadol, and it shares with Iznik the processing of the fruit grown on this south shore of Marmara.

Founded around 200BC by Prusias, King of Bithynia, Prusa was at first favoured. The Byzantine emperor Justinian developed the thermal baths at nearby Çekirge, and established a silk industry. But the Seljuks captured the city in 1075, the First Crusade recaptured it in 1097, it briefly passed to the Empire of Nicaea, and was finally captured by the Ottomans in 1317 when it became their first capital until that status passed to Edirne in 1402.

Bursa today The modern town's tourist sights are mostly mosques and associated buildings, but it's more interesting to visit the thermal baths at Çekirge or climb the 2,643-metre peak of Uludağ. Or do both.

Çekirge Çekirge is a suburb of Bursa, 4 km to the west in easy reach by dolmuş from the bus station to the north of town. The Yeni Kaplıca, 'new bath,' was new in 1522 when Süleiman had it built on the site of a Byzantine bath, and the Kaynarca, 'spouting,' has some particularly hot water. Facilities differ. Some places offer private baths while others expect you to muck in together, which can be fun on Friday, the busiest day.

Uludağ The 'Great Mountain,' Turkey's most popular ski resort, is temptingly close to town. One of several mounts Olympus of the ancient world, hence its 'Olympus of Mysia' tag, it offers splendid views across Marmara to Istanbul provided you catch it on one of those rare days when industrial pollution is low.

You can walk up. You can go all the way by dolmuş. You can even go much of the way by cable car, which is undoubtedly the most exciting; it takes half an hour and costs 3,000TL return. Catch a dolmuş from Cumhuriyet Alanı on Atatürk Cad either for the teleferik station, or all the way. *See the skiing and thermal baths sections for more details.*

Mosques and Museums The Atatürk and the Archaeological museum are on opposite sides of Çekirge Cad, midway between Çekirge village and Bursa; the latter is in the Culture Park. From here and stretching across the southern flank of town is a string of mosques of which the most important is the Yeşil Cami or Green Mosque to the east.

The building you see is of 1864 vintage but it authentically replicates the original of 1424, destroyed by the 1855 'quake. That 1424 mosque was the work of Mehmet I and marks a transition from the Persian to the emergent Turkish style; its name came from the colour of the interior tiles. The grounds contain Mehmet's tomb (türbe) which is open to the public — by that, I mean you can actually go inside. It's an eerie experience.

Uphill from the Green Mosque is the Mosque of Yıldırım Beyazıt, Beyazıt I, who pushed the Ottoman boundaries deep into Europe and east towards Persia, only to be be defeated by Tamburlane and his stinking camels. After the interregnum, his successor and son Mehmet I began the Green Mosque.

The town centre, between Atatürk Cad and Cumhuriyet Cad, contains the tourist office (tel 12359; there's another in Tophane to the west, tel 13368), plus the Grand Mosque and the covered bazaar, both the work of Yıldırım Beyazıt. The mosque is impressive mainly for its size, but the bazaar is more interesting even though it's a copy of the original which was destroyed in that 1855 earthquake.

HOTELS

The best are in or near **Çekirge;** the 5-star, 173-room Çelik Palas, Çekirge Cad 79 (tel 61900) and the 4-star Anatolia, Çekirge Mey (tel 67110). King Idris of Libya was taking the waters in the Çekirge Palas when Col Ghaddafi overthrew him.

Two-star near Çekirge include the Akdoğan (1 Murat Cad, tel 60610); the Ada Palas (1 Murat Cad, tel 61600) and the Büyük Yıldız 2 (Selvınas Sok, Çekirge, tel 66605). Cheapest in Çekirge is probably the Şifa, near the Ada Palas (tel 11483).

Town-centre places include the Kent (Atatürk Cad 119, tel 18700) and the Artıç (Fevzi Çakmak Cad 123, tel 19500).

There are others at **Uludağ** village. Most cater for skiers but a few stay open all year, including the Büyük Panorama (tel 1237), the Merih (tel 18101) and the İbo Oberj (tel 1140).

EDIRNE

Edirne, the Adrianople of old, is the frontier town, 6 km from Greece and 18 from Bulgaria, and it has belonged to both those countries, and others, in its turbulent history. It was the Ottoman capital from 1402 until the conquest of Istanbul in 1453.

The old town, Kale İçi ('inside the fortress'), is built on the grid system and has several narrow, cobbled streets lined with fairytale houses, but the main inducement to break a journey here is to see the mosques, of which the most impressive is the **Selimiye Mosque,** north-east from the town centre along Talat Paşa Cad. The dome is around 35 m in diameter, its weight carried by pillars and buttresses to such an extent that the wall could be pierced with windows: the total is supposed to be 999.

Built by Sinan, Süleiman's great architect, the interior is among the most impressive you'll see outside İstanbul, and the location on a slight rise makes it an impressive building from the outside. A nearby statue of grease wrestlers is a reminder that Edirne has a wrestling festival each July.

Eski Camii The Eski Camii or 'Old Mosque,' back towards the town centre, was the work of Mehmet I in 1414 and has a small forest of pillars supporting a roof made of small domes. Behind the mosque is the 16th century Rustem Paşa Kervansaray, now a hotel. The name of the 15th century town-centre **Üçşerefeli Mosque** means 'with three balconies,' but this is true only of one of the four minarets. The large dome, 24 m in diameter, marks another stage in the transition between Seljuk and Ottoman architecture. Across the Tunca River, the **Beyazıt II Mosque** has one of the largest Külliye (associated buildings) in Turkey. Completed in 1488 and restored in 1978, it has a canteen, hostelry, hospital, theological school, and formerly an asylum for the insane. Islam certainly had its charitable side.

HOTELS

The Balta (Talatpaşa Asfaltı, tel 5210) is the only 2-star hotel. One-star places in town are the Park (Maarif Cad, tel 4610); Kervan (that converted caravanserai at Talatpaşa Cad 134, tel 1355); and the Sultan (Talatpaşa Cad, tel 1372). As Edirne is on the trunk route between industrial Europe and the Near East, it has plenty of cheap pensions. Ask at the Tourist Office at Hürriyet Meydanı, Londra Asfaltı 48 (tel 1518). And if an overnight stay in Edirne begins your holiday in Turkey — welcome!

TURKEY IN HISTORY

Çatal Höyük to the Dardanelles

Recorded history in Turkey took over when the Trojan Wars closed the era of gods coming down to live and love alongside mortal man. But there are thousands of years of unrecorded history that go back to the dawn of civilization a hundred centuries ago when early man in northern Europe was living in caves, dressing in animal skins and using axes of flint.

Çatal Höyük At that time Çatal Höyük was already a mud-hut town covering some 30 acres (15 ha) whose people had domesticated their animals and cultivated their crops. In 8,300BC they traded in obsidian with the people of Jericho, wove wool into cloth, built square houses with flat roofs, carved religious figures and painted their walls. And then, 5,000 years before Christ, they quietly faded away.

Hatti Around this era Stone Age man, using a little copper from Cyprus, developed a community at Hacilar near Burdur, giving way to the true Bronze Age when the Hatti peoples, the ancestors of the Hittites, made their home at Kültepe — 'ash hill' in Turkish — near the modern Kayseri, and at Alaca Höyük south-west of Çorum.

The Hatti kept written records of their trading; it's our problem that we can't yet decipher them. And they built two-storey houses on stone foundations.

Hittites The next invaders came from the ever-dangerous east around 2,200BC, absorbed the Hatti lands and culture and called themselves the Hittites, with their capital at Hattuşaş, south of Alaca Höyük.

The Hittites were workers in clay, iron, and gold, who settled on the Anatolian highlands, striking east to capture Syria and west to glimpse the Aegean.

Peoples of the Sea Beyond the Aegean, where Greece now thrives, the Dorians whom we remember best for their Doric architecture, had come down from the Balkans and were driving the native peoples before them until they, too, reached the Aegean.

This coincided with the Trojan Wars around 1,200BC, the defeat of the outpost city of Troy leaving Asia Minor open for the invasion of the 'peoples of the sea,' the refugee tribes fleeing the Dorians.

The Aeolians came first, settling the coast from Troy to Myrina (Smyrna, later Izmir). Two centuries later came the Ionians, taking the next stretch of coastline south and extending to Miletos on the Menderes River. Soon the flood was unstoppable as Greek exiles came down from Thrace to seize the Hittites' western lands, creating Phrygia with its capital at Gordion near the modern Polatli, 135 km south-west of Ankara. The Hittites began their slow retreat to the eastern Taurus where they faded into history.

Midas and Mausolus In the 8th century BC Phrygia's ruler was King Midas, the man with the golden touch, while in the new Caria King Mausolus was designing his Mausoleum at Halicarnassos (Bodrum). Lycia and Pamphylia occupied the Mediterranean coast, and Lydia arose from nothing around the city of Sardis, inland from Izmir.

Urarti Meanwhile, the Urarti (also known as the Chaldians but not to be confused with the Chaldeans), were moving down from the Caucasian steppes and establishing their civilization on the shores of Lake Van, and the Cimmerians (whose name lingers on in 'Crimea') came through the Balkans and conquered Phrygia.

Croesus The Lydians' King Ardys destroyed these new invaders, and his successor Croesus, the richest man in the world now that his people had invented coinage, destroyed Smyrna and seized all the coastal cities except militant Miletos.

Persians Ambitious Croesus turned his attention to the wandering Persians in 547BC, going into battle with his best troops on horses. But Cyrus of Persia came with camels, knowing that their smell would be so offensive that the horses would desert the field, which they did. The now humiliated Croesus jumped onto his own funeral pyre.

The Persians seized the other member-states of the Ionian League and installed puppet rulers, satraps. Aristogoras of Miletos decided that the Persians' tax bill was too much and in 500BC he led the Ionian revolt. The Persians under Darius suppressed it in 494 by sacking Miletos though pardoning the other cities.

Darius King Darius, of whom his people chanted 'Live for ever!' moved on to attack the Greek homeland but in 490BC the Athenians defeated him at Marathon and Phaedippides, who ran the 26 miles back to Athens with the news, dropped dead from the exertion.

Alexander the Great In 334 Alexander the Great crossed the Hellespont and attacked Persian Asia Minor, conquering it within two years. When he reached the old Hittite capital of Gordion he was confronted by a piece of wood tied to the yoke of a sacred wagon by a rope of tree-bark. Whoever untied the knot would rule Asia, a fortune-teller had declared. Alexander had no time to waste so he cut the Gordian knot with his sword.

Alexander died in Babylon in the year 323 at the age of 33, and his successors squabbled over the unexpected spoils, Lysimachus seizing western Anatolia and Seleucus the eastern part, which became the Seleucid lands.

Seleucids Smaller kingdoms managed to rise and to flourish briefly in the unclaimed territories that remained: Commagene at Nemrut Dağı; Bithnia, ruled by Prusias at Prusa (Bursa); the Kingdom of Armenia ruled from Van by Ardvates; and Pergamon under the eunuch Philetarus.

In 190BC Lucius Scipio Asiaticus defeated the Seleucid Antiochus III at Magnesia (now Manisa) and so began the notional Roman rule of Anatolia, called Asia from its conqueror. Actual rule began in 133BC when Attalus III bequeathed the vast Pergamene kingdom to Rome.

Rome moved relatively slowly into Turkey; in 67BC Pompey destroyed the pirate fleets at the Battle of Coracesium (Alanya) and by the 4th century AD the empire had reached the limit of its expansion in eastern Anatolia, but it was still some way short of Lake Van.

St Paul Christianity began influencing opinion in this new province of Asia when Paul of Tarsus carried the message on his travels along the Mediterranean coast and inland to Iconium (Konya) in the short-lived province of Galatia: his Letter to the Galatians is the ninth book of the New Testament. His third journey took him to the capital, Ephesus, which prompted him to write the tenth book, his Letter to the Ephesians.

St John the Evangelist and his sister the Virgin Mary lived, and died, in Ephesus, but Paul went on to Rome and martyrdom.

Goths The Goths sailed down the Dniestr River, through the Hellespont, and in 262 attacked Ephesus and other cities. The Persians came back, the Roman Empire split, and the new eastern empire set its capital at Byzantium, to be renamed Constantinople in honour of Constantine the

Great.

Emperor Justinian took Byzantium to its greatest power, his conquest of Egypt carrying Roman culture into three continents. But five years after his death, Mahomet was born in Mecca and the world was about to see the creation of another major religion.

The Arabs, carrying the word of Islam, swept across north Africa and, attacking Europe from the west, occupied Spain and reached Poitiers in France by 732.

Seljuks By 770 the Abbasid Caliphate had taken Adana and Tarsus and entered the territory of modern Turkey. Still the Byzantine Empire hung on, centred on Constantinople, but in 1092 the Seljuk Sultanate defeated the Byzantines at the Battle of Manzikert (north of Lake Van), and Christianity was doomed in Anatolia.

Turks The Seljuks had come from mystical Bokhara and Samarkand and were the descendants of the Tu-Kin who had been driven from their homeland by the Mongols.

They had ideas about the freedom of the individual which were centuries in advance of their time. Under Seljuk rule, trade, commerce, art and architecture flourished, a network of caravanserais was begun, and the state provided health care, hospitals and orphanages, all funded from general taxation.

Poets and philosophers The best-known of the Seljuks were Omar Khayyam, the poet and philosopher (c1071-1123) and Celaleddin Rumi (c1207-73), the founder of the Whirling Dervishes in Konya.

The Fourth Crusade (1202-04), which set out to attack the Islamic rulers of the Holy Land, chose instead to pillage and plunder Constantinople, the last outpost of Christianity. Meanwhile, Alaeddin — Allah ed Din — Sultan of Konya, had allowed other descendants of Tu-Kin, now known as Turks, to settle in almost empty Phrygia. But these Turks were different. Their second-generation leader was named Othman (1259-1326) and he gave his name to the Ottomans, soon to have an empire rivalling that of Rome at its height.

Gallipoli Othman's son Orkhan (1326-59) snatched Bursa from the Byzantines, made it his capital, and in 1354 crossed the Dardanelles to seize Gallipoli. It was Islam's attack from the east and the first foothold in Europe for the Ottoman Empire.

Orkhan's son Murad I took Adrianople (Edirne) in 1361 and later moved his capital there; in '63 he defeated the Hungarians, in '66 the Serbs, and by 1382 he was in Sofia — but Constantinople, now far behind him, was still in Byzantine hands.

Tamburlane Murad's son Bayazid I (Beyazıt in Turkish), marched into Bulgaria in 1371 and annexed the country in 1396. Meanwhile, he had turned his attention eastward, annexed the seven emirates of Anatolia who were the Seljuks' successors in title, and justifiably earned himself the title of 'the Thunderer.' He had begun a siege of Constantinople, one of the last strongholds of the Byzantines, when another Turk, Timur the Lame — Tamburlane — attacked Bayazid's eastern frontier at Ankara in 1402, took Bayazid captive and reduced the Ottomans in Asia Minor to Phrygia and Bursa. But Tamurlane never occupied the territory; his was the thrill of conquest without the boredom of subjugation.

Fall of Constantinople Murad II rebuilt the western part of his empire and extended hs influence into Greece; his son Mehmet (Mohammed) II, 'the Conqueror' continued his work and managed to seize Constantinople in 1453 after a siege of a mere 53 days. Bayazid II and Selim the Grim

Backwoods Turkey: this is Küçükdereköy, 'Village of the Little Valley'

continued the Ottoman expansion east and west, and south into Egypt by defeating the Mameluk Empire. And then in 1520 Selim died and the usual ritual of installing a successor went into action.

Strangulation Total secrecy hid the news of any sultan's death until his chosen successor could be contacted and brought to the capital. The new sultan's first act was to protect himself by having all his brothers killed, usually by strangulation with a silken bowstring as royal blood must not be spilled. Selim had slain his two brothers, nephews, 62 other relations, and even his father Bayazid, in order to reach the throne. Now his successor rode hard for three days to reach Üsküdar and install himself in office: Selim's 26-year old son Süleiman, soon to be called 'the Magnificent' in the west, and 'the Lawgiver' by his own people, was Sultan.

Süleiman the Magnificent The Prince of Manisa and Prince of Trabzon, Süleiman added a string of other titles during his 46-year reign: Sultan of the Ottomans, Allah's deputy on Earth, Lord of the Lords of this World, Possessor of men's Necks, King of Believers and Unbelievers, King of Kings, Emperor of the East and West, Emperor of the Chakans of Great Authority, Prince and Lord of the Most Happy Constellation, Majestic Caesar, Seal of Victory, Refuge of all the people in the World, and Shadow of the Almighty dispensing quiet on the Earth. For final glory, his name was also a corruption of the Biblical 'Solomon.'

Süleiman's first act was to order a mosque for his father, free 1,500 prisoners, and compensate merchants whom his father had cheated. Then he attacked Europe and took Belgrade after a 20-day siege.

In 1522 he sent 300 ships and 100,000 men to drive the Knights of St John of   171

Jerusalem from Rhodes, and four years later with 80,000 men and 300 cannon he set out for Hungary. His army had engineers to build bridges, sappers to mine castle walls, spahis (cavalry, often on camels), scouts, a military band, and the Janissaries (*Yeni çeri* or 'new soldiers,' stolen in infancy from Christian homes). Budapest withstood the onslaught for just two hours.

Vienna In 1529 Süleiman attacked Vienna, but had to withdraw. It was the first of only two defeats, the second being from the Knights of St John who resisted him in Malta in 1565. But following the Viennese incident his admiral Barbarossa took Algiers and the empire extended from there to Aden, from Buda to Basra, up the Don and down the Nile.

Topkapı Between campaigns, Süleiman lived in opulence in the Topkapı Palace in Istanbul where, four days a week, he presided over a Diwan, his court of viziers who sat on couches and ultimately gave the English language the word 'divan.' There were 3,000 residents at Topkapı, except on diwan days when there were 8,000.

Malta The defeat at Malta was the turning point in Ottoman fortunes. Six years later his successor Selim II lost the Battle of Lepanto and the great decline began. For two centuries the empire gradually contracted its influence and its boundaries as its enemies grew stronger and its subject peoples fought for independence. The Janissaries revolted several times, usually in demand for long-overdue pay, while the countries of western Europe were conquering distant lands and bringing home untold wealth.

Vienna again The Turks attacked Vienna again in 1683, but were ignominiously defeated. Now Europe lost its fear of the terrible Turk, and Russia was at last ruler of the Black Sea.

Janissaries Selim III revised taxation in the late 18th century and in 1826 Mahmut II slaughtered all the Janissaries in their barracks with gunfire, then introduced wide-ranging reforms in education, brought in printing presses, and rebuilt the armed forces which the Europeans promptly destroyed.

Russian threat The west was beginning to recognise a new threat from Russia. Europeans agreed that the Dardanelles were Turkish waters, and refused Russia access to the Mediterranean. This led to the Crimean War of 1854-56 in which Britain and France sided with Turkey against mighty Russia. The Treaty of Paris in 1856 guaranteed the integrity of the Ottoman Empire, but its decline could not be reversed. Nor did Europe want to try. By 1876 Turkey's territory in Europe covered what are now Bulgaria, Yugoslavia, Albania and northern Greece — and Syria in Asia — but under Abdul Hamid, the 'Red Sultan,' Bulgaria and Yugoslavia emerged as free states.

World War One The Ottomans sided with the Axis Powers in the Great War and to the Allies the defeat of Germany was only marginally more important than the destruction of Ottoman rule.

The Gallipoli Campaign Russia was meeting stiff Turkish opposition in the Caucasus and in January 1915 the Tzar begged Britain to attack Turkey in the rear. Prime Minister Herbert Asquith was happy to oblige and on 19 February sent the Royal Navy to bombard Cape Helles (Ilyasbaba Burun). After heavy losses the British pulled back.

Britain and France decided together on the crazy scheme of landing at Gallipoli, at the tip of a long, narrow and mountainous peninsula with no roads, and marching to Istanbul. Britain appointed Sir Ian Hamilton to lead the combined force of 90,000 and Lord Kitchener declared the Turks would run at the sight of a submarine. He was wrong: he hadn't allowed for the courage of their commanding officer, Lt-Col Mustafa Kemal, soon to be

Turkey's first president.

Anzac Day On 12 March, Hamilton began landing his men. The Turks, who had yet to drop the Islamic for the Gregorian calendar, remember this date as 18 March and mark it accordingly in Çanakkale. Due to bad loading, the invasion was abandoned until 25 April when the troops were landed on an exposed beach with the fully-prepared Turks waiting in ambush. It was slaughter, yet this date in April is still remembered as Anzac Day in Australia and New Zealand, which sent many troops.

The Allies advanced a mile by 5 May, with British losses already totalling 13,979. The next day more French landed at Cape Helles and Anzacs came ashore 15 miles up the coast at Anzac Cove, a beachhead that had no contact with the original landing.

The strength of the Turkish attack showed the folly of dreaming of Istanbul, but the Allies countered from Cape Helles and took Krithia, now Alçitepe. And 100,000 reinforcements landed at Anzac Cove. Hamilton begged for more men — 45,000 conscripts and 50,000 regulars — but was refused. The result of the Gallipoli campaign was already obvious.

The Turks came in again in September and effectively defeated the Allies but failed to drive them into the sea. Çanakkale remembers 22 September as the day of victory and marks it with parades through the town.

Catastrophe Asquith was planning withdrawal and asked Hamilton for an estimate of the losses that might result. When Hamilton prophesied they'd be catastrophic, he was the first to go. The Allies, now down to 50,000 men and losing 1,000 a day, knew the Germans were advancing through Serbia with heavy artillery. Meanwhile, Bulgaria had seen the tide of events and joined the Axis.

Retreat On 20 December the Allies, including the surviving Anzacs, pulled out of Anzac Cove and early in January the remaining troops quit Cape Helles. The British had put in 468,987 men and lost 41,158 dead, 78,420 wounded, with French and Anzac losses proportionate. In retrospect the Gallipoli Campaign was a major disaster with the wrong number of troops

THE GALLIPOLI CAMPAIGN

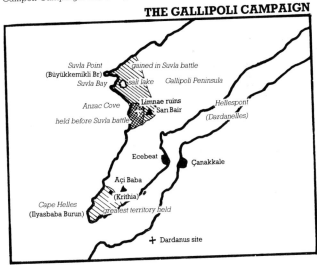

Suvla Point
(Büyükkemikli Br) — gained in Suvla battle
Suvla Bay — salt lake — Gallipoli Peninsula

Anzac Cove — Limnae ruins — Hellespont
San Bair — (Dardanelles)
held before Suvla battle

Ecebeat — Çanakkale

Açi Baba
(Krithia)

Cape Helles
(Ilyasbaba Burun) — greatest territory held

+ Dardanus site

with the wrong weapons going to the wrong spot at the wrong time for the wrong reason. And yet we won the war.

Carve-up The Allies had promised the post-war carve-up of Ottoman lands but in 1918 found they'd offered more than they could deliver. So they decided to carve the turkey as well.

Italy took Rhodes and the Dodecanese, Greece took the remaining Aegean islands and then, while the Allies stood by and applauded, seized Smyrna (Izmir) on 15 May, 1919 and began the invasion of Anatolia, determined to create a modern Byzantium.

Mustafa Kemal As far back as 1906, the general Mustafa Kemal had seen the way things were going and decided Turkey's only salvation was through westernisation. On 19 May, 1919, Kemal landed at Samsun on the Black Sea and began the revolution.

Revolution The Turkish War of Independence began in 1920 at the gates of Ankara. In 1921 Kemal's friend drove the Greeks back at Inönü and took the name for himself; later that year Kemal was tasting victory and on 9 September 1922 he led his troops in triumph into Izmir.

The war was finished; now peace had to be created. Kemal gave himself the name *ata Türk*, 'father of the Turk,' and began the major reforms of which he'd dreamed and which he knew were essential to turn modern Turkey from an introspective, defeated and eastward-looking land to the pro-European state it is today.

Çanakkale celebrates victory at the Dardanelles

INDEX